REVOLUTION AND
WAR IN SPAIN
1931–1939

Methuen
London and New York

REVOLUTION AND WAR IN SPAIN 1931–1939

Edited by
PAUL PRESTON

First published in 1984 by
Methuen & Co. Ltd
11 New Fetter Lane, London EC4P 4EE
Reprinted 1985

Published in the USA by
Methuen & Co.
in association with Methuen, Inc.
29 West 35th Street, New York, NY 10001

Printed by Richard Clay (The Chaucer Press) Ltd
Bungay, Suffolk

British Library Cataloguing in Publication Data
Revolution and war in Spain 1931–1939.
1. Spain – History – Civil War, 1936–1939
I. Preston, Paul, 1946–
946.081   DP269

ISBN 0–416–34960–9
ISBN 0–416–34970–6 Pbk

Library of Congress Cataloging in Publication Data
Main entry under title:

Revolution and war in Spain, 1931–1939.

Includes index.
1. Spain – History – Civil War, 1936–1939 – Causes –
Addresses, essays, lectures.   2. Spain – Politics and
government – 1931–1939 – Addresses, essays, lectures.
I. Preston, Paul.
DP257.R38   1984   946.081   84–1070
ISBN 0–416–34960–9
ISBN 0–416–34970–6 (pbk.)

This book is to be returned on or before
the last date stamped below.

- 4 OCT 89

29 NOV 89

2 5 JAN 1990

1 1 OCT 1993

LOA
ACK

1998

Contents

List of contributors

Paul Preston. Reader in Modern History, Queen Mary College, University of London. Author of *The Coming of the Spanish Civil War* (1978).

Shlomo Ben-Ami. Professor of History, Tel Aviv University, and author of *The Origins of the Second Republic in Spain* (1978) and *Fascism from Above: The Dictatorship of Primo de Rivera* (1983).

Frances Lannon. Fellow and tutor of Lady Margaret Hall, Oxford, and author of several articles on the history of Spanish Catholicism and a forthcoming book on the politics of the Spanish Church.

Martin Blinkhorn. Senior Lecturer, University of Lancaster, and author of *Carlism and Crisis in Spain 1931–1939* (1975).

Norman Jones. Principal Lecturer in Spanish, Oxford Polytechnic, and author of several articles on Catalan history.

Adrian Shubert. Research Fellow, Stanford University, and author of several articles on Spanish social history and a forthcoming book on social conflict in Asturias.

Santos Juliá. Professor of Sociology at the Universidad Nacional de Educación a Distancia, and author of *La izquierda del PSOE* (1977), *Orígenes del Frente Popular* (1979) and *Madrid, 1931–1934: De la fiesta popular a la lucha de clases* (1984).

Juan Pablo Fusi. Professor of Contemporary History, University of Santander, and author of *El problema vasco en la segunda República* (1979) and (with Raymond Carr) *Spain: Dictatorship to Democracy* (1979).

Michael Alpert. Principal Lecturer in Spanish, Polytechnic of Central London, and author of *El ejército republicano en la guerra civil* (1977) and *La reforma militar de Azaña* (1982).

Ronald Fraser. Freelance writer and author of *In Hiding: The Life of Manuel Cortes* (1972), *The Pueblo* (1973) and *Blood of Spain* (1979).

Denis Smyth. Lecturer in Modern History, University College, Cork, and author of several articles on inter-war diplomacy and a forthcoming book on Britain and Spain 1936–1945.

Angel Viñas. Professor of Economics, University of Madrid; senior adviser to the Spanish Foreign Minister and author of *La Alemania nazi y el 18 de julio* (1974), *El oro de Moscú* (1979) and *Los pactos secretos de Franco con Estados Unidos* (1981).

List of abbreviations

ACNP   Asociación Católica Nacional de Propagandistas – the political vanguard of the legalist right associated with Catholic Action.

ASM   Agrupación Socialista Madrileña – the Madrid section of the PSOE.

BOC   Bloc Obrer i Camperol – Workers and Peasants Bloc, Trotskyist organization which fused with the Izquierda Comunista in 1935 to create the POUM.

CEDA   Confederación Española de Derechas Autónomas – the Spanish Confederation of Autonomous Rightist Groups, the largest political organization of the legalist right.

CNCA   Confederación Nacional Católico-Agraria – a conservative, Catholic smallholders' organization which provided much mass support for the CEDA.

CNT   Confederación Nacional del Trabajo – anarcho-syndicalist trade union.

DRV   Derecha Regional Valenciana – the Valencian component of the CEDA.

FAI   Federación Anarquista Ibérica – the insurrectionary vanguard of the anarchist movement.

FNTT   Federación Nacional de Trabajadores de la Tierra – the landworkers' section of the UGT.

FPFR   Federación de Propietarios de Fincas Rústicas – a landowners' organization devoted to blocking the reforms of the Republic.

HISMA   Hispano-Marroquí de Transportes S.L. – the company founded in Morocco on 31 July 1936 to act as a cover for the entry of German aid to the Nationalists.

ORGA   Organización Republicana Gallega Autónoma – Galician regionalist party founded in 1930 and fused into Azaña's Izquierda Republicana in 1934.

PCE   Partido Comunista de España – the Moscow-orientated Communist Party.

PNV   Partido Nacionalista Vasco – the Christian Democrat Basque Nationalist Party.

POUM   Partido Obrero de Unificación Marxista – an amalgam of left Communist dissidents and Trotskyists from the BOC and the Izquierda Comunista who united in 1935 to create a revolutionary vanguard party.

PRC   Partit Republicà Català – the middle-class Catalan Nationalist party led into the Esquerra by Lluis Companys.

PSOE   Partido Socialista Obrero Español – the Spanish Socialist Workers' Party.

PSUC   Partit Socialista Unificat de Catalunya – the Catalan Communist Party.

ROWAK   Rohstoff- und Waren- Einkaufsgesellschaft – export agency set up in Germany in October 1936 to channel German supplies to Nationalist Spain.

SMA   Sindicato Minero Asturiano – the Asturian miners' section of the UGT.

SOV   Solidaridad de Obreros Vascos – the Basque workers' organization linked to the PNV.

UCD   Unión de Centro Democrático – centre-right party founded in 1977 which ruled Spain until its collapse in 1982.

UGT   Unión General de Trabajadores – the trade-union organization of the Socialist movement.

UME   Unión Militar Española – ultra-rightist army officers' society.

UMRA   Unión de Militares Republicanos Antifascistas – union of anti-fascist officers set up to counteract the influence of the UME.

Acknowledgements

I would like to thank a number of friends whose help made this book possible. Paul Heywood read the proofs and compiled the index. Nancy Marten of Methuen was the perfect editor, balancing efficiency with understanding. Herbert R. Southworth encouraged the project from its inception. A book which aims to demonstrate the most important trends in recent Spanish historiography is diminished by his absence. In their different ways, Raymond Carr and Joaquín Romero Maura helped in the intellectual formation of several of the contributors. I trust that none of them will be too disappointed.

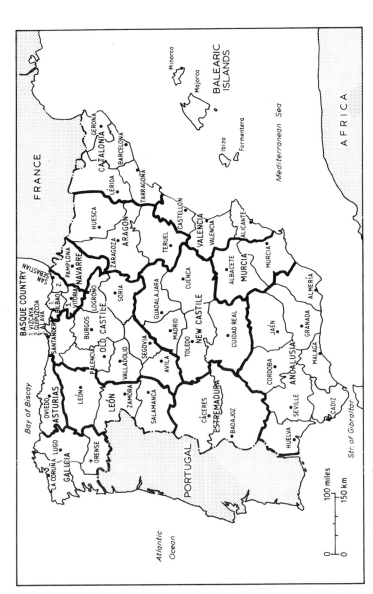

Regions and provinces of Spain

Introduction
War of words: the Spanish Civil
War and the historians

Paul Preston

The student of the Spanish Civil War and its immediate origins has,
until very recently, been at an enormous disadvantage by comparison
with colleagues concerned with the comparable experiences of Italy,
Germany or Austria. The defeat of the Axis dictatorships permitted a
wholesale opening of archives which was the basis not only for research
into the fascist period but also for investigation of the social and political
conflicts which preceded it. One of the side effects of the fact that
General Franco failed ultimately to join his erstwhile Axis backers in
declaring war on the Western allies was that archives remained closed.
In any case, much documentation was destroyed during the Civil War

either by accident or by those who feared reprisals. Thereafter, thirty-six years of dictatorship provided ample opportunity for the elimination of material likely to shed light on the repression and corruption which characterized the regime, especially in its early years. Only with the death of the dictator did the lamentable situation of Spanish archives begin to improve. Even then, it remained common for certain privileged individuals to gain exclusive access to closed archives and then use them for their own benefit while simultaneously criticizing others for their failure to use the same sources. However, thanks to the efforts of a number of Spanish scholars, perhaps most notably Professor Angel Viñas, there was gradual progress which, with the coming to power of the Socialist Party in 1982, has become quite dramatic.[1]

The obstruction of scholarship, like many other aspects of the regime's censorship machinery, was a continuation of the war by other means. In victory, the dictatorship sought to impose its own view of the nature of the war as a struggle between the barbaric godless hordes of the proletariat and the guardians of traditional Christian values. The benefits accruing from the deliberate distortion of the war and its causes were many. The presentation of the war as a religious crusade aimed above all at obscuring its class origins and obliterating the revolutionary achievements of the working classes between 1936 and 1939.[2] The landowners and industrialists who supported Franco, and in whose interests the war had been fought, did not wish to be reminded that they had wanted the Republic destroyed because its moderate reforms could not be carried out without some redistribution of wealth. The big estates and many industrial enterprises depended for their economic validity on the existence of a surplus labour force which could be paid starvation wages. The reforms of 1931–2 challenged that situation and the events of 1936–7 in the Republican zone indicated that its solution lay in rational collectivization. It is hardly surprising that Franco's backers preferred an apocalyptic and religious interpretation of the war.

The 'crusade' historiography was produced by policemen, who also seized and suppressed historical documents,[3] by soldiers, by government propagandists and by priests. By dwelling on, and exaggerating, anti-clerical atrocities without examining the background of social oppression from which they sprang, by pretending that working-class excesses had been inspired and manipulated by Communists and freemasons, the

Francoist 'historians' helped cement the alliance between the regime and the Catholic Church.[4] Similarly, they helped inflate the army's pride in its achievement in defeating other Spaniards. Even when the 'crusade' school of thinking had been rejected with repulsion by many sectors of the Church and regarded as an embarrassment by the more progressive servants of the regime, it continued to hold sway in the military academies. Under Franco, the army was the poor relation in economic terms but no efforts were spared to inflate its sense of being victorious over the bad Spaniards of the Republican zone. Its pride and its nostalgia were the basis of its loyalty to Franco.[5]

Outside the hermetic world of the military, Francoist historiography was not entirely monolithic. Changing political needs led eventually to a move away from the hysterical denunciations of the crimes of the red rabble and the semi-religious veneration of Falangist martyrs. After the fall of the Axis, the central necessity of the Franco dictatorship was to wipe away the opprobrium of its fascist connections. With survival dependent upon the regime's ability to ingratiate itself with the Western allies, historical writing on the Civil War undertook the task of portraying Franco as a clairvoyant pioneer in the war against communism. The fact that he had fought against liberalism and parliamentary democracy was forgotten; instead he became the bulwark of the Western defence against the Soviet threat.[6] Throughout the 1950s, the evil machinations of communism became the dominant theme of Francoist historiography, especially in the works written and edited by three policemen, Eduardo Comín Colomer, Mauricio Carlavilla and Angel Ruiz Ayúcar.[7]

A more thoroughgoing change began in the 1960s when a major operation to streamline the regime's image took place under the dynamic Minister of Information, Manuel Fraga Iribarne. The task of modernizing official historiography fell to an ex-Jesuit official of the Ministry, Ricardo de la Cierva. The operation was in large part a response to modernization in Spanish society as a whole. Higher standards of education and the growth of a militant student body which travelled abroad made the old propaganda untenable. The Church, in particular, was in the throes of a painful reassessment of its role during the Civil War, was pulling away from the regime and found the official historiography increasingly distasteful. However, La Cierva's Centre for Civil War Studies set up at the Ministry of Information was also a response to the success of an exiled leftist publishing house, Ruedo Ibérico, established in Paris by a libertarian, José Martínez, and a number of collaborators from the entire anti-Francoist spectrum. In June 1965, with the ex-Communist, Jorge Semprún, Martínez began to publish the journal *Cuadernos de Ruedo Ibérico*. Always economically precarious, it nevertheless quickly established a position of enormous intellectual prestige from which it set about dismantling the lies and distortions of the regime concerning both its present and its past.

Great damage to the regime's highly tendentious account of Spain's recent history was delivered by Ruedo Ibérico's translation of Hugh Thomas's *The Spanish Civil War*. Smuggled across the border by the thousand, it became the bible of the Spanish left, seized in hundreds of police raids on the homes of anti-regime activists. By comparison with regime historiography, Thomas's ostentatious objectivity rang truer and was devoured avidly. An even more devastating, if less well publicized, blow to the regime's credibility was delivered by what was to become a classic of Civil War historiography, Herbert R. Southworth's *El mito de la cruzada de Franco*. Astonishingly never published in its English original, it was a painstaking demolition of the untruths on which the Francoists had built their history.[8] La Cierva's stream of books was directed vainly at discrediting Thomas and Southworth, for whom he reserved the most vicious and virulent personal insults in lieu of serious intellectual argument. None the less, his works were highly readable, occasionally scholarly and a significant departure from crusade historiography.[9] In the writing of history, as in all other aspects of the regime's existence, it was the beginning of the end. In taking up the position that the war was the result of left-wing extremism driving moderate men reluctantly to take up arms in self-defence, La Cierva was opening doors which could never be fully shut, although he was to try hard to do so from his position in the censorship apparatus.

The fact that the Francoists continued to fight the war through the manipulation of history had its parallel on the other side. Of course, not having a regime to defend and chastened by defeat, the writings of the exiled Republicans were less blatantly propagandistic. Partisan and self-justificatory, the urgent need to explain defeat prevented a total disregard for truth and indeed produced some of the best work on the war.

However, a large proportion of the post-war production of the Spanish left was devoted to an ultimately sterile polemic between the Communists and most of the rest of the Republican camp as to whether the crushing of revolution in return for Soviet aid had hastened or delayed final defeat. In any case, writing in the hardship of exile, the Republicans can hardly be blamed for not producing major works of historical scholarship.

The Francoists in contrast not only carry the responsibility for turning history into propaganda but, much more seriously, are guilty of trying to annihilate history as an academic discipline. The great historians of pre-war Spain were hounded into exile. Those who remained were forced into a kind of inner exile, compelled to take up other jobs or else to work on periods earlier, and therefore less 'political', than the ones which interested them. The consequence of this has been that, until after Franco's death, the main burden of writing the history of twentieth-century Spain has fallen on foreigners, particularly Anglo-Saxons. They had access to exiled Republican publications denied to Spaniards and to pre-war and wartime newspapers whose scrutiny was not encouraged within Francoist Spain. Inevitably, the strength, and perhaps the weakness, of the foreigners was their tendency to broad generalization. Their own interests, and the exigencies of the publishing trade, led them to attempt to explain the central event of modern Spanish history, the Civil War. In the best of such works, this led to interpretations of great insight; in the worst, to the most ludicrous constructions based on wildly erroneous views of the Spanish character.[10]

The foundations of all modern scholarship on the Spanish Republic and Civil War were laid by Gerald Brenan in 1943. Parts of *The Spanish Labyrinth* have been challenged by subsequent investigations but the book remains unequalled for its authenticity and 'feel'. It was not a conventional work of scholarly research but Brenan had lived in the Andalusian countryside since the end of the Great War, read the newspapers regularly and was familiar with the work of the great social commentators of the day, Joaquín Costa, Juan Díaz del Moral and Constancio Bernaldo de Quirós. While most contemporary writers were still playing with the simplistic notion that the Spanish war was a battle between fascism and communism, Brenan perceived that it was a fundamentally Spanish affair, rooted in the agrarian question and comprehensible only in terms of the previous hundred years of Spanish development.

A similar perspective illuminates an equally significant English contribution to the historiography of the Civil War, that made by Raymond Carr. In two works, his monumental Oxford history of Spain and *The Spanish Tragedy*, Carr has presented Spain's twentieth-century disasters in terms of the failure of Spanish liberalism to break the power of the old landed oligarchy in order to carry through the political and economic modernization of the country.[11] Carr's work inspired a major leap forward in the sophistication of research into modern Spain, a fact reflected in the emergence of an Oxford 'school' of contemporary Spanish history. Six of the contributors to the present volume can, in one way or another, be considered to have been part of that group, influenced by Carr or by his one-time associate, Joaquín Romero Maura. Between them, Carr and Romero Maura instilled an intellectual rigour into modern Spanish historiography which had previously been conspicuously lacking.[12]

Despite its importance, the work of Carr, and indeed that of Brenan, has been overshadowed, commercially at least, by the enormous popular success of two general accounts of the war itself. The highly colourful narrative account by Hugh Thomas emphasized the role of British intellectuals, the wider diplomatic dimension and the activities of the International Brigades, to the detriment of the 'Spanishness' of the Civil War. Thomas's work did an enormous amount to popularize the subject but it constitutes a readable compendium of information about the war rather than a major historiographical landmark.[13] Its immediate rival, the account of the 1930s in Spain by Gabriel Jackson, was a well-written and humane account from a left liberal point of view. Jackson's use of the Spanish press, especially the Republican daily, *El Sol*, pointed the way forward to the need for sources other than memoirs and parliamentary debates to be exploited. In this, his own work, while remaining valuable, was soon superseded as a new generation of historians began to compensate for closed archives by exhaustive examination of local and party newspapers and bulletins.[14]

It would be wrong in any survey of academic contributions to the development of the historiography of the Spanish 1930s to ignore the remarkable works of the Englishman Burnett Bolloten and the American

Herbert Rutledge Southworth. Each have been accused of being obsessive when in reality they have pursued their subjects unimpeded by any need to publish or perish. Bolloten's account of the Communist Party's suppression of revolution in the interests of a conventional war effort and of Soviet foreign policy is based on tenacious scholarship but tends to be developed within an interpretative vacuum. Communist policy can be assessed seriously only in the light of its efficacy within the Republican war effort. By effectively concluding his story in May 1937, Bolloten permits himself to examine the dictatorial nature of Communist methods without having to assess the realism of their policies once they had gained the upper hand. His book remains, however, among the most important produced on the Spanish war.[15] Even more significant is the work of Herbert Southworth, not least because it contributed to the creation of the La Cierva government department in Francoist Spain dedicated to modernizing regime historiography. His masterpiece is his massively erudite study of the Francoist political manipulation of the destruction of Guernica. As the doyen of French hispanists, Pierre Vilar, pointed out in his introductory essay, Southworth's unswerving quest for truth, exposing how journalists, censors, propagandists and diplomats rewrite history, has implications far beyond the historiography of the Spanish war. In a field in which truth has consistently been a casualty, Southworth's 'passionate objectivity' stands as a salutary beacon.[16]

In their very different ways, Bolloten and Southworth stand outside the mainstream of recent Spanish historiography. With some important exceptions, its trend has been in the direction of the longer-span structural interpretations pioneered by Brenan and Carr. The exceptions were constituted by a number of conservative historians whose work was greeted by La Cierva with the most profound relief. Five books published in 1970 and 1971 by British and American historians so delighted Ricardo de la Cierva that, dropping all pretence of objective scholarship, he declared the Fraga face-lift operation to have been a total success, the initiative to have been recaptured and 'the enemy left without history'.[17] The books which occasioned his excitement were a biography of Franco by J. W. D. Trythall, an account of the agrarian problem in Spain by E. E. Malefakis, a survey of the Spanish left up to 1939 by Stanley G. Payne, a book on the right during the Second Republic

by Richard A. H. Robinson and a collective volume edited by Raymond Carr, containing essays by La Cierva himself, as well as Payne,
Robinson, Malefakis and others.[18] In his euphoria, La Cierva did not
stop to check whether the authors in question were happy about the
propagandistic use that he was making of their work. All that concerned him was that they were critical of the left during the 1930s.

With archives closed in Spain and many major works banned, La
Cierva's loud celebration of a new 'universal consensus' was hypocritical in the extreme. None the less, despite his exaggerations, it could not
be gainsaid that the collective tendency of the works in question was
supportive of the neo-Francoist position that the war was the fault of
the extremisms of the left. Malefakis, for instance, isolated the failure of
agrarian reform as one of the central features of the failure of the Second
Republic and then went on to blame that failure, not on the intransigence of the big landowners, but on the ineptitude of Republican politicians. The historians who went furthest in this direction, and who
were consequently most lauded by La Cierva, were Payne and Robinson.[19] Payne's denunciation of the Spanish left owed more to the earlier
work of the Francoist Comín Colomer than to any fresh investigations
of the social misery of Spain during the depression. Robinson, too, was
indirectly influenced by traditional Francoist historiography. The
crusade school had untrammelled admiration for those members of the
extreme right who set out to destroy the Republic from its inception and
a corresponding contempt for those on the moderate right who had been
prepared to work within the democratic regime. On this post-war
Francoist hostility to Gil Robles and the CEDA, Robinson built a
picture of a genuinely moderate Christian Democrat Party driven to
abandon its moderation by leftist extremism.

The emergence of this conservative orthodoxy and La Cierva's
shameless exploitation of it led to an immensely fruitful debate. A series
of articles by Joaquín Romero Maura and a number of other Oxford-
trained historians pointed out that, for the sweeping conclusions of the
new conservatives to be proved or discredited, it was necessary to move
away from generalizations about Madrid politics and towards a deeper
understanding of the realities of the rest of Spain in the 1930s.[20] All were
in agreement that Malefakis's work was, its political conclusions aside,
a substantial advance in this regard. Henceforth, political analysis

without consideration of the social background of Spanish industrial and agrarian conflicts was untenable. The first results of this new stage of the historiography of the 1930s were Martin Blinkhorn's lucid study of how rural anti-modernism was the basis of mass Carlist hostility to the democratic regime and my own attempt to explain the extremisms of national politics in terms of local social conflict in mining districts and in the big estates of the south.[21]

This new trend towards social history on the part of English-language historians coincided with a veritable avalanche of work which began to emerge in Spain towards the end of the Franco regime. In part, it was the fruit of the labours of the Spanish historians Miguel Artola and José María Jover and of the sociologist Francisco Murrillo Ferrol, many of whose pupils now began to publish their research. It was also the consequence of the remarkable annual seminar held at the University of Pau under the auspices of the exiled Manuel Tuñón de Lara. Tuñón was the catalyst of a vast array of studies in labour and social history.[22] In the face of this resurgence of Spanish scholarship during the twilight of the Franco regime, the vanguard position of the Anglo-Saxons was definitively eroded. The new outpourings were not without their problems. There was an alarming tendency to ideological studies which effectively meant little more than laboured exegesis of the thought of minor leftists whose main characteristics had been their simplicity. There was above all an apparent belief that only the truly unreadable could really aspire to the status of science. Massive theses crammed with interminable quotations and other raw material ironically kept the English-language writers, with their preoccupation with economy and style, in a prominent position.

The present situation is one of substantial rethinking. The general works of the last fifteen years are under threat from wave after wave of detailed local research. It will be some time before a new synthesis is possible. In the meanwhile, much of the best work remains in thesis form or, if published, unlikely to be translated into English. The purpose of the present volume is to make available to a wider audience some of the best examples of the revolution in the study of contemporary Spanish history which has taken place in the period since the death of Franco and the collapse of the La Cierva streamlining operation.

It has long been a commonplace of writing on the Spanish Civil War that it involved religious, regional and class conflicts. Yet despite the pioneering efforts of Carr and Brenan, and until the milestone of Edward Malefakis's work, the central trend has been to conventional political analysis of struggles within and among the parties of left and right throughout the 1930s. Recent research has tried to provide a more richly delineated picture of the interactions between religious, regional and social confrontations. From the variety of contributions to this volume there emerges the central argument that the Spanish Civil War was not one but many wars.

The book opens with a chapter by the Israeli historian Shlomo Ben-Ami which stresses the extent to which the Republic was in large part the culmination of a lengthy process of modernization and urbaniz-ation. He shows that it had a sufficiently wide social base to ensure that on 14 April 1931 everything was possible, even peace. The following seven chapters demonstrate how the new regime was shipwrecked on the rocks of the most varied and long-standing social problems. Frances Lannon examines traditional clerical education and attitudes, the econ-omic dependence of the Church and the implicit sociological and politi-cal definition of Catholicism within Spanish society in order to explain clerical hostility to the new regime. That an armed rising of the most disparate elements should be transformed into a 'holy crusade', blessed by a Church oblivious to the incongruity of Moorish and Nazi involve-ment, is taken by Dr Lannon to indicate that the scope, ferocity and pretensions of the Francoist war effort can only be fully understood through their religious dimension. It has long been accepted that religious fanaticism was nowhere more intense than among the Carlists of Navarre. In chapter three, Martin Blinkhorn illustrates the indissolu-bility of religious, regional and social issues, with the province's Carlists fighting a war on two fronts against Basque autonomists and the social reforms of the Republic.

The extent to which purely local issues came to have an impact in terms of national politics is a theme common to the regional studies contained in chapters three to eight. In chapter four, Norman Jones shows the ruling Catalan Republican party, the Esquerra, trapped in a triangle of the incomprehension and hostility of Madrid to local aspir-ations, the obstructionism of the Catalan right and the semi-permanent insurrectionism of the anarchists. In October 1934, the Esquerra fatally miscalculated the consequences of action against all three at once and embroiled Catalonia in a short-lived regionalist uprising with disastrous results for the Republic. The Asturian revolutionary insurrection of 1934 is the subject of chapter five. Adrian Shubert stresses the local origins of the social militancy of the miners as well as outlining the immediate political reasons for their defeat in a struggle which foreshadowed the Civil War. Just as Dr Shubert emphasizes the radicalizing influence of young miners, so too Santos Juliá, in chapter six, relates a parallel story. He examines the urban development of the capital, the consequent changes in its demographic structure and the growing militancy of unemployed youths, as sources of the class war which exploded in 1936. In chapter seven, I present an account of what I believe to be the central conflict of 1930s Spain, the southern agrarian war, how it spilled over into national politics and how the Francoists' Andalusian campaign revealed the priority that they gave to crushing rural revolution. Professor Juan Pablo Fusi, in chapter eight, charts the protracted process whereby the Basque Nationalists progressed from a position of ultra-Catholic anti-Republicanism in 1931 to one of firm support for the regime in 1936. This development is shown to have involved a major effort by the Socialist Party to bring the Basque Country into the Republican orbit and necessarily led to the engendering of bitter hatreds on the part of the most reactionary elements in both Basque and Spanish society.

These chapters provide a convincing picture of the multiplicity of conflicts which made up the Spanish Civil War. The remainder of the book is concerned with the external conditioning of the war, the way in which it was fought and how it was perceived. Ronald Fraser, whose pioneering oral history of the war constituted one of the most important historiographical advances of recent years, examines in chapter ten the issues for which ordinary people fought in the Republican zone. His chapter is preceded by Michael Alpert's analysis of how professional soldiers reacted to the upheaval of July 1936 and how different methods of mobilization in each zone produced different armies with different levels of performance. In chapter eleven, Denis Smyth's account of the deliberate and calculated nature of German intervention shows how Spain's internal conflicts were exploited and kept alive by external factors. Finally, in chapter twelve, Angel Viñas examines the ingenious improvizations by which both the Nationalist and Republican governments financed their war efforts. Again, the development of the Spanish war is shown to have been conditioned by outside forces, in this case by the Axis powers and the international financial circles who worked to influence the outcome of the war.

In a collection whose aim is to show the richness of the latest historiography of the Spanish crisis of the 1930s and whose theme is the variety of sometimes separate, sometimes intertwining, factors which made up the Civil War, there can be no uniformity of approach. In one thing the authors are, however, agreed: that the reality of Spain in that period is much more complex than has hitherto been allowed. Taken together, and as a representative sample of work that is now being carried out, the chapters in this volume indicate that the war of words may now be over. With the dictatorship's manipulation of history at an end and with archives now opening, the dialogue of historians can now supersede the propaganda battles of that war.

Notes

1 For a view of the situation in the late 1970s, see *Los archivos para la historia del siglo XX* (Madrid, 1980).

2 The central work of this school is Joaquín Arrarás, *Historia de la cruzada española* (8 vols., Madrid, 1939–43).

3 Papers belonging to Manuel Azaña were recently discovered at the Escuela de la Policía in Madrid, where they had been taken by its director, Eduardo Comín Colomer. *El País*, 28 January 1984.

4 See, *inter alia*, Aniceto de Castro Albarrán, *La gran víctima, La iglesia española mártir de la revolución roja* (Salamanca, 1940) and *Este es el cortejo. Héroes y mártires de la cruzada española* (Salamanca, 1941); Tomás Borrás, *Checas de Madrid, epopeya de los caídos* (Madrid, 1940); Juan Tusquets, *Masones y pacifistas* (Burgos, 1939).

5 Julio Busquets, Miguel Angel Aguilar, Ignacio Puche, *El golpe: anatomía y claves del asalto al Congreso* (Barcelona, 1981), 13–16.

6 The most extreme example of this tendency is Luis de Galinsoga and Francisco Franco Salgado Araujo, *Centinela de Occidente: (semblanza biográfica de Francisco Franco)* (Barcelona, 1956). See also Joaquín Arrarás, 'La clarividencia de Franco', *ABC*, 1 October 1953.

7 See, for example, Eduardo Comín Colomer, *Historia secreta de la segunda República* (2 vols., Madrid, 1954) with a prologue by Mauricio Carlavilla; Indalecio Prieto, *Yo y Moscú* (prólogo, comentarios y notas de Mauricio Carlavilla) (Madrid, 1960).

8 Herbert Rutledge Southworth, *El mito de la cruzada de Franco* (Paris, 1963). An expanded French version, *Le mythe de la croisade de Franco*, was published the following year.

9 The work of La Cierva has been subjected to merciless examination in Herbert R. Southworth, 'Los bibliófobos: Ricardo de la Cierva y sus colaboradores', *Cuadernos de Ruedo Ibérico*, 28–9 (December 1970–March 1971) and *Guernica! Guernica! A Study of Journalism, Diplomacy, Propaganda and History* (Berkeley, 1977), 252, 267, 278–98, 301–23 and *passim*.

10 See, for example, James Cleugh, *Spanish Fury* (London, 1962).

11 *Spain 1808–1939* (Oxford, 1966) and *The Spanish Tragedy* (London, 1977).

12 Romero Maura's work is little known to English readers. His most important book is '*La Rosa de Fuego*', *el obrerismo barcelonés de 1899 a 1909* (Barcelona, 1974).

13 Hugh Thomas, *The Spanish Civil War* (London, 1961, 1965 and 1977).

14 Gabriel Jackson, *The Spanish Republic and the Civil War* (Princeton, 1965). See also Santos Juliá, 'Un lejano resplandor', *El País*, 25 January 1981.

15 Burnett Bolloten, *The Grand Camouflage* (London, 1961 and 1968); revised as *The Spanish Revolution* (Chapel Hill, 1979). See also Paul Preston, 'The tactics of amnesia', *New Statesman*, 8 August 1980; and Herbert Southworth, 'The divisions of the left', *TLS*, 9 June 1978.

16 Southworth, *Guernica!*, ix–xvii.

17 Ricardo de la Cierva, 'La historia vuelve a su cauce', *El Alcázar*, 15 January 1972.

18 J. W. D. Trythall, *Franco: A Biography* (London, 1970); Edward E. Malefakis, *Agrarian Reform and Peasant Revolution in Spain* (New Haven, 1970); Stanley G. Payne, *The Spanish Revolution* (London, 1970); Richard A. H. Robinson, *The Origins of Franco's Spain* (Newton Abbot, 1970); Raymond Carr (ed.) *The Republic and the Civil War in Spain* (London, 1971).

19 Interview with Ricardo de la Cierva, *Criba*, 22 April 1972.

20 J. Romero Maura, 'Unas palabras sobre el debate historiográfico acerca de la segunda República'; Paul Preston, 'El accidentalismo de la CEDA: ¿aceptación o sabotage de la República?'; José Varela Ortega, 'Reacción y revolución frente a reforma', all in *Revista Internacional de Sociología*, 3/4 (July–December 1972); Martin Blinkhorn, 'Anglo-American historians and the Second Spanish Republic: the emergence of a new orthodoxy', *European Studies Review* 3, 1 (1973).

21 Martin Blinkhorn, *Carlism and Crisis in Spain 1931–1939* (Cambridge, 1975); Paul Preston, *The Coming of the Spanish Civil War* (London, 1978).

22 For an indication of the scale of this work, see Manuel Tuñón de Lara *et al.*, *Historiografía española contemporánea* (Madrid, 1980) and Santiago Castillo *et al.* (eds.), *Estudios sobre historia de España: obra homenaje a Manuel Tuñón de Lara* (3 vols., Madrid, 1981).

1
The Republican 'take-over': prelude to inevitable catastrophe?

Shlomo Ben-Ami

In their search for an explanation to the débâcle of the Second Spanish Republic, some historians and writers of memoirs have frequently resorted to medical metaphors; others have fallen back on fatalism. The Republic, as 'one of the most remarkable experiences of political pathology known to the contemporary world', must have been born, some say or imply, with 'discernible seeds of self destruction'.[1] Born with obvious 'congenital defects', Spain's incipient democracy was from the very outset 'an impossible Republic' and, due to Spanish idiosyncrasy, nothing but a skin-deep, 'false' political transformation.[2] On a somewhat different level it is also argued that as a premature parliamentary democracy devoid of the advanced social structure necessary to sustain it, the Republic's ultimate failure was inevitable. Rather than being the creation of a solid movement of opinion, it was the almost accidental outcome of the natural demise of the monarchy. But, 'civically uneducated' as they were, the Spaniards had no durable political option other than monarchy or anarchy.[3]

The coming of the Second Spanish Republic represented not a 'mysterious shift of opinion'[4] but the culminating point of a process of social evolution that had been gaining momentum since the Great War. In the decade of the 1920s alone, Spain's population had increased by 10 per cent,[5] and it had been, moreover, urbanized to a very great extent. Thus, for example, towns of over 10,000 inhabitants increased their population by an impressive figure of two million, and those of over 100,000 inhabitants by a not negligible one million, provincial capitals, whose population increased during the dictatorship by 30 per cent getting the lion's share of the growth. In 1930, 42 per cent of the population of Spain lived in towns of more than 10,000 inhabitants.[6] It was in such centres that the Republic was to achieve its greatest electoral gains in 1931. Primo de Rivera himself was not unaware of the socially and politically disturbing impact that the 'frightening dimensions of the desertion of the countryside',[7] which he viewed as responding to 'an excessive desire to satisfy earthly appetites', could have.[8] He might not have envisaged a rapid return to parliamentary democracy, but the defenders of the 'old order' would have been right in assuming that the flight from the countryside, or its 'increasing depopulation', as a leader of the National League of Farmers alarmingly put it,[9] meant that, once the people were called again to the polls, the grip of electoral *caciquismo* would be severely loosened, and the politics of immobilism seriously challenged.

In fact, by 1923, the once almost legendary electoral omnipotence of the Ministry of the Interior had already been seriously eroded.[10] The decade that preceded the Republic was likewise to witness a discernible modernization of Spain's social structure. Thus, for example, the proportion of the working force employed in agriculture decreased from 57.3 per cent to 45.51 per cent while that employed in industry and the service sector went up from 21.9 per cent to 25.61 per cent and from 20.81 per cent to 27.98 per cent respectively. By comparison, the

Portuguese Republic, brought about by a *pronunciamiento* rather than elections, rested on a far more archaic professional structure (57 per cent agriculture; less than 20 per cent industry; 5.5 per cent services).[11] In fact, in proportional terms, the intense transformation of the social fabric in the years that preceded the Republic almost matched that which took place during the Francoist boom, and in some aspects even surpassed it. Surprisingly, the twenties witnessed an increase of 4.57 per cent in the proportion of the workforce employed in industry, that is 1.35 per cent more than during the thirteen years of the Francoist boom (1960–73). Moreover, in the twenty years that preceded the Republic, the active population engaged in agriculture decreased by 20.49 per cent, in industry went up by 10.69 per cent and in the service sector by 9.8 per cent as compared with, respectively, 18.9 per cent, 4.72 per cent and 13.08 per cent in the fifteen years that preceded the advent of post-Francoist democracy.[12] Likewise, the fall in the rate of illiteracy in the 1920s was the highest of the century until the 1960s: 8.7 per cent for men and 9.15 per cent for women.[13] The dictator's expansionist economic policy had undoubtedly encouraged the upsurge of the middle classes and helped to consolidate the position of the organized proletariat.

The monarchy thus stepped down, entangled in a painfully obvious dilemma: either it democratized itself or it passed into oblivion. Primo de Rivera's dictatorship had unleashed modernizing processes that helped to erode the non-democratic foundations of the monarchy. The monarchy was doomed by its inability to absorb the processes of modernization by adapting itself to the democratic imperatives inherent in them. The growth of wealth, technological potentialities and urbanization, as well as the steady process of de-archaization of the social structure, were simply becoming incompatible with autocracy. This is how a sharp-eyed contemporary observer saw it:

> The new status of the town worker and the effect on the peasants of the building of thousands of miles of roads and railways were bound to have a great effect on the future. Roads meant motor buses, this meant more movement and freedom for the country people. It meant also that they would want a higher standard of living. . . .
> Nothing could be the same in Spain again after General Primo fell.

He had launched great schemes of modernization . . . and there
would be much political fruit in addition to economic changes.[14]

It was precisely this relation between socio-economic and political
change which Gregorio Marañón had referred to when he wrote late in
1929, without Buckley's advantage of hindsight, that 'the time is ripe
in Spain for the most profound transformations that the country's social
and political structure has ever undergone'.[15]

The republican movement was not just an anti-monarchist, negative
protest.[16] The significance of republicanism as it emerged after 1929 was
that it reflected a determined drive to establish the politics of mobilization in place of the system of patronage and clientele.[17] It was the
vehicle by which the masses were to be drawn into politics; it represented a wide and heterogeneous public both in its struggle against
the political immobilism of the monarchy, and in its hope of finding a
remedy to particular social and economic grievances.

Republicanism was not devoid of the support of the so-called *fuerzas
vivas* of Spanish society. One of the best-informed people in Spain, the
Chief of the Security Police, General Mola, observed in dismay that

the revolutionary spirit has invaded everything, absolutely
everything, from the humblest up to the highest social classes:
Workers, students, civil servants, industrialists, merchants,
rentiers, men of liberal professions, the military and even priests.[18]

It is this startling readiness of 'vested interests' to face 'the unknown
without apprehension' that had been the most salient feature of republicanism in the months that preceded the Republic. To the alarmed
monarchist organ *ABC* this phenomenon called to mind 'the same spirit
that prevailed in France on the eve of the Revolution'.[19]

Republicanism embraced, and gave expression to, the urban petty
bourgeoisie, small entrepreneurs throughout the country threatened
with the breakdown of their business under the burden of taxation and
the dictatorship's favouritism towards the big monopolistic concerns. It
did the same for merchants and shopkeepers who had to reduce the scale
of their businesses because of the excessively high tariffs.[20] Significantly,
the advocacy of free trade – to make possible cheaper food for the working class, and to help defend the smaller concerns against the protectionist

priorities of big business – was standard on the platforms of most republican parties.[21] Republican meetings were held and branches were opened not only in the major cities, but also in remote towns and villages and in working-class quarters. The Radical-Socialist Party, for example, was present in the working-class district of Chamartín,[22] and in the most remote provincial towns.[23] Appeals were made not only to dogmatic provincial intellectuals, but also to workers and small peasants whose land tenure was to be protected from both 'red' demagogy and the 'appetite' of the big landowners.[24] Another republican group that was thought to be exclusively concerned with intellectuals and the professional classes, Acción Republicana, went out also to make some gains among the lower classes. Its representative in Almería spread among the local working class his party's message: to curb rising prices by a cut in indirect taxes – of which merchants and small entrepreneurs were also highly resentful – to improve wages and to divide the big latifundia.[25]

Indeed, republicanism had also spread into typically rural districts. The Derecha Republicana made some gains among the vine-growers of Alicante through its campaign against the importation of French wines, which hit local agricultural interests.[26] In 1926, the Catalan tenants' association, Unió de Rabassaires, with its 14,000 members, had joined Alianza Republicana, which by then claimed a membership of 99,043 spread in 450 branches throughout the country[27] (in August 1929, membership rose to 150,000).[28] Alianza's effort to strike roots in rural areas continued through a display of interest in agrarian issues by its leaders. Lerroux, Azaña and lesser figures attended meetings in support of small tenants and landowners in rural districts in Almería, Cáceres, Badajoz, Ciudad Real and Old Castile.[29] Stability of tenancies, the creation of rural co-operatives and of centres for rural education were the core of the 1930 propaganda campaign of another party affiliated to Alianza, the Autonomous Republican Party of Córdoba.[30] The republicans of Palencia and Burgos, both wheat-growing areas, campaigned against the importation of wheat as likely to ruin Castilian farmers, a platform also subscribed to by the Agrupación Republicana de la Provincia de Zamora.[31] In the region of Valencia, the powerful Unión Republicana Autonomista de Valencia (112 branches throughout the region) espoused the cause of the orange growers in the area, and campaigned specifically for trade agreements that would boost the export of oranges.[32] A certain amount of headway was also made by republicanism in poverty-stricken, rural Galicia. The Organización Republicana Gallega Autónoma (ORGA), founded in March 1930, concerned itself with issues such as the abolition of the *foro* (a *minifundista* land tenure) and the need to uproot the notorious influence of the *caciques* of Bugallal in the area.[33]

The republican parties were certainly attractive to the professional classes, especially in the provincial capitals where the teacher, the physician, the engineer and the lawyer simply did not earn enough to make a decent living. As was the case under Italian Fascism, lawyers were especially shocked by the lawless practices of the Spanish monarchy in its later years, as were teachers by the clerical hegemony in the educational system, and engineers by the sudden end of what would long be remembered as an era of cement, dams, roads and bridges, which, given the popular appeal of republicanism, they had every reason to expect would be resumed by the Republic. But, no less important, republicanism for members of the liberal professions was the vehicle by which they could manifest their political independence after years of stifling autocracy.[34]

The Spanish 'Republic of students and professors'[35] had its roots in the fear of 'vocational prospectlessness' that stemmed from the strain on job opportunities for academics after 1929, and in a revulsion against the striking incompatibility between clerical obscurantism, social backwardness and political paternalism on the one hand and the trends of modernization on the other. The liberal intelligentsia, not just the lesser intellectuals but the greatest names of Spanish thought and letters, supported the Republic in its search for the culture of freedom. As for the student rebellion with its liberal Republican, sometimes even *Marxisant*, subculture and its challenge to orthodox values, it was a largely bourgeois phenomenon that, fed as it was by 'a renaissance of political literature',[36] responded to the widening generational gap that has been everywhere a concomitant of modernization and change.[37]

The crisis of confidence in the old order was shared as well by many in the so-called higher, 'respectable' classes. Indeed, as in France where the Thiers and the MacMahons had made possible the advent of the Third Republic, so in Spain republicanism came to mean for many in the upper classes of Spanish society, the institutionalization of an orderly democracy as a barrier against the 'red menace'. Alcalá Zamora, the grand Andalusian *cacique*, whose conversion to republicanism 'increased in geometric progression the enthusiasm for the Republic' especially among the *clases acomodadas*,[38] indeed viewed himself and other conservatives such as Miguel Maura as the Spanish Hindenburgs and Thiers who had made possible the Republics in their countries.[39] Support for the Republic from the upper middle class was evident also in Catalonia. There were those who defected from the Lliga – a leader of this party, Vallés i Pujals, shocked his listeners when he declared that 90 per cent of Lliga members were actually republicans[40] – to find in republicanism an outlet for their frustration at the monarchy's failure to accept cultural and political Catalanism. The incorporation of middle and upper middle-class republican Catalanism (Acció Catalana and Acció Republicana) as well as its more popular brand (Estat Català) into an all-Spanish revolution was a major achievement of the republican movement. It had thus neutralized the threat of an all-out separatist rebellion and had at last created the most credible preconditions so far for an institutional solution to Catalonia's grievances.[41]

However, republicanism was not just a petty bourgeois concern or a comfortable refuge for upper-class defectors from the monarchy. It was keenly attentive to, indeed allied with, the cause of the working class, which in Catalonia meant resurgent anarcho-syndicalism. It was no mean achievement for the republican movement to have harnessed the CNT to a peaceful transition to democratic government.[42] The Portuguese Republic had also initially enjoyed the support of the working class, but this was due mainly to the messianic belief of the urban masses in the Republic as a panacea for all maladies.[43] To be sure, such a Messianic myth was also widespread in Spain.[44] The Portuguese Republic, however, came into being devoid of the solid basis provided to its Spanish counterpart by a well disciplined republican Socialist movement, which had just emerged from the dictatorship strengthened and confident in its possibilist tactics.[45] Rather than a diffuse drive for change, the republican revolution in Spain was embodied in a rational, attainable, coalitional consensus of views and interests. The very heterogeneity of the republican alignment constituted, to use an expression of Miguel Maura, 'the mattress' upon which the Republic was to land softly.[46] In Portugal, in contrast, the declaration of the Republic was accompanied by an explosion of passions, a wave of crimes and even vandalism.[47]

Nevertheless, it can be argued that a potential threat to the future of the Republic lay in the fact that the republican movement was not heterogeneous enough. Thus, for example, the agrarian workers in the south, who suffered most from unemployment and the economic depression,[48] played too small a role in the political revolution that brought about the Republic. The Socialists, who provided the republican movement with a solid and responsible working-class *point d'appui*, had now returned to the countryside to reorganize, through the FNTT, their rural sections. But they did not seek to stir up passions among day-labourers, nor did the latter engender, in the early days of the Republic, the overwhelming protest that would have brought home to the Socialists and to the provisional government the inadequacy of gradualism in the countryside. The Socialists, therefore, believed that the extension to the countryside of the social legislation they had been able to wrest from the dictatorship and a non-violent agrarian reform would be absolutely compatible with the progressive Republic to which they lent their support.[49] In 1931, as Largo Caballero's early legislation was bringing about a substantial improvement in rural wages and in lease conditions,[50] there was no reason to doubt the validity of this prognosis; it was only later, well into the Republic, that agrarian reform seemed to be incapable of parliamentary solution.

But Socialist moderation was not just a piece of social-democratic doctrinairism. In 1931 Spain had just emerged from what would long be remembered as an era of relative prosperity and full employment. And though in the aftermath of Primo de Rivera's dictatorship, Spain would by no means escape economic maladies, it would be wrong to accept the alarmist view that the Republic's destiny was conditioned by the fact that it was born straight into the unfriendly arms of a catastrophic world economic crisis. The Spanish crisis of 1929 was not a catastrophic 'crash'. Throughout, the Spanish depression was a 'notably less profound phenomenon than the world depression. It neither paralleled the latter in its beginnings nor in its end, nor in its most substantial and typical vicissitudes.'[51]

Undoubtedly, a challenge to the viability of the future Republic lay in the fact that before it even started it was denied the support of the agrarian middle classes, let alone of the latifundist magnates. Unlike the case of the Third French Republic where democracy was based on the peasants who, as Jules Ferry noted, became republican precisely because they were conservatives,[52] the bulk of the Spanish middle and small land-holders (like the German Farmers' League at the turn of the century)[53] had already been drifting away from mere conservatism towards un-mistakable pre-fascist postures before the declaration of the Republic.

   True, the republicans' anti-clericalism, however it might have been played down on the eve of the municipal elections, could not be expected to be palatable to the members of the Confederación Nacional Católico-Agraria, the Liga Nacional de Campesinos or the Secretariado Nacional Agrario. But, it was these organizations' fundamental, unyielding denial of the precepts of parliamentary democracy, a denial made abundantly clear before any tangible threats to their religious sensi-bilities were evident, that lay at the root of their refusal to lend their active support to the Republic, however conservative this might be.[54] In the April municipal elections no threatening language was used by the republicans. A moderate Republic was proposed, the Church was assured that religion would not be persecuted, order was promised to capitalists and investors, and the working class was presented as the guardian of a bourgeois Republic.[55] Employers were indeed said to be delighted with the admirable discipline shown by the working class in the process of transition to the Republic.[56] But in spite of the remarkable moderation of the republicans, a coalition of Catholic agrarians, monarchists, and authoritarians who had served the dictatorship made it clear that, in their view, the forthcoming Republic would be the avenue to inevitable disaster. They portrayed the Republic as a barbarian invasion that would eliminate hispanic civilization and would enthrone 'the darkest instincts of man'. They laid the ideological foundations of a crusade against the 'anti-Spain' by rejecting in advance any unfavourable verdict at the poll. It was the very acquisition of power by democratic means, before any 'sectarian' legislation could even be promulgated, that constituted an invitation to civil war.[57] The Agrarian-Catholic organ *El Debate* viewed the municipal elections as 'a communist assault on the established order'.[58] The conservative *ABC* had warned, as early as 7 April, of an 'imminent civil war' if the Republic was declared, and before the new ministers had even time to settle firmly in the saddle, Acción Nacional labelled the new regime as 'a class dictatorship'.[59]

But in the euphoric days of April, the violence of the right could only be verbal as its institutional, as distinct from its socio-economic, power was almost non-existent. The Spanish Republic was the result of a peaceful nationwide plebiscite, preceded by a surprisingly sophisticated electoral campaign.[60] Not only did the republicans win a landslide victory in 45 out of 52 provincial capitals,[61] where they drew their votes from proletarian, middle-class, and even upper-class quarters,[62] but they also managed to win the day and shatter the grip of *caciquismo* in the more populated villages of such typically *caciquista* strongholds as the provinces of Jaen, Seville, La Coruña, Lugo, Orense, Cáceres and Badajoz, for example.[63] The student who cares to take the trouble of going through the papers of the Ministry of the Interior in the months that preceded the elections would be struck by its absolute disorientation and by the extent to which this once omnipotent ministry had lost control of the electoral machine.

Those who claim that the Republic was doomed because Spain was not republican in April would surely have to accept that it was not positively monarchist either. Neither the government nor the king found any consolation in the monarchist victory in rural districts (the overall results show in fact that the monarchists had outnumbered the left by a proportion of 3 to 1)[64] which represented, as the Minister Gabriel Maura put it, nothing but a sheep-like obedience orchestrated by *caciquismo*.[65] The Duque de la Mortera was probably more aware of the false nature of the monarchy's support than the believers in 'the mysterious shift of opinion' of April which implied that the monarchy had lost a public support which, in reality, it had never possessed. The view that regimes fall less because of the overwhelming strength of the opposition than because of their own weakness should not be elevated to the status of a dogma. In the present case, at least a shift of emphasis should be allowed. It was the strength of the opposition that lay at the root of the monarchy's loss of nerve. The Republic, according to the Minister of War, General Berenguer, was the result of 'the logical course imposed by the supreme national will'.[66] In similar vein, the Chief of Police, General Mola, saw it as 'an undisputable expression' of that will.[67] In 1923, Primo de Rivera had staged a last-ditch defence of

the authoritarian monarchy when it seemed to be challenged by democratic pressures. Now, however, it was defeated by them. 'The Mauser
gun', as Romanones acknowledged, was 'no longer the adequate
response to the manifestation of suffrage.'[68] Rather than as the result of
a temporary, or even accidental, loss of nerve by the monarchist establishment, the Republic was the culminating point of a process of civil
awakening and modernization that had been constantly eroding the
foundations of autocratic politics since, at least, the Great War.

The Second Republic was undoubtedly made possible by the attitude
of the army. Azaña had nothing but praise for the 'patriotism and discipline' displayed by the military in the process of transition to democracy.[69] The army, or rather its officer corps, had definitely lost the
'monarchist cohesion of the past'.[70] Neither among the generals, nor at
the level of local garrisons would volunteers be found to stage a last-
ditch defence of the monarchy. The army was certainly not united in a
positive attitude towards the new regime. Therefore, 'abstentionism'
seemed to be the best way to avoid not only a confrontation with the
people – a fairly new factor in the considerations of potential *coup*-
makers in Spain – but also the possibility that soldiers might have to fire
upon their brothers-in-arms. Moreover, the experience of the dictatorship had shown the military that, at least for the time being, the philosophy of the barracks was an inadequate instrument of government, and
head-on policies would not solve complex economic and social problems. It was, indeed, during the dictatorship and its immediate aftermath that important sections of the army had definitely renewed the old
nineteenth-century alliance between liberalism and the military.[71] In
1931 the military looked at their recent authoritarian model, Primo de
Rivera's dictatorship, as a highly discredited affair. In short, if the
military aspect is seen in isolation, all the conditions were there in 1931
for welding a durable alliance between the new regime and the army. It
is in subsequent decisions and policies that the cause for the wrecking of
this fragile understanding should be looked for.

One cannot condemn the Republic for its sectarianism and at the
same time argue that the heterogeneity of the republican movement
heralded inevitable catastrophe once the Republic was faced with the
need to reconcile opposing interests.[72] The provisional government
represented a prudent drive to substitute a coalitional consensus for the

rule of an authoritarian monarchy that was strikingly out of tune with a rapidly changing society. Not even the fact that the working class 'filling' of the republican 'mattress' consisted of two antagonistic organizations, the UGT and the CNT, can be seen as inherently self-destructive. The CNT had long abandoned its political virginity, assuming it had ever possessed it. It had in the past collaborated with the Socialists and with bourgeois republicans, and its masses were much more 'rational' and syndically oriented than is sometimes assumed.[73]

The process of immediate transition to republican government cannot be seen as heralding inevitable catastrophe. It has been frequently said that the new regime was doomed because, among other things, it was a 'Republic without republicans'.[74] Indeed, many who joined the Republic after it had been established were superficial converts to republicanism, thirsty for jobs and official favour. It was largely this phenomenon of *a posteriori* republicanism (the new republicans were sometimes called *adherentes* or 'the quarter-past zero hour republicans')[75] that accounts for the spectacular growth of the republican parties after April 1931.[76] But there is nothing unique in the inundation of the institutions of new regimes by last-minute converts. Such a phenomenon has been a concomitant of virtually every political transition. How would one otherwise explain the growth of such parties as the UCD in present Spain and Christian Democracy in post-war Italy and Germany? Ex-monarchists like Santiago Alba and Chapaprieta, together with their political clientele, joined the Republic in an attempt to make it acceptable to conservative opinion.[77] The threat to the viability of new democratic regimes does not lie in the understandable, indeed 'inevitable', influx of *a posteriori* converts to its institutions. It might lie, however, in the espousal of the clamorous demands of militants of all sorts to turn the new regime into an exclusive club in which the spoils should be shared by the 'authentic revolutionaries'. The response of the Spanish Republic to the pressures of self-styled 'authentic' republicans was altogether pragmatic.[78]

The much debated issue of the 'republicanization of the Republic' was approached by the provisional government in such a way that maintained the accessibility of republican institutions to non-republicans while at the same time trying not to lose the goodwill of the masses. One can even argue that, like Weimar, the Spanish Republic had seriously undermined its prospects of survival by doing so little, if anything, in the way of a political purge of the civil service. Admittedly not always faithfully executed, Miguel Maura's circular letter explicitly prohibiting the dismissal of civil servants on grounds of political allegiance[79] was nevertheless an accepted guideline.[80] Even an organization such as the Confederación Nacional Católico-Agraria, which made no secret of its contempt for the Republic, received ample representation in the institutions of the newborn Republic.[81] The May municipal elections represented Maura's most determined attempt so far, indeed under popular pressure, to 'republicanize' the rural strongholds of the old regime (7612 republicans and only 951 monarchists were elected in the May by-elections).[82] Nevertheless, the fact that the composition of hundreds of *ayuntamientos* in which about 18,000 monarchist councillors had been elected in April under Article 29 was not altered in May, and the evidence of many republican branches opposing Maura's insistence on new elections in their respective councils, indicates that the elections were not intended to undermine the possibility of working out a political framework that could be acceptable to the majority of Spaniards. That republicans had assured their predominance in hundreds of rural *ayuntamientos* by substituting for monarchist *caciquismo* their own brand of electoral management is clear.[83] But it is also evident that the ground gained by the republicans in May and later in the June general elections was owing to the appearance of what the understandably amazed monarchist politician, Romanones, called 'a truly admirable mass of voters';[84] in other words, it resulted from the fact that the transition from a system that rested on political apathy to one which relied on democratic mobilization had enhanced the politicization of the masses in a way never achieved before.[85] In that sense, at least, it would not be right to accept the view held by some Spanish writers that the Republic was nothing but 'the last disguise of the Restoration'.[86]

However, mass politicization was to underline one of the Republic's greatest problems and one that has been shared by virtually every political revolution in its initial stages, that is, how to reconcile the high expectations of its popular base with the compromising imperatives of power. The attribution by the masses of almost magical powers to what was essentially a political revolution undoubtedly heralded a grand disillusion. The seizure of power by a coalition of gradualist social democrats and bourgeois republicans whose energy was disproportionately devoted to the religious issue, not only could not be expected to usher in the millennium, but also hardly indicated that it was about to radically remodel Spanish society. Disappointment with *La niña bonita*, 'the pretty girl,' as the Republic was nicknamed, was 'extremely probable' also because it represented for many, especially among its intellectual supporters, a belief in an ideal government which could not exist. The promotion of friends and relatives and the discrimination against political opponents was seen as a reprehensible return to the practices of the old regime.[87] These practices and such disappointments were not peculiar to the Spanish Republic; they constitute the anticlimax of many political revolutions, including some that outlived the Second Republic.

It is now an established truism that the first *bienio* failed in a most tragic way to provide the Republic with 'social content'; its obsession with orthodox economics was strikingly incompatible with its professed intentions to improve the lot of the destitute masses. It may even be that the issue of agrarian reform was not susceptible at all to parliamentary solution. It is also obvious that the Republic's unnecessarily harsh approach to the religious issue was self-defeating. Notwithstanding its unmistakable apprehension at the coming of the Republic, the Church called for 'obedience to the constituted power' and was looking for some kind of accommodation with the new regime.[88] The dialogue between the Church and the Republic was not intrinsically 'impossible'.[89] It became so only because the Republican left worked under the deceptive premise that the secularization of Spanish society had reached the stage where an incisive nationalistic reaction could be discarded. The Republic thus awkwardly fed the build-up of the forces of its enemies.

In the first months of the new regime the provisional government did not seem to be conducting suicidal policies in any sense, or committing the Republic to an irreversible course of disaster. Unlike its counterpart in the Portuguese Republic, Alcalá Zamora's government followed throughout a compromising yet optimal policy of reforms on labour, agrarian and military questions, while relegating issues of a structural and constitutional nature to the sovereignty of parliament.[90] Even the sudden outbreak of mob anti-clericalism in the second week of

May was not allowed to wreck the unity of the government over such a sensitive issue as Church–State relations; nor did the evident pressure of the extremists for an outright radicalization of the Republic divert the government from its consistent, albeit uneasy, path of compromise.[91] It was likewise no mean achievement of the provisional government to have been able to curb the separatist flare-up in Catalonia in the days following the declaration of the Catalan Republic.[92] Basque regionalism was far less of a burning question in 1931. Moreover, contrary to what the founders of the Republic initially feared, it soon became clear that there was no intrinsic or inevitable contradiction between the democratic Republic and Basque nationalism.[93]

The pragmatism of the provisional government, however, could not be maintained for long. A great threat to the viability of the young Republic lay perhaps in the high degree of doctrinal commitment that permeated its parties and personalities. Nor was the right's Manichaean view of the Republican take-over likely to enhance the prospects of survival of the new regime. What enabled the Third French Republic to live for so long was perhaps the consensus of pragmatism, even cynicism and corruption that characterized its body politic. In Spain, the Republic was to be torn apart by issues and ideologies. The passing, by the politicians of the Third Republic, of an appalling amount of legislation without much debate or discussion and the cynical gap between their professed principles and their practical politics would have been inconceivable in the Spanish milieu.

Spanish conservatives were formed from a clay different from that of their French counterparts, who were ready to provide the Republic with a stable rural backbone. The new constitution was unacceptable to them not only because it was anti-religious, but also because it was liberal and democratic. Gil Robles fulminated in the summer of 1933 that 'hardly an article of the Republic's legislation will be saved when the rightist reaction comes, a reaction that every day promises to be more terrible and intense, a total rectification will be carried out; nothing will be left as it is'.[94] Gil Robles and his ilk did not come to politics just to defend threatened interests but rather to impose eternal values. From the very early days of the Republic, when the provisional government was painfully entangled in a struggle for a 'possible' Republic, the fight against the new regime was being conceived by the

Catholic-Agrarian right as a battle against a foreign invader, the agents of which in Spain were, as the Agrarian deputy Domingo de Arrese put it, 'Judaizing' and 'bolshevizing' parties. The Republic was viewed as the 'tyrannical empire of a class dictatorship',[95] for the destruction of which, 'like in war', a leveé en masse of the forces of the right should be called for.[96] An 'unyielding repugnance', to put it in Gil Robles' words, was what they felt towards the new regime.[97] It was not just the constitution that was 'born dead for them', it was the Republic itself. One can argue that the rejection by the Catholic-Agrarian right of the possibility, brought forward by Maura in the early days of the Republic, that they might join forces with the Derecha Republicana in order to hold in check the 'impetuousness' of the left, was a decision which prevented the 'balanced' Republic they allegedly fought for, from being forged at all.[98]

Yet notwithstanding the tragic indifference of the left to the religious sensibilities of the right, and the latter's Manichaean vision of politics, it would be inadequate to dwell excessively on the presumed 'pathological' or inherently self-destructive roots of the Spanish Republic as an explanation for its eventual collapse. Unless they want to spare themselves the trouble of going through the sometimes labyrinthine crises of the Republic, historians do not have to resort to a priori reasons in order to explain its eventual breakdown. On 14 April everything was possible, including 'peace'. The Republic had certainly inherited severe social, religious and regional cleavages. But the mere existence of these problems cannot be taken as a recipe for inevitable disaster. The coming of the Republic and its initial consolidation represented the most determined and the most widely representative attempt so far to create a framework in which Spain's fundamental problems could be made susceptible to democratic solution.[99] The Republic's ultimate failure was not irreversibly conditioned by structural imperatives or by any intrinsic incapability of the Spaniards for self-government. It was caused by policies, some obviously bad and highly inadequate, and by the reaction to them. No democracy can survive for long the challenge posed by the insistence of an important section of society – either on the right or on the left – to substitute the politics of conspiracy and retraimiento for that of participation.

Notes

1 Stanley Payne in *Journal of Modern History*, LI, 4 (December 1979), 831.
2 R. de la Cierva, *Historia de la guerra civil española*, 1 (Madrid, 1969), 145–9.
3 Duque de Maura y Melchor Fernández Almagro, *¿Por qué cayó Alfonso XIII?* (Madrid, 1948), 396–8. For a summary of the 'inevitability' theses, see Santos Juliá, 'El fracaso de la república', *Revista de Occidente*, 7–8 (November 1981), 196–7.
4 E. Malefakis, *Agrarian Reform and Peasant Revolution in Spain* (Yale, 1970), 396.
5 Amando de Miguel, *La pirámide social española* (Barcelona, 1977), 26.
6 Juan Díez Nicolás, *Tamaño, densidad y crecimiento de la población en España* (Madrid, 1971), 19; *Anuario Estadístico de España* (1929), pp. XX–XXI; J. A. Lacomba, *Ensayos sobre el siglo XX español* (Madrid, 1972), 46.
7 An Assembly member from Palencia, quoted in Miguel Primo de Rivera, *Intervenciones de la Asamblea Nacional* (Madrid, 1930), 157. The flight from the countryside developed as follows:
   1901–10 – 949,000; 1911–20 – 878,000; 1921–30 – 1,169,000; 1931–40 – 804,000; 1941–50 – 1,054,000; 1951–60 – 2,295,000.
   See Alfonso Barbancho, *Las migraciones interiores españolas, Estudio cuantitativo desde 1900* (Madrid, 1967), 43.
8 Primo in his *Intervenciones*, 146–51.
9 Antonio Monedero in *Diario de Sesiones de la Asamblea Nacional*, (23 November 1927).
10 Gabriel Maura, *Bosquejo histórico de la Dictadura* (Madrid, 1930), 9; J. Martínez Cuadrado, *Elecciones y partidos políticos de España 1868–1931* (Madrid, 1969), II, 799–816, 820.
11 Douglas Wheeler, *Republican Portugal* (University of Wisconsin Press, 1978), 62–3.
12

	Agriculture	Industry	Services
1910	66%	15.82%	18.18%
1920	57%	21.94%	20.81%
1930	45.51%	26.51%	27.98%
1960	39.70%	32.98%	27.32%
1973	23.80%	36.20%	39%
1975	20.80%	37.70%	40.40%

   Cf. *Estadísticas Básicas de España, 1900–1970* (Madrid, 1975), 369; Instituto de Cultura Hispánica, *La población activa española de 1900 a 1957* (Madrid, 1957); *Anuario Estadístico* (1976), 285.
13 Javier Ruiz Almansa, 'La población de España', *Revista Nacional de Economía* (Madrid, January 1930), 347.
14 Henry Buckley, *Life and Death of the Spanish Republic* (London, 1940), 26.
15 *El Socialista*, 16 December 1928.

16 La Cierva, op. cit., 146.
17 Cf. José Antonio Maravall, 'Todos éramos republicanos', *Historia-16*, 60 (April 1981), 94.
18 E. Mola, *Obras completas* (Valladolid, 1940), 480.
19 *ABC*, 4 April 1930.
20 For the agitation among small entrepreneurs and its political implications, see for example *Boletín de la Cámara de Comercio de Madrid*, January–April 1931; *Boletín de la Camara Oficial de Industria de la Provincia de Madrid*, April 1931; *El Mercantil Patronal*, September 1930, February 1931; *Nueva España*, 14 November 1930.
21 See, for example, *El Progreso*, 20 June 1930; *ABC*, 20 July 1930 (Estat Català); *El Progreso*, 3 October 1929; 1 January, 10–12 July 1930 (Radicals).
22 *Heraldo de Chamartín*, 20 February 1930.
23 For meetings across the country, see *Alianza. Boletín de Alianza Republicana*, April 1930. For branches, see *El Sol*, 7, 9 May; 16, 28 August; 3, 9 September 1930.
24 Salamanca Archive: *PRRS; Ideario aprobado por unanimidad en el congreso nacional celebrado los días 25–27 de Septiembre de 1930*.
25 *Nueva España*, 14 November 1930.
26 *El Luchador*, Alicante, 16 October 1930.
27 *Alianza Republicana, El 11 de Febrero de 1926* (Madrid, 1926).
28 *El Progreso*, 23 August 1929.
29 Archivo Histórico Nacional, Gobernación, serie A, leg. 45: 'Actos celebrados en provincias por republicanos en 11 de febrero 1930; *Alianza*, February–October 1930.
30 *Alianza*, May 1930.
31 *El Norte de Castilla*, 12 June 1930.
32 *Nueva España*, 1 March 1930; *Alianza*, June–July 1930.
33 *Nueva España*, 28 November 1930; *Alianza*, April, June–July 1930. See also Vicente Risco, *El problema político de Galicia* (Madrid, 1930), 189–90, 229–30.
34 For the professional classes, see 'La república: el sentido de una evolución social' in *La Voz de Galicia*, 25 April 1931. Cf. Félix Huerta, *Sombre la Dictadura* (Madrid, 1930), 75. The minimum wages decreed in 1928 for the industrial workers were higher than those earned by teachers: AHN, Presidencia del Gobierno, leg. 320: Rufino Carpena to Primo de Rivera, 7 December 1928. *Boletín del Colegio de Abogados de Madrid* (1930–1). Cf. Q. Saldaña y García, *Al servicio de la justicia. La orgia aurea de la Dictadura* (Madrid, 1930).
35 S. Ben-Ami, 'La rebellion universitaire en Espagne (1927–1931)' *Revue d'Histoire Moderne et Contemporaine* (July–September 1979), 365–90.
36 *La Epoca*, 12 March 1929.
37 Jiménez de Asúa, *Al servicio de la nueva generación* (Madrid, 1930); and his

Juventud (Madrid, 1929). Cf. 'El estudiante como fuerza social', *Nueva España*, 2 January 1931.

38 ibid., 1 September, 18 October 1930.

39 Alcalá Zamora in *El Sol*, 15 April 1930.

40 *El Imparcial*, 27 March, 6 July 1930.

41 Ben-Ami, *The Origins of the Second Republic in Spain* (Oxford, 1978), 61–7, 76–84.

42 José Peirats, *Los anarquistas en la crisis política española* (Buenos Aires, 1964), 27–31; *Solidaridad Obrera*, 12 April 1931; Mola, *Obras*, 760.

43 Douglas Wheeler, op. cit., 64–7.

44 Cf. Simon Sánchez Montero, 'La fuerza arrolladora del pueblo', *Historia-16*, 60 (April 1981), 62.

45 Ben-Ami, *The Origins*, ch. III.

46 *El Sol*, 30 May 1931.

47 V. de Bragança-Cunha, *Revolutionary Portugal* (London, n.d.), 142–52.

48 See, for example, Ministerio de Trabajo y Previsión, *La Crisis agraria andaluza de 1930–31* (Madrid, 1931), 15–16 (about 100,000 unemployed).

49 This view was constantly reported in the debates of the UGT's national executive. *Boletín de la UGT* (1930–1).

50 Malefakis, *Agrarian Reform*, 166–71.

51 Banco de España, *Ritmo de la crisis económica española en relación con la mundial* (Madrid, 1934). The quotation is on p. 35.

52 T. Zeldin, *France 1848–1945* (Oxford, 1973), I, 629.

53 Cf. Hans-Jurgen Puhle, 'Conservatism in Modern German History', *Journal of Contemporary History*, vol. 13, no. 4, October 1978, 702–7.

54 Juan José Castillo, *Propietarios muy pobres* (Madrid, 1979), 197–20, 255–64. For the SNA see their organ *España Agraria*, 1929–31.

55 See the left's electoral manifestos in *El Liberal*, 8 April 1931; *El Socialista*, 7, 10, 11 April 1931.

56 *El Eco Patronal*, 1 May 1931.

57 See extracts of the right's propaganda in *El Debate*, 7–11 April 1931; *ABC*, 10–12 April 1931; and *Propaganda electoral en contra de las candidaturas republicanas*, Hemeroteca Municipal de Madrid, A/1681.

58 *El Debate*, 10 April 1931.

59 ibid., 7 May 1931.

60 Cf. Ben-Ami, *The Origins*, 218–38.

61 1037 republican councillors; 522 monarchists; 64 constitutionalists; 77 unidentified were elected in the capitals. See AHN, Gobernación, serie A, legs. 29, 30.

62 Maura, *¿Por qué?*, 377, 389.

63 Cf. Ben-Ami, *The Origins*, 311.

64 A summary of the results as they reached the Ministry of the Interior until the evening of the 14th of April: 29,953 monarchists; 8,855 republicans; 1,787 constitutionalists; 1,322 others. The number of councillors whose

affiliation was still unknown when the Republic was declared was 38,715. See AHN, Gobernación, serie A, legs. 29–31.

65 Maura, ¿Por que?, 387,389.

66 D. Berenguer, De la Dictadura a la República (Madrid, 1975), 319.

67 Mola, Obras, 849.

68 Ben-Ami, The Origins, 242.

69 ABC, 15 April 1931.

70 Maura, ¿Por qué?, 395; Romanones, Las últimas horas de una monarquía (Madrid, 1931), 79–80.

71 S. Ben-Ami, Fascism from Above (Oxford, 1983).

72 La Cierva, op. cit., 146.

73 Cf. A. Pestaña, Lo que aprendí en la vida (Madrid, 1934), 103–5; L'Humanité, 23 September 1924.

74 For a feuilletonistic expression of this view, see Julio Camba, Haciendo de república (Madrid, 1968).

75 España Republicana, 1 June 1931; España Libre, 5 June 1931.

76 See the case of the Radical-Socialists in Texto taquigráfica del tercer congreso nacional ordinario del PRRS, 29–40; and the Socialists in Boletín de la UGT, May–December 1931.

77 El Norte de Castilla, 19, 23 May 1931.

78 For such pressures, see El Defensor del Extrarradio, 4 June, 8, 20 July 1931; El 14 de Abril, 30 May 1931; Alcalá Zamora, Los defectos de la constitución de 1931 (Madrid, 1936), 48–9.

79 AHN, Gobernación, serie A, leg. 16, circular no. 188, 14 April 1931.

80 Ben-Ami, The Origins, 264–5, 268–9.

81 Juan José Castillo, Propietarios, pp. 363–4.

82 AHN, leg. 29, 31; El Sol, 2 June 1931.

83 Ben-Ami, The Origins, 271–5.

84 Romanones to Lorenzo Feliz, 30 June 1931, in Romanones Archive, leg. 2, no. 8.

85 For a local case, see C. Lisón-Tolosana, Belmonte de los Caballeros (Oxford, 1966), 43–7.

86 E. Aguado, La República último disfraz de la Restauración (Madrid, 1972).

87 España Republicana, 16 July 1931; C.T.T., 20 June 1931; J. del Moral, Oligarquía y enchufismo (Madrid, 1933).

88 See, for example, Boletín Oficial del Obispado de Madrid-Alcalá, 1 May 1931; R. Muntanyola, Vidal i Barraquer el cardenal de la paz (Barcelona, 1971), 186–8.

89 Víctor Manuel Arbeloa, 'Iglesia y república: diálogo imposible,' Historia-16, 60 (April 1981), 79–7.

90 See a thorough account of the reforms in G. Picard-Moch and J. Moch, L'Espagne republicaine (Paris, 1933) 254–75.

91 Ben-Ami, The Origins, 256–60.

92 M. Maura, Así cayó Alfonso XIII (Barcelona, 1962), 236–9.

93 J. P. Fusi, El problema vasco en la II república (Madrid, 1979), 36–57.

94 *El Debate*, 19 August 1933.
95 ibid., 7 May 1931.
96 ibid., 28 April 1931.
97 J. M. Gil Robles, *No fue posible la paz* (Barcelona, 1968), 79.
98 The issue is discussed by José Montero, *La Ceda. El catolicismo social y político en la II república* (Madrid, 1977), 1, 223–43.
99 See an excellent and thought-provoking article on the favourable conditions in which the Republic came to be: E. Malefakis, 'Peculiaridad de la República española', *Revista de Occidente*, November 1981, 17–37.

2
The Church's crusade against the Republic

Frances Lannon

Historians who base their account of the Catholic Church's relations with the Second Republic firmly but narrowly on the legislative record experience little difficulty in presenting the Church as the victim of gratuitous attack between the summer of 1931 and the end of 1933.[1] While the separation of Church and state, the introduction of civil marriage and divorce and even the gradual ending of state subvention of the clergy might be regarded as the profoundly distasteful but inevitable, and therefore ultimately acceptable, concomitants of the new regime, other measures belonged to a quite different category. In particular the disbanding of the Society of Jesus, the proposed introduction of a uniform state system of secular education and the prohibition of all members of religious congregations from teaching, constituted a direct assault on the ordinary rights of the Church and its members – an assault made all the more radical and indefensible for being mounted in and through the constitution itself.[2] Juxtaposing the legislation of the Constituent Cortes with executive decisions from the very early days of the Republic, most dramatically the irresponsibly slow and evidently unwilling reaction to the burning of churches and convents in May 1931,[3] gives added sharpness to this version of events. The Church, itself willing to negotiate and to accommodate – as demonstrated by the Vatican, the nuncio Tedeschini, and the acting head of the Spanish hierarchy Cardinal Vidal i Barraquer – was provoked into a defensive hostility to the sectarian governments and dominant parties of the first *bienio* which led naturally to its later general opposition (with conspicuous but limited exceptions) to the whole Republican side in the Civil War.[4]

It is not necessary to deny the accuracy of some parts of this version in order to disagree with its conclusions. The Vatican's unusual readiness to force the resignation of the primate of Spain, the inflexible and unrepentant monarchist Pedro Segura, cardinal archbishop of Toledo, was indeed a costly conciliatory gesture;[5] Tedeschini and Vidal i Barraquer carefully pursued loyal agreement with the new state in unpromising circumstances;[6] the collective pastoral letters of the hierarchy in December 1931 on the new constitution and in May 1933 on the proposed law regulating the religious congregations, expressed the necessary and expected protests with measured serenity.[7] All of this is beyond controversy. Nor does the interpretation of Church as innocent victim fail simply because it dismisses too easily the counter-evidence. Segura, for example, indulged in notoriously provocative actions while still cardinal primate: a pastoral letter of May 1931 praised the fallen monarchy; the supposedly collective pastoral letter written by him alone in the name of the hierarchy in July was a stridently worded reaction to the comparatively moderate clauses on religion in the first, doomed draft of the constitution; and his disastrously impolitic plans to safeguard Church property, if necessary by exporting capital, were discovered in August.[8] The problem is not the simple one of positivist accuracy, but the much more complex methodological one of the choice of appropriate material and time-scale as the basis for historical judgement. Legislation on the one hand and pronouncements by Church leaders on the other are too narrow a base. Equally, any interpretation of the Church under the Republic which begins with the fall of the monarchy in April 1931 establishes a chronology which in itself renders impossible a proper assessment of the Church's position.

If one compares Catholic reactions to the proclamation of the Republic with those in 1923 to the *coup* of Primo de Rivera, the widespread sympathy for autocratic government is undeniable.[9] At the level of the hierarchy, even the most sober, serene and apolitical statements on the need for Catholic loyalty to the Republic (let alone the apocalyptic tone of bishops like Segura, Gomá and Irurita) seem damning when set beside the enthusiasm of 1923. Cardinal Reig of Toledo called for prayers to help the task of 'regeneration', a response echoed by many bishops, including for example Cardinal Ilundáin of Seville who wrote of the patriotic aims of the new government, and its laudable desire to regenerate national life.[10] When the Catholic reforming conservative and monarchist Angel Ossorio y Gallardo repudiated the dictatorship as 'immoral and illiterate' he was not so much articulating an alternative Catholic response as embarking on his painful and often almost solitary career as apologist for a conservative but democratic and socially reforming Catholic option in Spanish politics.[11] It is true, of course, that Catholics found themselves in respectable and varied company in their welcome of Primo, since few at any point of the political spectrum – socialist, liberal, authoritarian, regionalist – lamented the demise of an ineffective and corrupt parliamentary system. Nevertheless, ecclesiastical rejoicing in 1923 throws into relief the misgivings of 1931.

It is apparent that Church leaders expected trouble under the Republic well before the convent and church burnings of May, and before the June elections returned a clearly anti-clerical majority of Socialists and Republicans to the Constituent Cortes.[12] It would be naive to imagine that these justified premonitions of attack could be traced simply to the known anti-clerical stance of some of the political parties. Just such a naive explanation was dismissed proleptically in 1930 by the pioneer in social Catholicism Canon Maximiliano Arboleya Martínez. Reviewing the years since his own enthusiastic reception of Primo's *coup* in 1923 he lamented the passivity of Catholics who had treated the dictatorship as an invitation to rest rather than an opportunity for mobilization for political and especially social reform. Not only had Catholic unions with their paternalism and *amarillismo* (blacklegging) continued to serve as instruments of torture rather than liberation for workers, thereby pitting workers against the Church, but more generally Catholics had gained a reputation as enemies of democracy.[13] Arboleya's reflection is a useful reminder that any realistic assessment of the Church's position during the Republic must explore not only hierarchical statements, but the more complex question of Catholic attitudes and alignments within Spanish society on a whole series of issues which were not specifically religious. Among these the most crucial, because most central in the aspirations associated with the proclamation of the Republic, were democracy and social reform.

More revealing of attitudes to democracy than the sceptical comments of Catholics, both lay and clerical, on the futility of parliamentary talking-shops, which could be quoted in abundance, is the evidence of the programmes, propaganda and actions of the most powerful political grouping committed to the defence of the Church in the Republic, the CEDA (Confederation of Autonomous Right-Wing Groups). Acción Nacional, (later Acción Popular) which formed the basis of that later, massive confederation, defined its objectives as early as 7 May 1931 as the defence of religion against atheism and communism, of the fatherland against 'crazy' extreme local nationalisms, of the family against free love, of order against a 'class dictatorship', of work against a controlled labour market, and of private property against collectivization. Claiming to be an anti-revolutionary movement of social defence rather than a political party, it promised no more in constitutional terms than that it would act within the established political regime.[14] From the beginning, therefore, the political defence of the Church as ostentatiously championed by Acción Popular and then the CEDA stood in an ambiguous relationship to democratic commitment. The *acatamiento* or acceptance of the democratic system never even approximated to any declaration of loyalty to its principles, and indeed the vaunted 'accidentalism' of the parliamentary Catholic right deliberately left participation open to many whose monarchist and/or anti-democratic preferences were known to all.[15] Angel Herrera, the leader of the Catholic lay association that formed the nucleus of Acción Popular – the Catholic

National Association of Propagandists – apparently found no contradiction in calling for loyal acceptance of constituted authority in December 1931 while in the same speech arguing that 'radical democracy' was inappropriate in Spain and that the constitution should be substantially reformed along corporatist lines with a powerful executive more in keeping with the new style emerging in Europe.[16] By the end of 1933 the CEDA leader Gil Robles was more forthright: in an election speech he declared that

> We are about to put democracy to the test, perhaps for the last time. It does not matter to us. We are going to parliament to defend our ideals, but if tomorrow parliament is against our ideals we shall go against parliament, because in politics, not the forms, but the content is what interests us.[17]

'Acceptance' of the regime merely signified, at most, a formal tactical agreement to use Republican institutions, particularly parliament, to effect desired changes. It never included any declaration of sympathy for those democratic principles without which, in the eyes of its supporters, the Republic was emptied of its identifying content.

The Jesuit founder of the Propagandists Angel Ayala, affirmed unhesitatingly in an interview in 1952 that the political movements which had grown from Propagandist initiatives – Acción Popular and then the CEDA – had collaborated with the Republic but *not* in order to consolidate it.[18] Sharing that judgement from a different perspective, Ossorio y Gallardo found the inclusion of three CEDA ministers in the government in October 1934 intolerable, and concluded that the appointment of Gil Robles as Minister of War in 1935 virtually marked the demise of the Republic.[19] In the innovatory Catholic intellectual journal *Cruz y Raya*, José Bergamín denounced the demagogy and violence of the CEDA in its pitiless reaction to the rising of 1934, a demagogy and violence which he regarded as destructive of the state.[20] It was by no means only the revolutionary left in Catalonia and Asturias that considered CEDA objectives to be incompatible with the idea of a democratic Republic that attempted to be something more than just a regime without a monarch. And an analysis of CEDA programmes, CEDA accidentalism and Gil Robles's speeches reveals clearly that the parliamentary Catholic right remained unencumbered by democratic loyalties.[21] Since this political organization which held an accidentalist view of democracy was, by contrast, unwaveringly committed to promoting the institutional security of the Catholic Church in Spain, and through Herrera enjoyed close links with the nuncio and the Spanish hierarchy,[22] the relationship between Catholicism and democracy appeared, at best, fragile.

Fragility gave way to frank opposition among those Catholics who viewed Gil Robles's accidentalism as a perilous shilly-shallying likely to enervate the right's capacity to fight the Republic. In the dramatic parliamentary debates of the night of 13–14 October 1931 on the principal constitutional article on the Church, the Basque priest deputy Pildáin justified and threatened armed resistance.[23] Armed bands of Traditionalists were known to be training in militantly Catholic Navarre as early as 1931: by the spring of 1935 their numbers (including some trained in Italy) approached 6,000. Some local priests formed a junta to keep watch during clandestine, subversive meetings, and then graduated to small-scale bomb manufacture. Equally notorious is the meeting in March 1934 between Mussolini and representatives of the Traditionalists and Renovación Española which produced Italian arms and money for the planned rising.[24] While the interlocking groups of Traditionalists, Renovación Española and Acción Española remained sceptical of even an accidentalist acceptance of the democratic regime, they simultaneously challenged Gil Robles's right to be regarded as political spokesman for Catholic Spain. From 1933 to 1936 Renovación Española kept the Vatican informed of its view of events through almost monthly visits to Secretary of State Pacelli by Pedro Sáinz Rodríguez. This informal ambassador made no secret of his disapproval of Herrera, the CEDA, the nuncio Cardinal Tedeschini (memorably recalled later as resembling an Italian tenor taking the part of a cardinal) and cautious Vatican policy, all of which he regarded as relegating Catholics to the status of second-class citizens in Spain under a constitution there was no need to tolerate, even in the hope of gradual or eventual change.[25]

It is not surprising, then, that Sáinz Rodríguez in 1934 gladly contributed the prologue to a controversial book by Castro Albarrán, a canon of Salamanca, written to demonstrate the theological propriety of an armed rising. Castro Albarrán praised Segura, criticized Miguel Maura, the nuncio and the bishops for being in league with the revolution, introduced the section on rebellion with a provocative echoing of the Spanish Falangist hymn, scorned Herrera's *El Debate* and Gil Robles for the futility of their programme of opposition within legality, gloried in the fascist youth of Spain who 'were not prepared to weep like women for what we did not know how to defend like men', and invoked the grandeur of a patriotic and religious crusade.[26] This lengthy work appeared with the customary ecclesiastical licences guaranteeing doctrinal orthodoxy. Although an appeal to the Vatican by Vidal i Barraquer succeeded in having these removed, Gomá told a group of eminent Traditionalist and Renovación Española leaders who consulted him that in his opinion – he was by then archbishop of Toledo – it was theologically sound.[27]

However irenic and moderate the reception given to the Republic by many of the Church hierarchy, especially under the guidance of Vidal i Barraquer from 1931 to 1933, numerous Catholic voices loudly repudiated the democratic regime from the very beginning while many others, equally insistent on their Catholic credentials, continued to describe democracy as one option among many, to be judged by results. It was inevitable that Catholics should find some of the constitutional articles on religion deeply repugnant, and should conclude with Herrera's *El Debate* that 'The constitution . . . is not and will not be ours, of us Catholics. We are not within it. We are incompatible with it.'[28] But it was ominous that powerful political groups associated explicitly with Catholicism should have regarded democracy itself as, at most, a conditional commitment, instead of decisively accepting a democratic structure and campaigning for constitutional change within it.

There were some Catholic politicians whose democratic credentials were unassailable, but they were isolated. Miguel Maura, President Niceto Alcalá Zamora and Angel Ossorio y Gallardo, for example, remained leaders without followers, unable to rally a Catholic conservative democratic party. Groups with some claim to be classed as Christian Democrats (a title that is quite obviously inappropriate for the CEDA) were all regionally based and with restricted influence in Spain as a whole. Thus the Basque Nationalist party which had by the 1930s developed a firm democratic base and policy, could not hope to attract much interest or sympathy from Spanish Catholics who disliked its pursuit of Basque autonomy. Similarly the new Unió Democrática was of little significance outside Catalonia, and was not numerically strong even in Catalonia itself, where it had only one deputy in the Catalan parliament elected in 1932. Luis Lucía's party in Valencia owed much of its strength to its demand for regional autonomy, a preoccupation which necessarily limited its appeal to the area.[29] Moreover, this concern for regional autonomy taken to its logical and costly conclusion of opposition to the rising of July 1936 enabled hostile Catholic critics then and since to dismiss Lucía, the Unió Democrática and, most viciously, the Basque Nationalists, as misguided and perverse and so certainly disqualified as an alternative model of Catholic politics.[30] Away from a few peripheral areas, Catholicism and democracy seemed, when not mutual foes, easily separable allies.

The question of Catholic attitudes to social reform is highly complex. In 1935 the philosopher José Ortega y Gasset and the doyen of social Catholicism Severino Aznar formed part of the examining panel of a doctoral thesis on the meaning of social order according to St Thomas Aquinas, submitted by a canon of Córdoba cathedral, José Manuel Gallegos Rocafull. The successful thesis demonstrated lucidly that in Catholic moral theology derived from St Thomas, social order cannot be equated simply with the status quo. On the contrary, the central Thomistic argument that order means the adaptation of each thing to its proper end immediately implies a dynamic rather than static view. In the crucial case of private property, possessions have to serve a communal and not merely an individual purpose, and Thomas himself drew the inescapable conclusion of this instrumental view of wealth when he stated that 'in necessity, all things become communal'. In the light of such teaching, Gallegos Rocafull was able to argue that the true enemies of social order at the time he was writing were those who insisted on preserving an unjust status quo, while conversely the advocates of genuine order were precisely those who refused to accept the present economic regime. He was undoubtedly correct in claiming that for anyone who had not transcended a 'bourgeois' idea of order, St Thomas was a revolutionary.[31]

In February 1934 Bergamín's *Cruz y Raya* printed in full a translation of Emmanuel Mounier's presentation of his movement and journal *Esprit*, expressing his personalist philosophy with a clear dependence on Thomistic tradition. Opposing bourgeois individualism and fascism,

as well as total collectivism, Mounier lamented the way in which the
'bourgeois values' of money and private property had co-opted religion
to their defence, and called on Catholics in France to resist and change
the 'established disorder'.[32]

These theoretical formulations are useful in clarifying the decisive
issue in Catholic attitudes to social reform before and during the Republic, that is, the degree of willingness to identify desirable social order
with established property relationships. It was not enough for bishops
to go on quoting Leo XIII on workers' rights, the inequities of class
division and capitalism, and the Christian limits on property rights, in
appeals to the rich to act with charity and justice to undercut the
attractions of expanding Spanish socialism.[33] On social reform as on
democracy Catholics were necessarily judged by their actions rather
than by the sublimity of their aspirations. And the spheres of action
were clearly marked out in Spanish society in the first third of the
twentieth century, beginning with the all-important question of agrarian
reform and property relations on the land.

There is no dearth of material on the *latifundio* areas of central and
southern Spain that constituted the agrarian problem *par excellence*. The
work of the committee appointed in 1931 to prepare a project for
reform, especially the classic studies by one of its members, Pascual Carrión, and the detailed local investigations of the Institute of Social
Reform (founded in 1904) and the Central Junta for Internal Coloniz-
ation and Repopulation, provide all too clear a picture of widespread
misery and its causes.[34] Tracts of uncultivated land; a wasteful three-
field system (*tres hojas*) with only one-third cultivated at any one time;
scandalously low harvest yields; lack of fertilizers, irrigation and other
technical improvements; fertile land given over to raising fighting
bulls; absentee landlords; day-labourers living in appalling barracks
(*cortijos*) separated for months on end from their families; labourers
with little or no income in the winter months; emigration in despair of
landless labourers to seek a living elsewhere: the dimensions of the
disaster were well known. Ecclesiastical appeals to the large landowners
to take remedial action on their own initiative had proved futile. In
latifundio areas a series of reforms including compulsory cultivation,
higher and more regular wages, and at least some limited expropri-
ations by the state was obviously the minimum required if human

misery culminating sometimes in starvation was to be eradicated or even eased.

Those measures were entirely defensible on the basis of Catholic teaching on the right of workers to a wage capable of sustaining a family in decency, and on the social function of property. A self-proclaimed conservative like Ossorio y Gallardo argued on precisely that basis in 1920 for government intervention.[35] But Catholic organizations never faced the issue squarely. The CNCA (National Catholic Agrarian Confederation) enjoyed only slight and ephemeral success when in 1919 it attempted to establish syndicates in Andalusia. Its component federations, built up with the aid of Herrera's Propagandists and their Jesuit advisers, had flourished in the preceding years among the poor smallholders and tenant farmers of the north and centre, who were helped to maintain a precarious relative independence by its characteristic activities of providing cheap credit and fertilizers, and co-operatively owned machinery. But these ameliorative measures were irrelevant to the plight of landless labourers in the south.[36] This Catholic federation, although often critical of the egoism of large-scale landowners,[37] was unable to advocate expropriation or any other serious threat to existing property relations because of its own anti-socialist roots, its total commitment to the defence of private property and the dominating presence of rich landlords in its ranks. On the contrary, it was active in the local committees of Primo de Rivera's Patriotic Union in the 1920s, bolstering the regime's reactionary passivity in the *latifundio* countryside. When this passivity was modified in 1928 with the attempted introduction into the agrarian sector of worker participation in wage-fixing committees, the CNCA helped thwart the initiative.[38] CNCA parliamentary deputies opposed the Republic's agrarian reform of 1932 with its cautious use of strictly limited expropriation. Moreover its wealthy *latifundista* vice-president, the Traditionalist Lamamié de Clairac gained a shameful celebrity in December 1934 when he helped mutilate an already modest reform bill on agrarian leases presented by his fellow Catholic Giménez Fernández, while crudely proclaiming his preference for schism, if the alternative were the implementation by the Minister of Agriculture of social principles derived from papal encyclicals.

The agrarian record of the Catholic politicians grouped in Acción Popular and then the CEDA during the Republic – some of whom belonged to the agrarian federation – has been thoroughly scrutinized in recent years.[39] Although their leaders claimed an interest in social reform, they opposed the 1932 agrarian bill, demanded its repeal after the 1933 elections, and notoriously failed to close ranks in support of the CEDA minister Giménez Fernández during his attempts at significant but minimal reform in 1934–5. Defence of property rights brutally overrode all other considerations and the Minister of Agriculture's citing of Catholic moral theology proved ineffective, especially as Gil Robles, secretary-general of the Catholic agrarian federation as well as leader of the CEDA, declined to risk his political skin over the issue.[40] With fervent and proud defenders of the Church – if not of its teaching – in the CEDA, the Traditionalists and Renovación Española refusing to countenance even modest changes in the provocatively cruel and inefficient system of property relations in *latifundio* areas, it is a barren exercise for historians to claim that the Church itself was not anti-Republican. For its supporters, the Republic was a political shorthand for democracy and social reform, just as the monarchy it replaced had long been a political shorthand for government by élites in the interests of the propertied classes. Whatever the technically apolitical stance of the Church as an institution, Catholic politicians and Catholic voters behind them spelt out the equation in deeds: defence of the Church equals the defence of landed property rights, whatever the social cost, which in turn equals rejection in real terms of the necessarily reforming Republic.

No other social issue in Spain in the first third of this century rivalled in urgency or in violence the conflict over the land in the *latifundio* regions. Catholic intervention in industrial relations, however, followed a similar pattern to its role in the agrarian sector. Well-established basic principles of a just wage able to support a family, and decent living conditions, were reiterated in pastoral letters, in the Catholic Congresses at the turn of the century and Catholic Social Weeks from 1906 to 1911 and again in the 1930s. But, although the Catholic trade unions and their forerunners have still not been adequately studied, it is quite clear that from the time of Fr Vicent's Valencian workers' circles in the 1890s onwards, Catholic unions were primarily a defensive reaction against socialism. They were often involved in strike-breaking, were reluctant to jettison a paternalist structure for a more militant workers-only organization, and remained wary of the language and tactics of class conflict, even in circumstances where industrialists' policies rendered conciliatory methods quite useless.[41] Respect for order and property prevailed. It is not surprising that, with the local exceptions of the Basque Solidarity movement and the Catalan free unions, Catholic unions were puny in comparison with the anarchist CNT and the socialist UGT. The more radical stance of some priests involved in the unions, especially Gafo and Arboleya, was an inadequate counterweight to the long tradition of hopeful but ineffective co-operation with employers. Similarly, the startlingly direct adoption of the terminology, at least, of the class struggle and of direct, coercive and revolutionary action in industry by the small Unió Democrática in Catalonia in 1933[42] scarcely represented a serious Catholic alternative to the CEDA's insistence on dismantling recently enacted labour legislation after the 1933 elections. And *Cruz y Raya*'s bitter denunciations of the right's anarchic abuse of power and killing without cause in the brutal repression of the Asturias rising in October 1934 could not counteract Catholic approval of the repression as expressed by many Catholic representatives in parliament. While Catholic organizations in industry, in agriculture and in parliament combined defence of the institutional Church with the preservation of the established order, Catholic concern for social reform was bound to seem both vacuous and suspect, however sincere the subjective commitment of many lay people, priests and bishops, and however generous their dedication in countless kinds of welfare work.

Because so many Catholics in Spain both before and during the Republic were at best dubious democrats and unwilling to disturb the established disorder, an interpretation of the democratic and socially reforming Republic of 1931–3 as a gratuitous aggressor in relation to the Church rings false. Fears of the intrinsic antipathy of Catholics towards the political and social innovations embodied by the Republic were far from being mere spectres conjured up by anti-clerical fever. This is not to claim that the controversial articles on religion and the subsequent legislation were either wise or just. The brusque ending of state support of the clergy without adequate time for the Church to devise alternative methods of financing, invited epithets such as vindictive, soon supplied by the right – though I have seen no evidence to support the frequent suggestion that potential Republican loyalty existed among the poorer lower clergy and was alienated by this decision.[43] The dissolution of the Society of Jesus and the attempted appropriation of its sometimes already alienated property proved dangerously double-edged. Most difficult of all to justify on the Republic's own democratic principles was the legal assault on the religious congregations and especially the ban on their teaching activity. The law of June 1933 rapidly became a perfect illustration of the Spanish saying, 'hecha la ley, hecha la trampa' ('once the law is made, the evasive tricks follow'), as religious schools changed their names and their management and religious personnel donned lay dress while behind the new appearances life continued much as before.[44] This over-ambitious and ineffective law was necessarily intolerable to Catholics of all political persuasions, including those prepared to accept as inevitable the general de-confessionalizing of the state. But wider motives than dogmatic anti-clericalism, undoubtedly a powerful factor in the political creed of many groups on the left, inspired such sweeping measures. Catholic institutions and Catholic practice in Spain had a notoriously well-defined sociological and political shape, largely conformed to the conservative outlines of property, large and small. The Catholic schools which fell under such bitter attack, for instance, were in many cases ineluctably conservative of class divisions, and although non-political in their own self-understanding, immersed in and propagating an explicitly anti-liberal, anti-democratic tradition.[45] Republican distrust especially of the secondary schools run by the religious congregations, of the political and social ideology they expressed and the Catholic social structure they reflected, did not lack justification, even though its legal expression eventually did more harm to the Republic itself than to the Church.

If, then, one looks beyond legislation on the one hand and hierarchical statements on the other, and behind the over-restrictive chronology of 1931–6 (or even worse, 1931–3), it is evident that the relationship between the Republic and the Church was not that of gratuitous aggressor and innocent victim. Indeed the argument so far suggests that the opposite is closer to the truth and that the official declaration by the Spanish Church in July 1937 in defence of the 1936 rising and in opposition to the Republican cause in the Civil War has to be traced back beyond both the appalling massacre of religious personnel in Republican territory in the first months of the war and beyond the legislation of 1931–3 into the longstanding political values and socio-economic structures of Spanish Catholicism.[46] The argument that near-consensus among Catholics in 1936 (always with embarrassing exceptions, especially on the Basque, Catalan and Valencian periphery) is explicable simply on religious grounds as a response to the Republic's sectarianism and the terrifying anti-clerical violence in the weeks after 18 July is misleadingly myopic in focus.[47] It is important to recognize that the Church's implicit and explicit anti-Republicanism in the 1930s, culminating in its enthusiastic and notorious baptism of the generals' rising into a religious crusade was no more improvised or gratuitous than the Republic's anti-clericalism. The Church was essentially concerned with its own institutional survival and vigour, and its options to achieve this were limited severely by its own recent past as well as by the stance of its critics and enemies.

When Azaña declared in the Cortes on 13 October 1931 that Spain was no longer Catholic, he was not telling Church leaders anything they did not already know, protests and repudiations notwithstanding. In tradition, of course, Spain was Catholic, but in almost every aspect of national life the Church saw itself progressively losing ground. The intellectual battle, for example, was all but lost. Apart from the polymath Menéndez y Pelayo, the outstanding figures of Spanish literature, philosophy and art from the late nineteenth century onwards were not orthodox Catholics. Manuel de Falla and Miguel Hernández in music and poetry are exceptions that prove the rule. From Pérez Galdós to Lorca, Spanish intellectual life was dominated by men the Church could not claim as its own.

The educational system in Spain left Catholic leaders far from sanguine about the prospects of challenging that dominance. Although both the concordat of 1851 and the constitution of 1876 had guaranteed ideological control of education for the Church, in practice this had not been fully implemented. As early as 1881 confessional control of the universities had been irretrievably lost; in 1901 religion became an optional instead of obligatory subject in the *bachillerato*; in 1913 exemption from classes in religion was granted to children of parents who declared themselves not Catholic. The decisive threat to Catholic cultural hegemony appeared in 1923 with the mooted revision of the

1876 constitution in the direction of complete religious liberty. It stimulated an alarmed protest to the government by the united hierarchy whose position was, however, saved for a while by Primo de Rivera's *coup* later that year.[48]

Patterns of Catholic practice were equally discouraging, especially in the expanding cities and the impoverished rural south. Some contemporary clerical observers were well aware of the catastrophic dimensions of the problem. Canon Arboleya entitled the famous analysis of the Church's failure, which he presented to the Madrid Social Week in October 1933, 'The apostasy of the masses'. A Jesuit writing in 1935 cited the example of San Ramón parish in the working-class district of Vallecas in Madrid. Of a ludicrously unwieldy total of 80,000 parishioners, only 7 per cent attended Sunday Mass, and even that 7 per cent included the children in the parish schools; 6 per cent made their Easter duty; 10 per cent died with the Church's sacraments; 25 per cent of the children were not even baptized; of those wishing to marry in church, 40 per cent could not recite the 'Our Father'. The comparable parish of San Millán presented a similar picture. Fr Peiró analysed the Church's poor showing in the working-class areas of the capital and identified inadequate and anachronistic parochial structures – too many people, too few priests in expanding *barrios* – as one cause. In comments reminiscent of similar investigations of church attendance patterns in nineteenth-century industrial England, he described families who declined to go to church without shoes or a clean shirt, which they did not possess. But he also detected a deep-rooted mistrust of Catholicism as an essentially bourgeois-phenomenon, committed to the defence of property against workers' revindications, and hypocritical in the social morality it preached. And he warned Catholics against relying on political means, whether a coup, a dictatorship, or election victory, to re-Christianize the masses.[49] Similar conditions in cities like Barcelona and Bilbao were no secret, and accorded ill with any comfortable notion of a Catholic society.[50] And although Fr Peiró, like many religious commentators then and since, was possibly unwilling to allow that simple disbelief and boredom accounted for some of the statistics he gathered, his comments on the Church's class alignment help explain why so often non-practice was accompanied by active hatred of the Church, its representatives and its institutions.

If industrial workers in the expanding cities were often lost to the Church, the same was true of agricultural workers in the south. Cardinal Ilundáin's *ad limina* report to the Pope in 1932 told of villages in which few women and no men attended Sunday Mass.[51] In Neva, in the Riotinto mining area of the province of Huelva, 300 people out of a population of 18,000 were Sunday churchgoers; but in agricultural El Rosal de la Frontera on the Portuguese frontier the figure was an even more desolating three per thousand. Moreover, parish priests reported undisguised dislike of Catholic schools, and a superstitious fear of the last sacraments as likely to hasten death. We do not yet know how far back these habits of non-practice and frank hostility can be traced. But Ilundáin's predecessors in the see of Seville had few illusions about attitudes to the Church and its liturgy in the villages of Andalusia. In 1898, for instance, Archbishop Spínola noted with obvious relief some encouraging statistics for confirmations and attendance at special missions, as proving that faith was asleep rather than, as it usually seemed, quite dead. In 1899, lamenting the stoning of mission priests by the inhabitants of one part of the diocese, he predicted that one day torrents of blood would be shed in a massive popular persecution of priests.[52] It would be foolish, then, to suggest any recent process of de-Christianization in an area where formal religious practice may never have been prevalent, and where other forms of popular religiosity – missions, processions, the cult of local statues – certainly continued to exist. But some of the priests, in their reports to Ilundáin, mentioned moribund or defunct religious associations and brotherhoods that had once enjoyed some vitality, and many asserted that radical political propaganda and mobilization by socialists and anarchists over a number of years had notably hardened the inhabitants' rejection of the priests and Church-centred activities. The Church's already insecure hold on agricultural workers in the south was seen as slipping away inexorably, leaving not indifference but hatred.

That Spanish intellectuals, industrial workers and landless peasants were, more often than not, not Catholic in any but a residual sense, was a well-known if unpalatable fact to Church leaders. Furthermore, before the birth of the Republic they were already doubtful about the adequacy of the Church's resources to reverse or even stabilize this situation. Hence the continuing though losing battle to activate that state backing of Catholic ideology promised in the concordat and the constitution, and the panic in 1923 at the prospect of the legal basis of the Church's privileged position being modified. Hence too the formal complaint addressed by the archbishops to the government in 1928 at the increasing inadequacy of state funding of the Church. With obvious foreboding they drew attention to churches falling into disrepair and ruin, and to villages with no church at all. But especially they criticized the level of clergy stipends which had not kept pace with rising prices nor with the proportional rise of other sectors of the state budget, so that in 1928 the great majority of the diocesan clergy received less than the lowest grade of janitors in government pay.[53] Hierarchical worries about the poverty of some of the clergy and parishes were exacerbated by the fact that the number of diocesan priests not only failed to match the rise in population between 1920 and 1930 but actually decreased absolutely from about 34,500 to about 32,500.[54] Whatever its wealth in buildings and art treasures, and however privileged its receipt of state funding seemed to its critics, the Church was perceived by its bishops as dangerously under-equipped in money and men, and in need of sympathetic government assistance.

The Republic, however, was not sympathetic. In the first *bienio* it rapidly intensified the Church's weaknesses and undermined its strengths. Both directly, as in the attempt to abolish the flourishing network of schools run by the religious congregations, and indirectly through the pervasive effects of a new political atmosphere, the Republic shook the foundations of the Church's far from robust institutional security. One repercussion to which the bishops were acutely sensitive was the marked fall in vocations to the priesthood. Between 1931 and 1934 the number of boys and young men in the seminaries dropped dramatically by, on average, over 40 per cent. Seminary rectors in Andalusia, for instance, watched their joint totals decline from 1,133 to 633 in just four years.[55] Other signs of impending collapse proliferated, particularly where Church structures were already shaky. Correspondence between the cardinal archbishop of Seville and his parish clergy gives a grim picture of the Church's struggle for survival in the southern villages. The 1932 correspondence is particularly revealing since this was the only full year in power of the Republican-Socialist coalition governing through the new constitution, and because 1932 was a relatively quiet year, lacking the national confrontations of the 1931, 1933 and 1936 elections, and the abortive revolution of 1934. In January Ilundáin instructed all parish priests to set up a parish committee to raise funds for the upkeep of clergy and church now that state support was to end. But just as Abraham had trouble finding a handful of just men to save Sodom, so twenty-three parish priests replied in despair that there were no adult, male practising Catholics of moral solvency available in their parishes to form any such committee, and that they could not possibly be self-financing. There were thirteen reports of explosions or fires in churches. Innumerable restrictions by new Socialist local councils were imposed on funeral processions, bell-ringing, church weddings, and the outdoor celebration of patronal feasts. Some wayside shrines were removed or destroyed, together with religious statues and plaques in village squares. A battle for the streets, for public places, was being waged – an important battle in a society with a strong street culture – and the Church was losing, in spite of appeals to the local civil governor when Socialist mayors and councils exceeded their legal powers. In the course of these bitter disputes various priests were imprisoned and roughly handled, while others received death threats or became the targets of angry public demonstrations. Not surprisingly, in this twelve-month period seven totally demoralized priests wrote, some of them repeatedly, to Ilundáin begging unsuccessfully to be allowed to resign or at least withdraw from their parishes for a while.[56] Nor was possession of the streets in dispute only in remote villages. In Seville itself only one of the traditional brotherhoods ventured onto the streets in Holy Week of 1932, and in 1933 there were no Holy Week processions in the city at all.[57]

With pressure on its schools, its churches and its priests, declining numbers in the seminaries and a many-pronged attack on its traditional public role in Spanish life, the Church needed to look to its defences. Viewed from the inside, the Church's problem under the Republic was nothing less than a problem of self-defence, of survival. But the terms for survival had been set long before 1931. With all of the privileges it enjoyed under the 1876 constitution the Church had proved unable to prevent the dominance of a non-Catholic and often anti-Catholic intellectual élite; nor could it claim much allegiance or even sympathetic tolerance from huge sectors of both the industrial and agrarian working population. In 1931 it was badly placed to cope with the access to power of a Republican-Socialist coalition representing just these groups and seeking, however ineffectively, to further those long-standing claims of landless peasants and industrial workers which the Church had been incapable of championing. It was tied inextricably to the fortunes of the propertied classes, a dependence evident on the land, in industry and in that urban proliferation of secondary schools for the bourgeoisie which constituted the major achievement of Catholic efforts at ideological reinforcement under the restored monarchy. It could scarcely avoid defending these classes in defending itself, just as they protected themselves in protecting the Church. It could not be anything but anti-Republican in real terms, just as the Republic of the first *bienio* and the popular front could not easily regard the Church as anything but an enemy.

Once the war began in July 1936, the settled conviction of Church leaders that nothing less than survival was at stake for Catholicism in the political confrontations of the 1930s was immediately confirmed. Although the original declarations of the rebellious generals did not mention the Church or religion,[58] their fateful initiative provoked anti-clerical violence wherever the insurgent cause failed. The barbaric hunting down and killing of thirteen bishops, 4,184 diocesan priests, 2,365 male religious and 283 religious sisters, mainly in the opening weeks of the war, provided evidence as terrible as could be imagined of the determination of some political groups, especially the anarchists, to wipe out the Church completely.[59] Violence against ecclesiastical personnel was accompanied by the wholesale destruction of churches and other ecclesiastical property. In Republican territory, the only exception to this dismal pattern was the Basque provinces, where the political and military alliance between the Catholic Basque Nationalists and the parties of the left safeguarded the Church. After the events of these opening weeks, it was extremely difficult for Catholic leaders to do other than throw in their lot with the Republic's enemies. An excellent example of this foreclosing of options was provided by some Catalan priests who had voted for the Republic in 1931 and warmly supported Catalan autonomy. However, witnessing the brutal massacre of their colleagues by Catalan defenders of the Republic in 1936, they felt compelled to conclude in bitter disillusion that an autonomous

Catalonia and the Republic were ineluctably their enemies and persecutors.[60]

Equally unenviable was the lot of those few Catholics who, in spite of the purges of Church personnel, retained their earlier Republican allegiance. Gallegos Rocafull, Ossorio y Gallardo and Bergamín all wrote scathing criticisms of the Church's role in covering with a religious mantle the political, military and class aims of the anti-Republicans.[61] Placing a priestly mask over the bloody terror of the hangman, was Bergamín's stark image for this ostentatious collaboration and blessing. After the war was lost, all three paid the high price of exile, as did Basque political leaders and priests. The most complete refutation of the 1937 collective pastoral letter in which the bishops (with a few notorious exceptions) justified both the military rising and their identification with it, was written during the war in Catalonia by a Catholic Republican, the ex-Jesuit Vilar i Costa.[62] His co-religionary, the Catalan democratic politician Carrasco Formiguera, was executed on Franco's orders in April 1938 because he too failed to agree with official Catholic views.[63] This tiny minority of Catholic Republicans – caught hopelessly between anti-clerical political allies and Catholic political foes – traced its rejection of reactionary Catholic political orthodoxy back to long before the war broke out. The various analyses of events offered by these men concur in emphasizing that the Church's anti-Republican alignment did not originate in, although it was certainly strengthened by, the slaughter of priests by uncontrolled groups on Republican territory.

It is beyond the scope of this essay either to detail the involvement of the Spanish hierarchy as gun-blessing apologist for one side in the war and examine its substantial victory spoils, or to investigate the much more cautious and complex policies of the Vatican between 1936 and 1939. Its purpose has been to demonstrate the validity of the arguments of that exiguous Catholic minority which saw in the Church's crusade against the Republic not a defensive holy war that began in 1936 and deserved their support, but a long series of class commitments on political and socio-economic policies which themselves powerfully helped to create the ruthless and desperate anti-clericalism unleashed by the war. The crusade had been waged for a long time by the Church for its own institutional interests, for survival. The cost of its survival was the destruction of the Republic.

Notes

1 For example, V. Palacio Atard, 'La segunda república y la iglesia', in Q. Aldea, T. Marín and J. Vives (eds.), *Diccionario de historia eclesiástica de España* (Madrid, 1972), II, 1179–84, reprinted in his *Cinco historias de la república y de la guerra* (Madrid, 1973), 39–60.

2 For the 14 September meeting between the nuncio, Vidal i Barraquer, the Minister of Justice and the President, in which the Church representatives recognized the virtual inevitability of the first measures while securing a (worthless) agreement that the second set would be avoided, see M. Batllori and V. M. Arbeloa (eds.), *Arxiu Vidal i Barraquer: Esglesia i estat durant la segona república espanyola 1931–36* (Montserrat, 1971), I, 313–23.

3 See especially M. Maura, *Así cayó Alfonso XIII* (Mexico, 1962), part 2, ch. 5.

4 See V. Palacio Atard, 'La iglesia y la guerra de España', in *Diccionario de historia eclesiástica*, II, 1184–8, reprinted in *Cinco historias*, 61–78.

5 The Minister of Justice thought that not even Philip II had ever extracted such a concession from the papacy. See R. Garriga, *El Cardenal Segura y el Nacional-Catolicismo* (Barcelona, 1977), 179–82.

6 Their activities can be followed in *Arxiu Vidal i Barraquer*.

7 Texts in J. Iribarren (ed.), *Documentos colectivos del episcopado español 1870–1974* (Madrid, 1974), 160–81, 189–212.

8 For a careful assessment, see V. M. Arbeloa, *La semana trágica de la iglesia en España* (Barcelona, 1976), 12–33.

9 See S. Ben-Ami, *Fascism from Above* (Oxford, 1983), chs. 2, 3 and 4.

10 Both in *Boletín eclesiástico del Arzobispado de Sevilla* (1923), v. 66, 277–80.

11 *La España de mi vida* (Buenos Aires, 1941), 96.

12 For Gomá's total pessimism on 15 April, see *Arxiu Vidal i Barraquer*, I, 19. For Vidal i Barraquer's forebodings, ibid., 20 and 30.

13 *Sermón perdido* (Madrid, 1930), especially 128–9, 154–9.

14 Text in J. R. Montero, *La CEDA. El catolicismo social y político en la II República* (Madrid, 1977), II, 593–4.

15 The term was derived from Leo XIII's writings to French monarchists under the Third Republic and Spanish Carlists under the restored monarchy of 1875, insisting that Catholicism was not tied to any one system of government. See especially *Immortale Dei* (1885), *Cum Multa* (1882), *Nobilissima Gallorum Gens* (1884).

16 Text in *El Debate*, 26 December 1931.

17 Quoted in R. Robinson, *The Origins of Franco's Spain* (Newton Abbot, 1970), 141.

18 Interview in *Ya*, 21 November 1952, quoted A. Sáez Alba, *La Asociación Católica Nacional de Propagandistas* (Paris, 1974), 7–8.

19 *La España de mi vida*, 134; *Mis memorias* (Madrid, 1975), 185.

20 No. 19 (October 1934), 109–19, and No. 20 (November 1934), 127–33, both reprinted in J. Bergamín (ed.), *Cruz y Raya. Antología* (Madrid, 1974).

21 See Robinson and Montero, both already quoted, and P. Preston, *The Coming of the Spanish Civil War* (London, 1978). Robinson defends the CEDA of charges that it resorted to violence, but admits that it aimed at a corporatist regime.

22 Some of Herrera's communications can be traced in *Arxiu Vidal i Barraquer*. In spring 1933 he was appointed director of Catholic Action in Spain, and therefore brought into even more direct contact with the hierarchy than through *El Debate* and the Propagandists.

23 *Diario de Sesiones de las Cortes Constituyentes de la República Española* (Madrid, 1931), 1706–8.

24 A. Lizarza Iribarren, *Memorias de la conspiración. Cómo se preparó en Navarra la Cruzada 1931–6* (Pamplona, 1953). Text of Mussolini agreement, 24–5.

25 P. Sáinz Rodríguez, *Testimonio y recuerdos* (Barcelona, 1978), 183–4.

26 A. de Castro Albarrán, *El derecho a la rebeldía* (Madrid, 1934).

27 R. Comás, *Isidro Gomá. Francesc Vidal i Barraquer* (Salamanca, 1977), 89.

28 *El Debate*, 15 October 1931.

29 J. Tusell, *Historia de la democracia cristiana en España* (2 vols., Madrid, 1974), H. Raguer i Suñer, *La unió democràtica de Catalunya i el seu temps (1931–9)* (Montserrat, 1976); for the Basque Nationalists as seen by their leader, J. A. Aguirre, *De Guernica a Nueva York pasando por Berlín* (Buenos Aires, 1943). Many of Lucía's own supporters abandoned his line in 1936. We still lack a full, detailed study of the DRV.

30 The classic case is Cardinal Gomá's complete rejection of the Basque Nationalists in the pastoral instruction he wrote for the bishops of Vitoria and Pamplona, August 1936 (A. Granados, *El Cardenal Gomá Primado de España* (Madrid, 1969), 127–31), and in his open letter to President Aguirre, January 1937 (I. Gomá, *Por Dios y por España 1936–9* (Barcelona, 1940), 54–69). M. L. Rodríguez Aisa, *El Cardenal Gomá y la guerra de España* (Madrid, 1981), disappointingly gives only extracts from these texts.

31 J. M. Gallegos Rocafull, *El orden social* (Madrid, 1935), 19, 31–4, 150–3.

32 *Cruz y Raya*, February 1934, suppl. 1–14.

33 E.g. Bishop Maura y Gelabert, *La cuestión social* (Madrid, 1902), and Cardinal Guisasola Menéndez, *Justicia y caridad en la organización cristiana del trabajo* (Madrid, 1916).

34 P. Carrión, *La reforma agraria. Problemas fundamentales* (Madrid, 1931), and *Los latifundios en España* (Madrid, 1932). Instituto de Reformas Sociales, *Los salarios agrícolas en Andalucía y Extremadura en el año 1905*, reprinted in *Revista de Trabajo*, 1 (1963), 187–294; and *Información sobre el problema agrario en la provincia de Córdoba 1919*, reprinted in ibid., 7 (1964), 97–268.

Memoria de la Junta Central de Colonización y Repoblación interior (Madrid, 1917), quoted in J. Cuesta, *Sindicalismo católico agrario en España 1917–19* (Madrid, 1978), especially 139–41.

35 *Una política de derechas* (Madrid, 1921).

36 For the CNCA, see J. Cuesta, op. cit., and J. J. Castillo, *Propietarios muy pobres* (Madrid, 1979).

37 E.g. Antonio Monedero Martín, *La Confederación Nacional Católico-Agraria en 1920* (Madrid, 1921), 85–92, where the CNCA president warned that if landlords should come to dominate the CNCA it would become an instrument of tyranny over the poor.

38 S. Ben-Ami, op. cit., ch. 8.

39 P. Preston, op. cit., chs. 2, 4, 6, and J. R. Montero, op. cit., especially II, 172–207.

40 See J. M. Gil Robles, *No fue posible la paz* (Barcelona, 1978), 172–8. *El Debate* did not share his toleration of the failure of Catholic social reform.

41 See A. Vicent, *Socialismo y anarquismo* (Valencia, 1893); J. N. García Nieto, *El sindicalismo cristiano en España* (Bilbao, 1960); M. Llorens, 'El P. Antonio Vicent S.I. 1837–1912. Notas sobre el desarrollo de la Acción Social Católica en España', in *Estudios de Historia Moderna* (Barcelona, 1954), IV; J. J. Castillo, *El sindicalismo amarillo en España* (Madrid, 1977); A. Elorza, 'El sindicalismo católico en la segunda república: la CESO 1935–8', in *La utopía anarquista bajo la segunda república espanola* (Madrid, 1973); D. Benavides, *El fracaso social del catolicismo español* (Barcelona, 1973); J. Andrés Gallego, 'La iglesia y la cuestión social: replantamiento', in *Estudios históricos sobre la iglesia española contemporánea* (El Escorial, 1979).

42 H. Raguer, op. cit., 170.

43 E.g. M. Tuñón de Lara, 'Iglesia y estado durante la segunda república', in *Estudios históricos sobre la iglesia española contemporánea*, 339.

44 For example, Salesians set up in each school an Asociación Escolar which assumed legal ownership while the religious teachers affected lay style in dress and nomenclature but continued as before; the Sacred Heart convent school in Bilbao became the Instituto de Cultura Feminina and the nuns went to school from the convent each morning in lay dress by a roundabout route; the De La Salle brothers exchanged the complete staff of their schools, and the new arrivals in each place introduced themselves in lay style.

45 See F. Lannon, 'The socio-political role of the Spanish Church – a case study', in *Journal of Contemporary History*, XIV, no. 2 (1979), and 'Modern Spain: the project of a national catholicism', in S. Mews (ed.), *Religion and National Identity* (Oxford, 1982), especially 571–80.

46 Text of July 1937 letter in Iribarren, op. cit., 219–42.

47 V. Palacio Atard, 'La iglesia y la guerra de España'.

48 Text in Iribarren, op. cit., 116–17.

49 F. Peiró, *El problema religioso-social de España* (Madrid, 1936).

50 E.g. on Bilbao, J. Azpiazu, 'La religiosidad del arciprestazgo de Portugalete' and J. Iñigo, 'La situación religiosa en la zona minera vizcaína', *Idearium* (1935), 92–101, and 327–36. In Catalonia, only 5 per cent of young people could be described as practising Catholics after leaving school: see *La federació de jovens cristians de Catalunya – contribució a la seva historia* (Barcelona, 1972), 12.

51 See J. Ordóñez Márquez, *La apostasía de las masas, y la persecución religiosa en la provincia de Huelva 1931–6* (Madrid, 1968), 219–22 for a summary of Ilundáin's report on the whole diocese, and *passim* for texts of all parish reports for Huelva province.

52 *Boletín Eclesiástico del Arzobispado de Sevilla* (1898), v. 30, 241, 209–10; (1899), v. 32, 402.

53 Text in Iribarren, op. cit., 125–8.

54 *Guía de la iglesia en España* (Madrid, 1954), I, 294.

55 S. Aznar, *La revolución y las vocaciones eclesiásticas* (Madrid, 1949), 43–9; *Razón y Fe* (1935), no. 466, 333.

56 Archivo de la curia diocesana de Sevilla, Ano 1932, Parroquial, leg. 1–4.

57 F. Gelán, *ABC* (Sevilla ed.), 3 April 1982.

58 See H. Raguer, *La espada y la cruz* (Barcelona, 1977), ch. 2.

59 See th. definitive study, A. Montero Moreno, *Historia de la persecución religiosa en Espana 1936–9* (Madrid, 1961).

60 Information from one of these priests, Joan Bonet i Baltà, Barcelona, 12 July 1982.

61 J. M. Gallegos Rocafull, *Crusade or Class War? The Spanish Military Revolt* (London, 1937); A. Ossorio y Gallardo, *La guerra de España y los católicos* (Buenos Aires, 1942); J. Bergamín, *Detrás de la cruz* (Mexico, 1941).

62 J. Vilar i Costa, *Glosas a la carta colectiva de los obispos españoles* (Barcelona, 1938).

63 H. Raguer, *La unió democrática*, 395–412.

I would like to thank the British Academy for a research grant to collect some of the material on which this chapter is based.

3
War on two fronts: politics and society in Navarre 1931–6

Martin Blinkhorn

In the immediate aftermath of the rising of 18 July 1936, Spain was the scene of numerous local struggles, the collective outcome of which strongly influenced the general conflict. One of these, as brief, decisive and predictable as its character was unique, occurred in the northern province of Navarre and along its borders with Guipúzcoa to the north-west and Logroño (Rioja) to the south. Here the Carlists of Navarre, heirs politically and, in countless cases, literally of those who in the nineteenth century had waged battle against Spanish liberalism, now mounted a war on two fronts – both militarily and ideologically speaking – against newer enemies: Basque 'separatism' and 'Marxism'.

Within a matter of days the Carlist militia, the *Requeté*, had established control over Navarre, encountering significant resistance only in the south of the province. Navarre thereby became a safe bastion of the rising and an important base for the conquest of Guipúzcoa, the securing of Rioja, the reinforcing of Zaragoza and the advance upon Madrid.

After the military conquest of Navarre came its political 'cleansing'. Some of Carlism's enemies fled into the temporary safety of the Basque country; others sought refuge with their conquerors: Basque Nationalists through recantation and reconciliation with Carlism, leftists within the suddenly expanding Falange; many, however, stood exposed to summary execution at the hands of the *Requeté* or lynching at those of right-wing mobs. How many died is unlikely ever to be satisfactorily determined, estimates varying from under 700 to over 15,000. That the former figure, admitted by post-war Carlist writers, is too low is suggested by the concern at the scale of bloodletting expressed during the summer of 1936 by the Navarrese Carlist authorities themselves.[1] What certainly is clear is that the province in which such antagonisms now exploded can hardly have been, before the war, the backwater of political uniformity and social peace that has so often been depicted in historical literature.

For most English-language writers, at least, Navarre before the Civil War was little short of a rural arcadia. A 'satisfied area', Gerald Brenan called it, with a 'self-subsisting economy, based on small but relatively prosperous farms, owned for the most part by their proprietors'.[2] Hugh Thomas paints an even cosier picture: the Navarrese, he declares, were 'a contented group of peasant proprietors nestling in the foothills of the Pyrenees', whose hostility towards the modern world inspired them to rise in 1936 against the Republic.[3] That parts of Navarre did conform more or less to this pattern is demonstrated by the description of the village of Echauri, a few miles west of Pamplona, given by one of Ronald Fraser's interviewees: a community in which a 'comfortably-off' peasant farmed 45 hectares, owning a cow, two horses and a pair of oxen; the majority got along adequately on between six and ten hectares; and everyone was a Carlist save the local bourgeois intellectual – the vet.[4] Echauri was not Navarre, however, nor such accounts as Brenan's and Thomas's the whole truth. Navarre is anything but a geographical unity, and whilst differences of topography, climate and economy within the province may not in themselves explain its politics, neither can the latter be properly understood without some awareness of them.

For the purposes of this essay it may be useful to regard Navarre as dividing into three broad zones: the northern *montaña*; the southern *ribera*; and a complex central zone displaying characteristics of the other two (see map 1).[5] The pure *montaña* extends southward from the French frontier to a line corresponding very roughly to the northernmost limit of the vine. Moist and temperate in the west, subject to harsh winters in

Districts of the *montaña*
1 La Barranca (Araquil valley)
2 Regata del Bidasoa (Bidasoa valley)
3 Baztán
4 Burguete-Roncesvalles
5 Aezcoa-Irati
6 Salazar valley
7 Roncal

Map 1 *The regions of Navarre*

the higher north-east, the *montaña* is fractured by numerous valleys in which the greater part of its population concentrates. The rivers of these northern valleys flow in a variety of directions, giving each one its particular character and outside contacts. In the 1930s many smaller valleys remained all but isolated, whilst the larger often rejoiced in their own institutions of self-government. In the far north-west the Bidasoa valley, Atlantic-facing, was physically and culturally closer to Guipúzcoa than to other districts of Navarre; neighbouring Baztán lay on the main road from Pamplona to France and possessed easy and longstanding contacts with both; the valley of the Araquil, west of Pamplona, connected with Alava province; and the north-eastern valleys of Salazar and Roncal possessed historic and economic ties with France and, in Roncal's case, with Aragon. The northern rural economy centred upon the production of timber, and mixed sheep and dairy farming.

Central Navarre is a region of more populated hills, intervening valleys and broader plains such as the *cuenca* of the capital, Pamplona, a city of 42,000 inhabitants in 1930. In the centre marked variations of climate and agriculture are evident, especially between the mild, damp north-western fringes of the zone and the arid south-east. As the climate changes, crops become progressively more important within a mixed rural economy, above all wheat and vines. The southern flank of the central zone and the basins of its mainly south-flowing rivers – the Ega, Arga, Cidacos and Aragon – mark the beginning of the *ribera*, a region truly 'Mediterranean' in both climate and economy, where in the 1930s extensive sheep and goat pastures alternated with equally large areas given over to wheat, vines, olives, sugar beet and, in the irrigated districts around Tudela, market-garden produce. The *ribera*, with its baking summers, is not merely quite different in character from the *montaña* a mere thirty miles north, but is also a region of extremes itself: only a few miles from Tudela begin the Bardenas, mile upon mile of parched semi-desert. Unlike the rest of Navarre, with its villages, hamlets and isolated farmsteads, but much like parts of southern Spain, the *ribera*'s countryside is largely empty of settlements but its towns and villages commensurately large.

The distribution of landed property in pre-Civil War Navarre is difficult to determine with any precision, since the Cadastral survey begun in 1906, on which the Republic's agrarian reform of 1932 was largely based, had still not reported on Navarre by 1936.[6] Although Navarre was one of the few regions of Spain where medium-sized holdings of between ten and 100 hectares played a major part in local agriculture,[7] this does not mean that the entire province was a peasant proprietors' paradise. In the first place not *all* holdings were medium-sized. In some southern districts partitive inheritance had produced concentrations of small-scale cultivators struggling to survive in the face of 'progressive' wine-producers' control of processing and marketing. At the other extreme, parts of southern and eastern Navarre exhibited characteristics more commonly associated with southern Spain, namely *latifundia* and a landless rural proletariat. A related though not identical feature of the Navarrese landscape was that of seigneurial estates (*señoríos*), in the possession of which the province, with 12,440 hectares, ranked thirteenth in Spain. In all, well over a hundred estates in Navarre extended to 300 hectares or more, the largest reaching thousands of hectares and encompassing entire villages.[8] Much of the land held by large-scale proprietors was leased out or sharecropped (*aparcería*); Navarre's numerous medium-sized farms were thus not necessarily the property of those who worked them. Tenancy and sharecropping terms varied widely from the farmer's point of view: from the relatively secure and generous throughout much of the centre and, where relevant, the north, where agreements were often long-term and virtually hereditary, to the decidedly insecure and exacting further south.[9]

In so far as Navarre, notwithstanding these variations, may be considered a socially harmonious region before 1931, this was in large part the result of nineteenth-century developments drawing her along different paths from most of Spain. In particular, during the liberal disentailment of civil property carried out in the 1850s and 1860s, the delaying and diversionary tactics of the Navarrese provincial and local authorities effectively averted, throughout much of the province, the speculation and the widening of socio-economic differences caused elsewhere. Close control of land sales ensured that such property as was released was relatively widely dispersed among Navarre's landholders and new purchasers, and that a higher proportion of common land survived than in most other regions. With approximately half the territory of Navarre still held in common, the small and medium farmer retained access to pasturage, fodder, manure, fuel, building stone and water: necessities of rural life of which his counterparts in other Spanish regions now often found themselves deprived. All this was nevertheless truer of northern and central Navarre than of the *ribera*, where the area of land available for common exploitation was significantly reduced, both by post-disentailment purchase and by the systematic encroachment of richer proprietors on what survived.[10]

Arcadia or not, Navarre in 1931 was certainly still predominantly rural and agricultural, with only one major town, Pamplona, and little modern industry. The single, small blast furnace of the Vera de Bidasoa ironworks and the much more important cement-manufacturing centres of La Burunda, both on Navarre's western fringes, were exceptional in a province otherwise short of mineral resources and ignored by major domestic and international road and rail links.[11] The rest of Navarrese industry chiefly involved the small-scale processing of local agricultural products, most importantly the wine, olives, sugar-beet, fruit and vegetables of the *ribera*.

An integral part of Navarre's apparently cohesive social order was the Church. Navarre north of the *ribera* had good cause to be regarded as the most Catholic region of Spain. The Church's strength, moreover, transcended mere statistics, though in terms both of church attendance and numbers of regular and secular clergy these were striking enough.[12] All sources agree on the genuinely popular (in both senses) character of the Church in Navarre, where mainly local-born parish priests were integrated into their communities in a manner unusual in, for example, Old Castile.[13] In Basque districts of the north and west, common culture and, less generally, language naturally tightened the bond between clergy and laity.

From the early years of the twentieth century, the Catholicism and conservatism of central and northern Navarrese rural society were further reinforced by the gradual construction of a network of Catholic farmers' and landowners' syndicates, which in 1914 merged into a large and powerful national organization, the Confederación Nacional Católico-Agraria (CNCA). Within the CNCA Navarre, with 156 syndicates, was by 1920 one of the most important regions.[14] The leading figures in such social-Catholic enterprises were usually reforming priests and paternalistic larger proprietors, anxious to maintain social stability and ward off possible 'socialist' threats to it by providing small and medium producers with such inducements to conformity as cheap credit, insurance, fertilizers and anti-pest chemicals, as well as encouraging some degree of carefully guided co-operation and rationalization of marketing. Such activities were infused with a system of values which stressed the indivisibility of the 'agrarian interest' and the social-Catholic principle of 'access to property' for tenants and the landless. Before 1931 the 'socialist' threat in Navarre was negligible. Inasmuch as social-Catholicism served to bolster the position of Navarre's landlords and wealthier peasants through maintaining the essential contentment of the rural majority, it therefore remained to be seen how this state of affairs would be affected by the more serious challenge from the left which now became likely.

It must already be evident that in a highly charged political atmosphere such as that of the Republic, the regional differences within Navarre were bound to become unprecedentedly significant. A further factor ensured this – the distinction, linguistic and cultural, between Basque and non-Basque Navarre. In the 1930s there were approximately 400,000 Basque speakers left in Spain, of whom some 80,000 were to be found within Navarre's population of just under 350,000. These were concentrated in the *montaña* and the western half of central Navarre. Basque had by now all but disappeared from the eastern *montaña*, save for its continuing outpost in the Salazar valley. Farther west, from Baztán down to Navarre's western corner, it remained more vigorous. Basque consciousness, and an accompanying tendency to regard Navarre as a Basque province, nevertheless survived in all those northern and western districts which remained culturally Basque whether or not the language lived on. Throughout most of the *ribera*, however, and in more southerly and easterly parts of the centre, Basque consciousness was largely absent. Here, any human contacts other than within the immediate locality or with Pamplona were more likely to be with Aragon or Rioja than with the Basque country; no Basque had been spoken in most of southern Navarre for centuries, and neither Basque language nor culture held any place in the popular consciousness.[15]

Although a strong sense of Navarrese identity was apparent throughout a province still described by many of its inhabitants as a 'kingdom', its essential components therefore varied widely. At one extreme stood those who saw Navarre as the heartland of a historic medieval Basque state, destined to form part of another Basque state in the future; at the other, those who, whilst sentimentally devoted to the idea of Navarrese autonomy based upon her historic but now largely defunct *fueros*, nevertheless stressed Navarre's separate development from the Basque region since 1200 and her crucial role in the creation of a Spain of which they insisted she must always form a part. Before 1931 these different conceptions of Navarre's identity and destiny were a matter for debate; in 1936 the issue was to be settled with bloodshed.

The change of regime in April 1931 affected Navarre no less dramatically than other regions, albeit in a manner that was unique. Since the Carlist defeat of 1876 the conservative and liberal parties of the old regime had maintained a stake in Navarrese politics, essentially through the use, especially in the *ribera*, of patronage and *caciquismo* (local 'bossism'), and helped by the Carlists' inconsistent attitude towards participation in 'liberal' politics.[16] Carlism's survival as a 'cause' rather than a party, able to command popular loyalties by means unavailable to its rivals – family bonds and traditions, local particularism, religious devotion – remained evident throughout, however, despite internal schisms and some loss of support to Basque Nationalism after 1900. Carlism's numerical and organizational revival began amid the uncertainty following Primo de Rivera's fall at the start of 1930 and by April 1931 was well under way. During the next few months the revival accelerated, giving Carlism a pre-eminence within the Navarrese right which it was to retain until the Civil War.[17]

   The advent of something approaching genuinely mass politics to Navarre in place of the manipulated sham of the fallen monarchy nevertheless provided opportunities for other popular forces besides Carlism. One was Basque Nationalism. Arising, in effect, out of a defection of some late nineteenth-century Carlists, dissatisfied with their movement's failure to defend effectively the Basque and Navarrese *fueros* against 'liberal' encroachment, Basque Nationalism drew much of its early inspiration and intellectual impetus from Navarrese Basques, without ever becoming, for reasons indicated above, more than a minority cause within Navarre itself. Nevertheless Basque Nationalism stood in 1931 as a 'popular' movement, poised like Carlism to seize any opportunities offered by the new situation.[18] So, too, did Navarrese Socialism and Republicanism: minority causes, certainly, but as elsewhere in Spain expanding appreciably by the late 1920s and sufficiently concentrated in certain parts of Navarre to possess greater potential power – especially in the context of a sympathetic regime – than mere total numbers might suggest.[19]

As to the latter, it is possible to state that between 1931 and 1936 around 70 per cent of Navarre's adult population appears to have aligned itself with the 'Spanish' right – Carlists and other, largely 'fellow-travelling' Catholics; some 20 per cent with Republicanism or Socialism; and a steady 10 per cent with Basque Nationalism. Navarre was therefore no mere Carlist fief during the Second Republic, for not all Navarrese stood on the right and not all who did were Carlists. It is time now to examine the distribution of these forces, since it is this which gave Navarrese politics in the 1930s their special character.

Despite the commonly held notion of Carlism as a movement of 'sturdy mountaineers' rooted in the Navarrese Pyrenees, it was not the *montaña* that was Carlism's greatest stronghold in the 1930s.[20] Carlism was unquestionably a presence, spiritual if not necessarily physical, in most northern valleys; even so, it was by no means generally dominant. The principal political feature of northern Navarre was rather an ostensibly non-party conservative Catholicism, sometimes genuinely independent but often inclining towards a 'fellow-travelling' relationship with Carlism or, in the north-west especially, towards Basque Nationalism. At local elections during the 1930s – those of April 1931 which precipitated the monarchy's fall and those of April 1933 – right-wing candidates throughout much of this area preferred to offer themselves not as Carlists but as 'Catholics', 'independents' or members of a 'Rightist Bloc'. The overall dominance of this conservatism in much of the *montaña* is clear: thus in the general election of June 1931, of something over seventy electoral districts located in this zone, forty-five returned a right-wing vote of 70 per cent or higher whilst no fewer than twenty-nine actually recorded 90 per cent or above. Moreover this dominance tightened, if anything, at subsequent elections.[21]

The political map of the *montaña* in the 1930s is nevertheless more chequered than might be inferred from these remarks. Not only did Basque Nationalism, understandably enough, make its presence felt electorally throughout much of this zone, but Republicanism and Socialism also commanded pockets of support – in the timber-producing districts of Roncal and the Irati forest[22] and, most notably, in La Burunda. Here, among the workers of the cement and asphalt industries and the Alsasua railyards, the Navarrese Socialists possessed their principal northern base. In June 1931 the Republican-Socialist alliance conquered five of La Burunda's six electoral districts with an overall poll of 77.5 per cent. This figure was exaggerated by right-wing abstentions and fell back sharply at the November 1933 election; even so, the Socialists remained the leading political group in La Burunda throughout the years of the Republic.[23]

Although Navarre's northern valleys were thus something more than mere nests of Carlists, it remains true that these pockets of Republicanism and Socialism were exceptional within a region of generally conservative character. And within this conservatism it would be unwise to take Carlism's organizational weakness too much at face value. By the middle years of the Republic, admittedly, only some thirty northern villages boasted any sort of Carlist organization, and that normally a mere committee requiring nothing more than enough individuals – five or six – to form it. The real signs of organizational vigour were the public clubs or 'circles', of which only half a dozen were to be found from Leiza on the Guipúzcoan border in the west to the strongly Carlist, partly Basque Nationalist Salazar valley in the east. As for the paramilitary *Requeté*, only in the Salazar valley could more than a handful be claimed.[24] Two points, however, must be borne in mind: first, that the *montaña*, with its difficult terrain, often inadequate communications, and dispersed population was a problematical area to organize and mobilize politically; second, that as a 'cause' as well as a movement or party, Carlism cannot be satisfactorily quantified in organizational or even electoral terms. Much of the ostensibly uncommitted Catholic population of the *montaña* was anything but *anti*-Carlist, and constituted a reservoir of passive sympathy upon which Carlism could expect to be able to call in the event of a renewal of the hostilities suspended in 1876.

During the Second Republic, however, it was in central Navarre that Carlism flourished most. The districts electing the greatest numbers of self-confessed Carlists to local councils in 1931 and 1933, possessing the most circles and ancillary organizations (youth sections, women's sections, etc.), and finally in 1936 sending the most – and best prepared – volunteers into the Carlist *tercios* were all situated in this zone: in the *cuenca* of Pamplona and the small valleys radiating from it; on the hillsides and in the valleys of the chain of *sierras* running south-west from Pamplona, through the old Carlist capital of Estella, to Viana and the point at which Navarre, Alava and Rioja meet; and in a crescent of mostly hilly territory, skirting the *ribera* and running from Estella, through Tafalla to the market town of Sangüesa and the borders of Aragon. Throughout this region Carlist traditions and loyalties, dating from the struggles of the nineteenth century, were widespread and devotedly nursed. Their survival was facilitated by a relatively harmonious social milieu, which nevertheless possessed a layer of richer proprietors and conservative professional men capable of putting such sentiments to practical use and of giving leadership to the Carlist cause. During the early twentieth century these Carlist notables succeeded in harnessing the energies of parish clergy and of rural Catholic syndicalism on behalf of Carlism's programme: that of installing in Spain a 'traditional', hierarchical and corporatist monarchy.[25]

The sheer solidity of opinion in central Navarre during the Second Republic was impressive. Only two towns detracted significantly from the right's monopoly: Pamplona, whose appreciable liberal tradition was now transmuted into Republicanism and whose electorate divided more or less evenly between a Carlist-led right and a Republican-led left; and the much smaller town of Tafalla, on the edge of the *ribera*. In a few small towns and larger villages such as Estella, Viana, Villava and the wine-producing centre of Puente la Reina there existed a pro-Republican, petty bourgeois minority of sorts, otherwise only in a sprinkling of *pueblos* throughout this mostly well-populated zone could the right command under 80 per cent of the electorate. Furthermore, as the declared affiliation of local councillors indicated, in central Navarre, save for some Basque-speaking villages in the *sierra* around Estella where

Basque Nationalism maintained a foothold, the right *did* mean Carlism.[26]

The Carlist consciousness of so much of central Navarre's population, especially in such strongholds as Artajona, San Martín de Unx and Sangüesa, was undoubtedly raised by close and easy contact with the *ribera*, where the social and political environment was so different as to seem, when viewed from the north in the atmosphere of the 1930s, positively threatening (see Map 2). South of a line Viana–Tafalla–Sangüesa the right, and Carlism in particular, found itself faced with a severe challenge from the left once the old regime's election fixing gave way to something resembling representative politics. Although the most dramatic Republican and Socialist triumphs in the April 1931 local elections, and those decisive in precipitating the downfall of the monarchy, occurred in cities and large towns, many parts of rural and small-town Spain also witnessed a pronounced shift in political power.[27] The *ribera*, where seventeen of Navarre's twenty-five largest centres of population were situated, was just such an area. It was here, in April 1931,

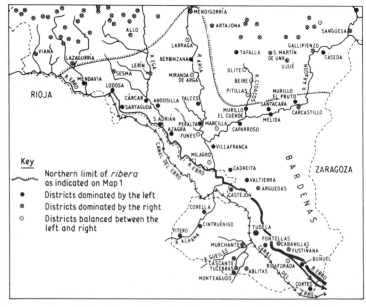

Map 2 *The Navarrese* ribera *and its northern margins, 1931–3*

that the Navarrese Republicans and Socialists elected a good proportion of their 643 local councillors – out of the province's total of 2088. Something under a hundred more were added in May when new elections were held in districts deemed by the Republican authorities to have been still under the influence of monarchist *caciques* on 12 April, all but a handful of these being in the Navarrese south.[28] At the general election late in June, the same alliance of Republicans and Socialists defeated the right in thirty-four out of forty-seven districts of the *ribera*, with 62 per cent of the poll. As in La Burunda further north, right-wing disorganization and abstentions exaggerated the left's strength in 1931; the 1933 and 1936 general elections demonstrated that, whilst the left's grip on the northern bank of the Ebro itself remained secure, elsewhere in the *ribera* the right did after all command majority support.[29] This made the control of local government by Republicans and Socialists all the more provocative from the point of view of southern Navarrese conservatives. From 1931 to 1933 left-controlled local councils in the *ribera* created a climate favourable to the growth of Socialist trade unionism among agricultural labourers and workers in the food-processing industries. In this they met little resistance from higher up; civil governors in Pamplona, appointed by Madrid, for the most part looked tolerantly upon anything tending to 'republicanize' Navarre, as did the 'temporary committee' installed by the Republican government in 1931 to replace Navarre's unacceptably monarchist *Diputación* (provincial council). The contrast with recent times was sudden and stark; not only had the conservative and propertied elements within the *ribera* itself every cause for concern but, owing to the simple sense of physical proximity to these novel and disturbing developments, so too had the inhabitants of the Carlist arcadia only a few miles to the north.

The left's emergence in southern Navarre materially affected the outcome of the issue which dominated Navarrese politics during the Republic's first year: that of regional autonomy. When, in April 1931, Basque Nationalists throughout the region launched a campaign for 'Basque-Navarrese' autonomy, Navarrese reactions varied widely. In the more Basque – and more conservative – north and west, popular enthusiasm was widespread; in much of the south, however, and especially among left-wing circles, apathy and even hostility were common.

The campaign initially won the support of Carlism's provincial leaders; outraged by Republican assaults on rightist power in Navarre, conscious of Carlist weakness elsewhere, and attracted by the vision of a Basque-Navarrese region sealed off from Republican anti-clericalism, these notables were quick to grasp the practical advantages of autonomy. The fruits of their collaboration with Basque Nationalism were an autonomy statute designed to give the region, among other things, power over religious affairs, and a provincial electoral alliance which won Navarre in the June 1931 general election. The Republican constitution approved in late 1931, however, made religious autonomy unattainable, whereupon a gulf rapidly opened up between the Basque Nationalists and the Carlist leadership. The former were prepared to accept a revised and more limited autonomy statute, and in order to obtain it moved towards an awkward embrace with the left of Vizcaya and Guipúzcoa which was to survive into the Civil War. The latter, deprived of autonomy's chief attraction and increasingly involved in other issues, swung decisively against autonomy.

So, ironically, did the Navarrese left. At the crucial assembly of local council representatives in Pamplona in June 1932, the revised statute was rejected by 123–109 with 35 abstentions. The left's representatives, who could have tipped the balance in favour of approval, mostly opposed or abstained. Grassroots sympathy for autonomy remained demonstrably higher on the right, but outside the most Basque districts many Carlists, like their leaders, had cooled towards the idea. Another factor was pressure from Carlist notables on councillors and their representatives to vote 'no': hence the dramatic switch from support to opposition among councils within easy influencing distance of Pamplona.[30]

The vote, which was mortally to damage the entire Basque autonomy campaign, indicated widespread *Navarrese* resistance, on left and right, to an excessively *Basque* conception of autonomy. Basque Nationalists nevertheless interpreted it as a right-wing betrayal of the *fueros*. Their bitterness was increasingly reciprocated as time passed and the Carlists recognized in their ex-allies the collaborators of Marxists and atheists. Some rank-and-file Carlists in Navarre's more Basque areas felt differently, but their voices were muted as their leaders and militants added 'separatists' to their blacklist.[31]

The position of the Navarrese Carlist notables in 1932 is easily understood, though Basque Nationalists could not be expected to sympathize with it. Most of the notables, plus a considerable proportion of an expanding, increasingly activist rank and file, were becoming daily more involved in other, wider issues for which autonomy seemed to offer no solution. Whether the abandonment of the autonomy statute's religious clauses was the reason or merely the pretext for the Navarrese Carlists' breach with the Basque Nationalists, their concern for the Church was sincere and their growing preference for conducting its defence in the national arena quite logical. Resistance to the Republic's anti-clerical legislation was only to be expected in Spain's most devout province. The Catholic press – especially Carlism's *El Pensamiento Navarro* and the independent *Diario de Navarra* – joined with the formidable apparatus of Catholic syndicalism, Catholic Action and such bodies as the Catholic Parents' Association, not to mention the local clergy themselves, to resist such legislation. Letters flooded the press and the Ministry of Justice; Carlist and fellow-Catholic deputies protested in the Cortes; even children demonstrated in Navarrese villages: but all in vain.[32]

The religious issue exercised a vital influence upon Navarre's political future. In the eyes of many Navarrese Catholics the Republic's anti-clericalism quickly became its salient feature and stamped it indelibly as an unacceptable regime. Even granted the Navarrese Carlists' hatred of the fallen monarchy, there was little likelihood of their accepting a Republic – as their willingness to ally with the monarchy's supporters in the April 1931 local elections indicated. What slender chance there was of this – or, somewhat less improbably, of the Carlist leadership's encountering difficulty in mobilizing mass support against the Republic – vanished amid the religious fervour of 1932–3. Instead it was the religious issue, skilfully exploited by press and pulpit, which more than anything else nourished the remarkable growth in Carlist numbers, organizations and activity apparent during these years. By mid-1933 Carlism's grip on the Navarrese right was all but total. Other movements, of both the Catholic and the radical right, did emerge: in 1933 the Navarrese version of the Catholic-conservative CEDA, Unión

Navarra; and in 1934 the Falange. Neither, however, could challenge Carlism's dominance.[33]

In the context of the Republic, the particular significance of the Navarrese Carlists' unanimity and combativeness on the religious question was the manner in which they were carried over into other issues: specifically the overriding social problem of the day, that of the land. For, within the framework of an ostensibly religious crusade against a 'Godless' Republic, the Navarrese Carlist élite began to show an increasing preoccupation with more material affairs, and in particular with the attempts of successive Republican governments to modify the distribution and use of various forms of landed property.

This concern was scarcely surprising. Although the main provisions of the Azaña government's agrarian reform, enacted in September 1932, did not apply to Navarre, this was due less to the absence of *latifundia* than to the limitations of the Cadastre; the warning remained clear. Far more relevant to most of Navarre, however, was the legislation on rural leases formulated and proposed both by the left-of-centre Azaña administrations of 1931–3 and, in 1934–5, by the social-Catholic CEDA Minister of Agriculture, Giménez Fernández. Proposals aimed at generally improving the lot of tenants and sharecroppers, and at extending ownership opportunities to long-standing tenants, implied for existing landlords and estate-owners the loss both of property and of their accustomed advantage over those tenants who remained. Ironically, a region of long-standing tenancies such as Navarre was liable to be affected sooner by any such legislation than those where tenancies were customarily short-term and insecure. Even if in much of central Navarre a move from tenancy to peasant proprietorship may have offered little immediate attraction to its potential beneficiaries, or threat to larger landowners, the latter could feel no certainty that this state of affairs would endure indefinitely. As for the *ribera*, both kinds of land reform held immediately serious implications for landowners.[34] Proprietorial uneasiness was all the greater owing to the interest taken in the question by the Socialists, both nationally and locally. The Navarrese Socialists, influenced increasingly by Ricardo Zabalza, a rising figure within the Socialist land-workers' union, the FNTT (Federación Nacional de Trabajadores de la Tierra), believed that sooner or later land reform should be applied to *all latifundios* those of the *ribera* included: hence their close interest in the 1932 Act's implementation and growing impatience with its shortcomings.[35] Moreover, between 1931 and 1933 especially, considerable attention was paid in the Socialist and FNTT press to tenant cultivators and sharecroppers, in the hope of curing these rural elements of the 'false consciousness' which commonly bound them to their social superiors and thereby to the political right.[36]

The Navarrese Carlist élite was not disposed to take such developments lying down. Its leading figure and from early 1932 to May 1934 Carlism's national political leader, the Conde de Rodezno, set the tone; a grandee of Spain, Rodezno owned extensive estates not only in Rioja but also in Cáceres, and thus *did* stand to suffer under the terms of the 1932 Act. Even if he stood literally in a class by himself, other Carlist notables owned considerable landed property within or outside the province and were liable to be hit by any serious legislation on rural leases; they included such prominent pillars of Navarrese social-Catholicism as Eugenio Sanz de Lerín, an early leader of the Navarrese *Requeté* under the Republic; José Sánchez Marco; and above all two of Navarre's deputies from November 1933, Javier Martínez Morentín and José Luis Arellano.[37] From 1931 onwards, moreover, Navarrese notables were drawn into close personal and political contact with their co-religionaries from other regions where the 'land question' was more immediate and explosive. Some of these, like Lamamié of Salamanca, Estévanez of Burgos, and the representatives of Andalusian Carlism, were large landowners whose dedication to social-Catholicism went hand-in-hand with their staunch defence of private property. Those Navarrese – Rodezno, Arellano, Martínez Morentín, and the prosperous lawyer Joaquín Beunza – who at one time or another between 1931 and February 1936 represented their province in the Cortes were likewise affected by the concerns of conservatives and landowners belonging to other parties.

As social issues more and more attracted their attention, leading Carlists in Navarre therefore came to embrace a resolute social conservatism of a flavour not previously characteristic of Carlism. This found expression not only on the political stage proper but also through Carlist participation in a variety of organizations, some social-Catholic in emphasis and others more frankly intended for the defence of established interests. As early as November 1931 Sánchez Marco presided over a meeting of Navarrese landowners in Estella, convened 'to defend proprietors' rights' in the face of Republican land-reform proposals and existing efforts to hold down rents and increase security of tenure.[38] Sánchez Marco, Arellano, Martínez Morentín and others remained active and influential both within the Navarrese components of the CNCA, which in the prevailing climate were employed to legitimate and protect the existing distribution and utilization of property, and in other organizations, newly created in order openly to defend the property and power of landlords. An early example of the latter was the Asociación de Propietarios Terratenientes de Navarra; from the summer of 1933 this was largely superseded by a distinctly more combative body, the Federación de Propietarios de Fincas Rústicas, which itself formed part of a powerful national landlords' and *latifundistas'* pressure group.[39] Between 1932 and 1935, Carlist deputies from Navarre joined Carlists and fellow-rightists from other regions in successfully resisting successive attempts at legislation on rural leases. Such proposals, as Giménez Fernández's advocacy demonstrated, were broadly in conformity with the social-Catholic principles to which all socially and politically conscious Carlists subscribed, which did not prevent them regarding the unfortunate minister as a 'white bolshevik'.[40] By the time the combined forces of the right had finished their work, Giménez Fernández's purpose had been all but reversed; by 1935 landlords were in a stronger position than ever, able now to reduce tenants to sharecroppers.

It is in the light of this rising pugnacity in defence of property that Carlism's 'push' into the *ribera* during the 1930s may best be understood. Although by Andalusian standards the Navarrese *ribera* may have been a haven of rural peace, by those of the rest of Navarre it was a social cauldron. By 1933 the growth of the FNTT, its parent organization the UGT (Unión General de Trabajadores), and in one or two districts such as Mendavia the anarcho-syndicalist CNT (Confederación Nacional del Trabajo), had created a state of alarm among larger landowners and employers. A climax was reached in autumn 1933, with Azaña's fall and the assumption of office by the Radical Lerroux. An immediate slowing down of the already sluggish implementation of land reform, and a general reversal of the predominantly pro-labour policies of the previous two-and-a-half years, provoked widespread demonstrations by small peasants and labourers throughout the *ribera*. The initiative had nevertheless shifted decisively; even before the general election of November 1933, the outcome of which was a conservative-supported Radical government, the Federación de Propietarios de Fincas Rústicas had instituted a concerted campaign of wage-cutting and a boycott of unionized labour from one end of the *ribera* to the other.[41] These developments passed unreported in the Carlist press, but suffice to indicate the social climate of the *ribera* and the tactics of organizations to which Carlists not only belonged but actually provided direction. They also illuminate other Carlist activities in southern Navarre.

These involved mainly propaganda and organization. From 1932 onwards, Carlist propagandistic activity in Navarre concentrated disproportionately on the *ribera* and its northern margins. Elsewhere in Navarre, Carlist sentiment was so widespread even when passive that the movement's strength expanded almost spontaneously in reaction chiefly to Republican anti-clericalism. In the south, hard work was necessary. In February 1934 Arellano, who was soon to be appointed national leader of the Carlist Youth, declared that since 1932 he had participated in over 200 acts of Carlist and social-Catholic propaganda, mostly in 'the plain of Navarre'.[42] The overlapping of Carlist and social-Catholic propaganda was further demonstrated later the same year, when the CNCA and Catholic Action jointly mounted in Pamplona a course for 'agrarian propagandists', the later fruits of which were borne mainly south of the provincial capital; the course was given not only by non-Carlist social-Catholics but also by two Carlists from *latifundista* areas, Lamamié from Salamanca and Jesús Requejo from Toledo, who expressed profoundly conservative views on property.[43] 'Agrarian propagandists' were prominent in February 1935, when Carlism's new national leader, the Andalusian Manuel Fal Conde, visited Navarre and held several public meetings, all in or close to the *ribera*.[44]

Carlist propaganda in the south was presented as a challenge to left-wing dominance: peasants and labourers were to be wooed away from 'Marxism' through the social message of the papal encyclicals *Rerum Novarum* and *Quadragesimo Anno*, the material safety-net of the CNCA, and if necessary the physical protection of the *Requeté*. Significantly, however, energies were not evenly expended across the region. Both effort and reward were least where the going was toughest – in the main left-wing citadels along the north bank of the Ebro between Mendavia and the railway town of Castejón. More attention was paid to the partially irrigated, agriculturally more mixed and generally more prosperous valleys of the Arga, Cidacos and Aragon, together with the fertile Alhama and Queiles valleys south of the Ebro – districts of greater social complexity than the Ebro bank itself, with a sizeable Catholic population ripe for recruitment. It was in such areas that Carlism made some progress in the April 1933 local elections and that the right as a whole advanced strongly in the general election of November 1933; that the membership of existing Carlist organizations expanded; and that new Carlist circles, indicating new concentrations of support, were still opening during 1935.[45] Especially important, given the *ribera*'s conflictive atmosphere, was the growth of the *Requeté*. By early 1935 its membership appears to have numbered some 120 in both Corella and Cascante; eighty each in Tudela, Peralta and Tulebras; over sixty in Murchante; and over forty in both Arguedas and Fustiñana. Recruitment continued at a high rate thereafter; within a few more months the membership in Corella, for example, was over 500.[46] Nevertheless there is little evidence that Carlist ranks swelled with day-labourers or poor peasants. The Carlists themselves would have been the first to publicize any such success, and it is noteworthy that when in 1933 attempts were made to launch an 'anti-Marxist peasants' front' in the *ribera* they sank without trace.[47] Instead, Carlism in the Navarrese south provided a rallying point for an assortment of smallholders, modest traders and businessmen, and devoutly Catholic professional people.

Although before 1933 Carlist expansion in southern Navarre may have represented defensiveness in the face of Republican policies and local left-wing advances, from late 1933 onwards this was no longer the case. From then until February 1936 the advantage lay once again with landowners and employers. Following the Asturias rising of October 1934 this situation was reinforced further, with Socialist *casas del pueblo* closed for months on end and the Carlist-led right recapturing the provincial government during 1935.[48] In a climate such as this, Carlism's intensified thrust into the *ribera* bore all the hallmarks of a counter-offensive.

If it was the Carlist notables who initiated and led a course which marked Carlism's development from a predominantly anti-liberal 'cause' into a far more rigorously organized movement of opposition to democracy and 'socialism', there was certainly little open reluctance among the rank and file to flow with the tide. Nor did a more ostentatious show of social concern on the part of a Carlist mean less hostility towards the left: just the opposite. Some younger Carlists briefly, during 1934–5, chilled their elders' spines with exalted talk of a 'Carlist Revolution' of poor against rich. Talk was all it was, however, and even for such self-conscious radicals as these sons of the Pamplona bourgeoisie it was the battle against the 'latter-day disciples of Karl Marx' which took priority over any war on capital. Well before 1936 Navarrese leftists were wounded and even killed by Carlist weapons, but the bankers of Pamplona and the landlords of the *ribera* survived unmolested.[49]

Carlism's role in the *ribera* and its increasing emphasis generally upon paramilitarism convinced Navarrese leftists that they were in the presence of fascism. The *Requeté*, by far the most visible and threatening manifestation of Carlism's revival, to the Socialists in particular seemed, in its style, behaviour and role, to resemble not so much the Carlist volunteers of the nineteenth century as the Italian *squadré* of the previous decade. More than once during the Republic the left warned the regime's leaders of the more than local threat posed by the *Requeté*; if fears of an imminent 'March on Madrid' as early as 1933 were premature, as an assessment of Carlist intentions they were anything but absurd.[50] From the Republic's earliest days the assumption was general among Navarrese Carlists, leaders and masses alike, that sooner or later violence would be needed to overthrow the Republic and that Carlism must provide a major part of that violence. Young Carlists carried concealed weapons from the start; paramilitary squads were being formed within the first few weeks; and throughout the next five years recruitment, training and the smuggling into Navarre of weapons steadily increased.[51]

Navarrese Socialists were correct to conclude that such preparations could have only one essential purpose. The Navarrese Carlist élite was working not only to oppose and obstruct secularizing and socially reforming policies but actually to destroy the very regime which made the pursuit of such policies possible. Most, like Rodezno, appreciated that despite its flourishing condition in Navarre Carlism lacked sufficient strength elsewhere to perform this task unaided. The Navarrese thus displayed a consistent willingness to collaborate, first politically and then conspiratorially, with other rightist parties – Alfonsist monarchists, Catholics and Falangists – and with anti-republican army officers. In March 1934 it was in this spirit that Rodezno, still – though not for much longer – Carlism's national leader, authorized Carlist participation in the joint monarchist-military mission to Mussolini which forged one link in the chain leading to July 1936, as well as giving members of the Navarrese *Requeté* the chance to receive training in Italy. Finally, in 1936 itself, Rodezno and his fellow-Navarrese bypassed their movement's hesitant national leadership in order to ensure the *Requeté*'s commitment to the imminent rising. That story, like that of the *Requeté*'s exploits in the Civil War, has been told at length elsewhere.[52]

As the Navarrese Carlist élite realized, joining a broad alliance of the right meant that Carlism's 'maximum' programme of a decentralized, social-Catholic monarchy was most unlikely to be the reward for the sacrifice of their followers' blood. With the authoritarian, centralizing officer corps all but certain to control the insurgent forces, and with 'fascism' in the air, Carlists might instead, in order to be rid of the Republic and of 'socialism', have to settle for a more 'modern' regime: one not entirely unlike some of those abroad – in Italy and Austria for example – for which many Carlists during the 1930s had more than a sneaking regard.

The best guarantee against too great a compromise in this direction was Carlism's impressive strength in Navarre, as graphically revealed in the numbers – perhaps 40,000 – of the Navarrese *Requeté* committed to the insurgent war effort. The military leadership of Nationalist Spain could not but be impressed; once Navarre had been purged of 'separatism' and 'Marxism', the local Carlists were therefore permitted to assume control over the province. Within its borders they proceeded to create a semblance of the social-Catholic utopia with which they had been beguiling their supporters during the Republic. Education and culture underwent wholesale clericalization; the Catholic syndicates largely run by Carlists before the war were extended and elevated into a corporatist governmental and social apparatus; and, of course, property was frozen in its pre-war state. Franco's arbitrary fusion of the Carlist and Falangist movements in April 1937, if not exactly popular with most Navarrese Carlists, was nevertheless accepted in the realization that whilst it might change the form of things in Navarre, so secure was Carlist control of the province that it was unlikely to change the substance. And so it proved; with Navarrese autonomy partially restored as a reward for her contribution to the 'Crusade', the province became, within Franco's Spain, a virtual fief of those Carlist notables prepared to collaborate with the regime.[53]

Without doubt, much of the Navarrese Carlist élite found this arrangement an acceptable one, if for no better reason than that it guaranteed the return to Navarre of that social harmony which had been so central a part of Carlist pre-war propaganda. The manner of its return nevertheless glaringly exposed the contradictory nature of the social-Catholicism to which most leading Carlists – and many of their allies – subscribed. For social harmony had been restored not by attacking the disease of social and economic inequality, present even in the arcadia of Navarre, but by eliminating its symptoms – what Carlists were wont to dismiss as 'socialism'; it was based not upon the religiously inspired consensus of which social-Catholics fruitlessly dreamed, but on the shedding of blood and the silencing of opposition; and it was protected not within a framework of decentralization such as Carlists advocated but under the auspices of an authoritarian, centralizing and oppressive state. The Navarrese Carlists thus solved the problem of the *ribera* as the Spanish right generally solved the problem of Spain. For the leaders of a supposedly backward-looking cause, it was a very modern kind of solution.

Notes

1 Hugh Thomas, *The Spanish Civil War*, 3rd edn (Harmondsworth, 1977), 260–5. Thomas's chief sources were Juan de Iturralde, *El catolicismo y la Cruzada de Franco* (Bayonne, 1960), II, and Fr Iñaki de Aberrigoyen, *Sept mois et sept jours dans l'Espagne de Franco* (Paris, 1938). For a post-war pro-nationalist account, see Jaime del Burgo, *Conspiración y guerra civil* (Madrid and Barcelona, 1970), 63–9, 87–107.

2 Gerald Brenan, *The Spanish Labyrinth*, 2nd edn (Cambridge, 1962), 97.

3 Thomas, op. cit., 97–8.

4 Ronald Fraser, *Blood of Spain* (London, 1979), 123.

5 For a useful examination of differing approaches to the regional divisions within Navarre, see Jaime del Burgo, *Historia de Navarra. La lucha por la libertad* (Madrid, 1978), 81–110. The divisions employed in the present essay are admittedly open to the criticism of exaggerating the breadth of the central zone in both a northerly and a southerly direction, but appear the most useful for the essay's purposes.

6 Edward E. Malefakis, *Agrarian Reform and Peasant Revolution in Spain. Origins of the Civil War* (New Haven and London, 1970), 25–8, 401–5.

7 Joseph Harrison, *An Economic History of Modern Spain* (Manchester, 1978), 7; Malefakis, op. cit., 15.

8 V. Huici Urmeneta, M. Sorauren, J. Ma. Jimeno Jurio, *Historia contemporánea de Navarra* (San Sebastián, 1982), 111–13. On the *señoríos* see also Jacques Maurice, *La reforma agraria en España en el siglo XX (1900–1936)* (Madrid, 1975), 93.

9 Brenan, op. cit., 96. On *aparcería* generally, see Malefakis, op. cit., 117–8, 122–3; also the valuable volume produced by the British Admiralty, Naval Intelligence Division, *Spain and Portugal, III: Spain* (London, 1944), 200.

10 On disentailment in Navarre see Javier María Donézar, *La desamortización de Mendizábal en Navarra* (Madrid, 1975) and more particularly Rafael Gómez Chaparro, *La desamortización civil en Navarra* (Pamplona, 1967), 136–9, 168–71; also José Andrés Gallego, *Historia contemporánea de Navarra* (Pamplona, 1982), 75–85.

11 British Admiralty, op. cit., 157, 167.

12 For figures relating to regular clergy, see Manuel Ramírez Jiménez, *Los grupos de presión en la segunda República española* (Madrid, 1969), 198–200.

13 Fraser, op. cit., 125.

14 Josefina Cuesta Bustillo, *Sindicalismo católico agrario en España (1917–1919)* (Madrid, 1978), 133–6; José R. Montero, *La CEDA. El catolicismo social y político en la II República* (Madrid, 1977), I, 82.

15 Ortzi, *Historia de Euzkadi: el nacionalismo vasco y ETA* (Paris, 1975), 207. On the state of Basque language and culture in the late 1920s, see Rodney Gallop, *A Book of the Basques* (London, 1930), especially 37–9.

16 Miguel M. Cuadrado, *Elecciones y partidos políticos en España (1868–1931)* (Madrid, 1969), I, 319–489 *passim*; II, 881–1001 *passim*.

17 Martin Blinkhorn, *Carlism and Crisis in Spain, 1931–1939* (Cambridge, 1975), 72–8.

18 On the early Carlist contribution to Basque Nationalism see Stanley G. Payne, 'Carlism: Basque or "Spanish" traditionalism', *Anglo-American Contributions to Basque Studies. Essays in Honor of Jon Bilbao*, William A. Douglass *et al.* (eds.) (Reno, 1977); and Blinkhorn, op. cit., 34–5.

19 Mariano Ansó, *Yo fuí ministro de Negrín* (Barcelona, 1976), 17–31; Octavio Ruiz Manjón, *El Partido Republicano Radical, 1908–1936* (Madrid, 1976), 612–4, provides some information on the Radical Party in Navarre during the 1930s.

20 The quote is from Brenan, op. cit., 97.

21 The fullest results of general elections in Navarre between 1931 and 1936 were published in the *Boletín Oficial de la Provincia de Navarra*, Pamplona, special issues of 1 July 1931, 22 November 1933 and 19 February 1936 (hereafter referred to as *BOPN*).

22 *BOPN*, 1 July 1931.

23 *BOPN*, 1 July 1931, 22 November 1933, 19 February 1936.

24 *Boletín de Orientación Tradicionalista*, Madrid, 21 October 1934; Antonio Lizarza Iribarren, *Memorias de la conspiración. Cómo se preparó en Navarra la Cruzada, 1931–1936*, 4th edn (Pamplona, 1969), 56–9.

25 On the evolution of Carlist ideology and policies, see R. M. Blinkhorn, 'Ideology and schism in Spanish traditionalism, 1874–1931', *Iberian Studies*, I (1972).

26 *El Pensamiento Navarro*, 13 April, 28 June 1931; 25 April 1933.

27 Shlomo Ben-Ami, *The Origins of the Second Republic in Spain* (Oxford, 1978), 310.

28 *El Pensamiento Navarro*, 13 April, 2 June 1931.

29 *BOPN*, 1 July 1931, 22 November 1933, 19 February 1936.

30 For a more detailed discussion of these issues, see R. M. Blinkhorn, ' "The Basque Ulster". Navarre and the Basque autonomy question under the Spanish Second Republic', *The Historical Journal*, XVII, 3 (1974), 595–613. Aspects of this article are modified by Mikel Button, 'The betrayal of Navarre: a study of the events leading to Navarre's exclusion from the Basque Statute of 1932' (unpublished M. A. thesis, University of Birmingham, 1980) and by José María Jimeno Jurio, *Navarra jamás dijo No al Estatuto Vasco* (Pamplona, 1977), especially 87–103. See also José Antonio de Agirre y Lekube, *Entre la libertad y la revolución, 1930–1935* (Bilbao, 1976), 289–305.

31 Agirre, op. cit., 305–16; Blinkhorn, *Carlism and Crisis*, 83–4, 105–6. Fraser, op. cit., 541, recounts an interview with a rank-and-file Carlist who believed the movement's masses would still have accepted autonomy had their leaders done so.

32 *El Siglo Futuro*, Madrid, 3 June 1931, 4, 6, 10 February 1932; *El Pensamiento Navarro*, 12 February 1932; Blinkhorn, *Carlism and Crisis*, 78, 99–100, 103–4.

33 Montero, op. cit., I, 408–9.

34 On the generally neglected subject of rural leases legislation, see Malefakis, op. cit., 269–73.

35 *El Socialista*, Madrid, 10 October 1933.

36 The most informative source on the Navarrese left and in particular its

activities in the agrarian sphere is the provincial UGT weekly ·
¡¡*Trabajadores*!!. See, among other issues, those of 15 September and 13
October 1933.

37 *El Pensamiento Navarro*, 12 October 1932.

38 *El Siglo Futuro*, 3 November 1931.

39 *El Siglo Futuro*, 8 August 1932; *Revista Social y Agraria*, Madrid, 30 September 1933.

40 Blinkhorn, *Carlism and Crisis*, 104, 194–5.

41 ¡¡*Trabajadores*!! 6 October 1933; *El Socialista* 10 October 1933.

42 *El Siglo Futuro*, 13 February 1934; *El Pensamiento Navarro*, 8 March 1934.

43 *El Siglo Futuro*, 29, 30 August 1935.

44 *Boletín de Orientación Tradicionalista*, 17 February 1935.

45 On the local elections of April 1933 and the general election of November
1933 see, respectively, *El Pensamiento Navarro*, 25 April 1933 and *BOPN*,
22 November 1933. For other Carlist activities see *El Pensamiento Navarro*,
31 March, 2 April, 15, 17 May 1935.

46 Lizarza, op. cit., 86.

47 *El Siglo Futuro*, 31 May 1933.

48 *El Pensamiento Navarro*, 25 August, 8 November 1934; 25, 29 January, 8
September 1935; *El Siglo Futuro*, 26, 29 January, 27 August 1935; *Boletín de
Orientación Tradicionalista*, 3 February 1935.

49 The mouthpiece for this revolutionism was the Pamplona weekly *a.e.t.*
Extracts appear in Jaime del Burgo, *Requetés en Navarra antes del Alzamiento*
(San Sebastián, 1939).

50 *El Siglo Futuro*, 7 August, 30 November 1933; Ansó, op. cit., 122–3. *El
Siglo Futuro* and other Carlist organs delighted in publishing and loudly
denying Socialist reports of what both sides knew to be substantially the
truth.

51 See Lizarza, op. cit.; Burgo, *Conspiración y guerra civil* and *Requetés en
Navarra*, both *passim*; and B. Félix Maíz, *Alzamiento en España. De un diario
de la conspiración* (Pamplona, 1952).

52 Blinkhorn, *Carlism and Crisis*, 207–70.

53 ibid., 251–95; also Burgo, *Conspiración y guerra civil, passim*.

4
Regionalism and revolution in Catalonia

Norman Jones

The proclamation of the Second Republic presented the Catalans with
an exceptional opportunity to loosen the constriction of unsympathetic
and inefficient rule from Madrid. Resentment of central government
had an economic base. Catalonia was the most prosperous part of Spain.
Constituting one-eighth of the Spanish population, Catalans argued
that they contributed nearly a quarter of total state revenue, while only
one-twentieth of this reverted to the region in the form of public
spending. It was hardly surprising, then, that Catalans greeted the
Republic as a way of breaking the centralist hold. Their initial success in
obtaining home rule was frustrated by the calculated dilatoriness of the

new regime's politicians in Madrid, by conflicts of interests among the autonomists themselves and by the violent radicalization of the region's labour movement. For the duration of the Republic, Catalan political life became introspective to a degree that largely precluded constructive participation on the wider Spanish scene.

The collapse of the Primo de Rivera dictatorship effectively placed the defence of Catalanist aspirations in the hands of the local republican left. The bourgeois Lliga Regionalista, led by the financier Francesc Cambó, had tacitly supported the dictatorship as a bulwark against the anarcho-syndicalist Confederación Nacional del Trabajo. When Primo had been revealed to be a traditional military centralist, the Lliga had been discredited. Moreover, the Lliga's monarchism was out of joint with the times and the various left Catalanist groups were able to reap the benefit. Inevitably, it was to these that the republicans of the rest of Spain turned for support in the movement against the monarchy. The price exacted by the Catalans was one of significant concessions of local autonomy. However, the Pact of San Sebastián of August 1930 was not to provide the springboard for Catalan resurgence that had been hoped for. Despite right-wing smears that republicanism meant separatism, the republicans of Madrid were in fact to work hard to claw back the concessions made in 1930.

Originally, the Spanish republicans were drawn to Acció Catalana as their Catalan interlocutor. Acció Catalana had been created in 1922 out of a defection of the Lliga youth section in protest at the conservative policies of Cambó. In style, it was a serious, responsible, soundly organized and well financed party. However, for all that its style appealed to Madrid republicans, its influence in Catalonia was dramatically overshadowed by that of two other groups which both had massively popular and charismatic leaders. The first was the separatist party, Estat Català, led by Colonel Francesc Macià, the grand old man of intransigent Catalan nationalism. The second was the Partit Republicà Català, led bythe labour lawyer, Lluis Companys, a man with considerable influence among the more moderate sections of the CNT. A third, albeit much smaller group, gathered around the weekly leftist journal, L'Opinió, published by a group of young Barcelona lawyers captained by Joan Lluhí. They had already made clear a number of doubts concerning the Pact of San Sebastián. The verbal agreement was apparently straightforward. Once a republic was established, the Catalan town councils would draft an autonomy statute which, after a regional referendum, would be ratified by the Cortes. However, doubts hinged on whether the republic would be federal and, if not, whether there was any guarantee that a Spanish Cortes would accept a Catalan statute without amendment.[1]

The *L'Opinió* group, known as the Lluhins, in loose association with Companys, had been trying since May 1930 to gather together the various elements of Catalan republicanism into a front well to the left of the middle-class Acció Catalana. To do so, they exploited something ignored by most politicians of metropolitan Barcelona: the potential organizational basis provided by hundreds of republican clubs that survived as down-at-heel social centres in provincial towns and villages. The key was Companys. He had been Catalan co-ordinator for the abortive Spanish plots against the dictatorship, suffering frequent imprisonment. Astute, if impulsive, radiating affability, he had contacts throughout the region: in the inland textile towns; among the 20,000 tenant farmers whom he had organized into the Unió de Rabassaires; among the federalists of Reus and Gerona and the Republican Youth of his native Lérida. For their part, the Lluhins had proselytized the provincial clubs since 1928 in successive lecture tours as exponents of an 'advanced' republicanism that admired Viennese social democracy and the British Labour Party.[2]

Realizing that Estat Català lacked the electoral machinery to take advantage of his own immense popularity, Macià enthusiastically led his followers to a 'Conference of the Left', organized by the Lluhins and held on 18 and 19 March 1931. Hurried debate of policy documents drafted by the Lluhins culminated in the foundation of a new party. Macià was elected its president, with a twelve-man committee reflecting its tripartite origins: two from Estat Català, three Lluhins and the remainder from provincial republican centres and Companys' PRC, which ceased to exist. The Lluhins wanted the party's name to include the word 'socialist', but the conference opted for the more moderate Esquerra Republicana de Catalunya, Republican Left of Catalonia.[3] With municipal elections only three weeks away, the Esquerra proposed a coalition with Acció Catalana but was rejected.[4] In contrast to Acció Catalana's restrained concentration on municipal issues, the Esquerra conducted an energetic campaign centring on the abuses of the monarchical regime. The voting on 12 April 1931 was the heaviest ever recorded in Catalonia, two-thirds of the electorate coming to the polls. The result, as elsewhere in Spain, was an overwhelming anti-monarchist plebiscite. In Barcelona the victory went clearly and un-expectedly to the Esquerra, with 36 per cent, followed by the Lliga and the Radicals, with 24 per cent each, and Acció Catalana, with 16 per cent.

For the first time in Catalonia, a majority of the working class had voted and did so mainly for the Esquerra. In Madrid, the suspicion was henceforth nurtured that the Esquerra had a secret electoral pact with the CNT, despite the fact that the anarcho-syndicalist leadership was unable to produce votes to order, even had they been so inclined. In fact, the CNT stood aside. 'The masses', wrote Joan Peiró, 'felt an irresistible urge to change the political décor of the State. . . . We never told the workers to go to vote, but neither did we tell them to abstain.'[5] They voted for political change, for the material improvements that the Esquerra optimistically promised in education, housing, health services and pensions, and, like the lower middle classes, for the 'party of Macià', for a Catalonia not administered from Madrid. To a surprising degree, the Esquerra retained their support until the war.

At 1.30 p.m. on 14 April, eight hours before the King left Madrid, Companys proclaimed the Republic from the balcony of the Barcelona town hall. As the news spread, Macià was hastily summoned. After briefly conferring, he made his own proclamation to a growing crowd of a 'Catalan State which we shall cordially endeavour to integrate within the federation of Iberian Republics'.[6] It was an act of oppor-tunism beyond the provisions of the Pact of San Sebastián, exploiting the power vacuum in Madrid to stake a maximalist claim for autonomy. Macià hoped, by this *fait accompli*, to commit the Republic to a federal constitution. For two days, the provisional government in Madrid was too preoccupied with consolidating its hold on central power to deal with the anomalous situation in Catalonia, but Macià's appointment of his own seven-man 'government' made it imperative to intervene. Three ministers were dispatched by air to Barcelona on 17 April. In the evening they issued with Macià a joint communiqué which recommitted Catalonia to the path marked out at San Sebastián.[7] However, under arrangements formalized in decrees of 21 April and 9 May, Macià's administration was recognized as the provisional government of the

'Generalitat', an inspired antiquarian *trouvaille*, since for Catalans it revived the title of their independent medieval government, while for Madrid it signified nothing. In reality, the Generalitat was permitted to run the four provincial councils of Catalonia (as the Mancomunitat had done), and to exercise powers of decree in matters not reserved to central government.

Macià's coalition cabinet included three Esquerra representatives and one each from the Radicals, Acció Catalana, and the two small socialist parties in Catalonia. He vainly invited Pestaña to represent the CNT as labour councillor. The Lliga was omitted, on the grounds that it was non-republican, and it consequently refused to collaborate in constituting a regional assembly, elected by town councils, which met in June to appoint the commission to draft an autonomy statute. The document that emerged from this body, the 'Statute of Núria', was nevertheless far from the maximalist claim Madrid expected: indeed it was similar, in its apportionment of central and regional prerogatives, to one proposed by the Lliga in 1919.[8] It was put to the Catalan people in a referendum on 2 August. All parties recommended it, from the Lliga to the Communists, and the result was its overwhelming approval by 99.4 per cent of the votes, or three-quarters of the electorate. Two weeks later Macià presented the statute to Alcalá Zamora, who laid it before the Cortes as a government bill. It had, however, to wait until the Cortes completed the prior task of debating a new Spanish constitution.

The impressive Catalan solidarity demonstrated in the referendum was due, in part, to a series of conflicts between the Generalitat and individual ministers in Madrid, prominently reported in the Barcelona press. Maura, Minister of the Interior, who from the outset had opposed legitimizing Macià's government, was its most uncompromising adversary. He took care to exclude Esquerra sympathizers from the region's four civil governorships – with the exception of Companys' brief tenure of that of Barcelona – and systematically thwarted the Generalitat by insisting on his right to designate all local functionaries.[9] Prieto, Minister of Finance, caused a furore in July when his ministry, in what was seen as 'an attack on Catalan financial institutions', vetoed Barcelona city council's plan to resolve its accumulated deficit and forced it into technical bankruptcy, provoked the collapse of Catalonia's biggest bank by withdrawing state deposits, and temporarily closed

Barcelona's independent stock exchange.[10] There were many similar incidents, though it was Largo Caballero at the Ministry of Labour, as we shall see, who caused the greatest friction. A general crisis in relations was prevented from developing only by Macià's almost daily telephone conversations with Alcalá Zamora – a lifelong friend – and the diplomacy of Hurtado, the Acció Catalana lawyer who acted as his personal envoy in the capital.[11]

Central government's refusal to tolerate any initiative on the part of Macià's administration could be seen simply as strict implementation of the San Sebastián agreement[12]; but it was also inspired by ministers' disdain for the Esquerra, whose leaders they regarded as inexperienced nonentities thrown up by the April revolution. They were convinced that the party's heterogeneous composition and social base made it unviable in the longer term. They persisted in this view despite the Esquerra's resounding victory in the June parliamentary elections, when it swept Catalonia taking 68 per cent of the votes and forty-one of the fifty-one seats. The ineffectual Nicolau, leader of the badly defeated Acció Catalana, was retained in the cabinet as Catalonia's 'representative'. In riposte to such 'Bourbon centralism', the Esquerra abstained from the vote of confidence in the government at the opening of the Cortes. During the debate, Maura and Largo accused the Esquerra of being the handmaid of the CNT.[13]

The Esquerra had indeed enjoyed a brief honeymoon, or tentative liaison, with the CNT. Peiró, in *Solidaridad Obrera*, praised Macià's 'equanimity and liberal spirit'.[14] In May, syndicalists helped guard Barcelona churches against possible incendiarist attacks in imitation of those in Madrid. Companys, as civil governor, pressed employers to concede workers' claims in the numerous industrial disputes of early summer. This provoked repeated public reprimands from Largo, intent on having all labour conflicts submitted to his ministry's 'new' arbitration boards – and, through them, promoting the growth in Catalonia of his own UGT.

The very idea of state arbitration was anathema to anarcho-syndicalists. Worse still, many of the chairmen of the boards, and the labour ministry's delegate in Barcelona, Pius López, had been retained by Largo from the old *comités paritarios* of the dictatorship. Companys, and the Generalitat, therefore turned a deaf ear to Largo's injunctions to refrain from interfering with his ministry's monopoly of labour affairs.[15] In the most serious dispute, Macià discreetly negotiated a return to work by the CNT dockers' union, which had paralysed the port of Barcelona in a fight for recognition by the employers, who engaged UGT blacklegs. However, when Companys resigned the governorship in June (to lead the Esquerra in the Cortes), Maura replaced him with an authoritarian Acció Catalana magistrate, Anguera de Sojo, who revoked the 'improper' docks settlement. The strike recommenced, with shooting incidents between CNT and UGT. Anguera's methods hastened the CNT's evolution towards insurrectionism. August brought a wave of industrial disputes in which he increasingly used his police powers to try to compel observance of Largo's labour legislation. If a union refused to go to arbitration, its strike was illegal; Anguera had its pickets and strike committee arrested, and encouraged the employer to resist and recruit fresh labour.

In August thirty of the best-known syndicalist leaders issued a warning – the 'Treintista Manifesto' – against jeopardizing the CNT's long-term goal of social revolution by involving it with the uncoordinated and counterproductive violence of the militant anarchists of the FAI. They were disregarded: *Faístas* were gaining positions of influence in the organization. On 3 September a general strike was called in protest against Anguera's detention of syndicalists. From early morning there was firing throughout the city as armed men prevented food deliveries to markets and halted public transport. Anguera ordered the police to react vigorously, and there were forty casualties and three fatalities in gun-battles. On the second day police stormed the *Faístas*' strongpoint in the building workers' union, and later shot dead three of their prisoners inside central police headquarters. The strike collapsed, but the Local Federation of Barcelona unions declared that its 'truce with the Republic' was ended.[16]

The Esquerra vociferously dissociated itself from Anguera. Its press conducted a campaign of denigration against 'the Acció Catalana governor' which finally provoked his resignation in December, with that of Acció Catalana's representatives in the Generalitat and Madrid. At rallies hastily organized in working-class areas, Macià pleaded for social peace until the Generalitat acquired powers to regulate labour affairs. But on 20 January 1932 miners on strike in the Pyrenean foothills, encouraged by *Faísta* agitators from Barcelona, occupied the surrounding townships and proclaimed a libertarian revolution. Azaña instantly dispatched army units; they occupied the mining zone without meeting resistance, but interior minister Casares nevertheless deported 119 detained miners to Spanish Guinea as exemplary punishment. A further general strike on 15 February, in protest against the deportations, was only partially supported by workers, but was marked by the most violent incidents: explosions, sabotage of railways, and the seizure of Terrassa town hall by *Faístas*. The new civil governor, Moles, closed all Barcelona unions. Six months of labour quiescence ensued, during which the rift between messianic and moderate leaders deepened and split the CNT.

The first anniversary of the Republic was celebrated by the Esquerra with an external enthusiasm that overlaid deep unease. Its hopes of a *modus vivendi* with organized labour were dashed and the Generalitat still lacked real power and finance. Yet the party enjoyed popular goodwill and local centres continued to affiliate: six hundred were represented at its first congress, in February.[17] If it was not allowed to govern, it could at least propagandize. Macià ceaselessly toured Catalonia with a stamina that belied his years, indiscriminately inaugurating primary schools, village fêtes and Esquerra centres with speeches stressing the fraternity between all Iberian peoples. If this was the 'incorrigible incendiarist' abhorred by Madrid,[18] his pyromania took a subtle and subdued form.

The draft autonomy statute that Macià had taken to Madrid in August went through report stage in the Cortes from January to April 1932. It was not merely 'harmonized' with the non-federal Spanish constitution, but substantially attentuated. In May debate on the floor of the chamber began. The bill's passage was rendered excruciatingly slow by the hostile procedural devices of forty right-wing deputies who filibustered and tabled two hundred amendments.[19] Lerroux allowed his party a free vote, and some thirty Radicals reinforced the obstruction by the right. The government's own supporters were lukewarm – half the left Republican and Socialist deputies regularly abstained from divisions – and Azaña avoided serious risk of defeat only at the cost of further curtailment of the statute. After ten weeks, only five of its forty-eight articles had been approved, and the Esquerra threatened to withdraw from the Cortes. Outside parliament, an inflamed public opinion mirrored the acerbity of the sessions. In Castile, the right fanned traditional anti-Catalan animosity into boycotts of Catalan products, and demonstrations attended by tens of thousands. In Catalonia, Macià expressed confidence in the final outcome, but lesser politicians and journalists unrestrainedly denounced 'Castilian oppression'. The ultra-nationalist nuclei – the largest of which, Estat Català's youth movement, kept its own identity within the Esquerra – made implausible threats of armed resistance, which Madrid's right-wing press reported prominently as the authentic separatist voice of the Esquerra.[20] However, it was finally the failure of Sanjurjo's rising on 10 August that convinced rightist deputies that further obstruction was futile. The remaining articles were passed without formal divisions, and on 9 September the entire statute was approved by 314 votes to 24, with 116 abstentions.

The statute of autonomy was not generous, though its implementation entailed a substantial organizational task. It created a Catalan parliament, whose legislative competence was limited to agriculture, the secondary transport network, public health and poor relief, regulation of municipal government, and Catalan civil law. However, the statute also authorized the Generalitat to *administer* (as agent for the central power, without any legislative competence) public education, major public works, labour conciliation services, and the police forces and law courts. In all these areas, nevertheless, amendments had introduced close state inspection and provision for unilateral intervention from Madrid. The gravest alteration inverted the draft statute's financial terms: barely one-third of Catalan taxation was allotted to the Generalitat, to be handed over to cover the costs of existing state services in the region as they were transferred from Madrid. The remainder – the direct taxation – was retained by the state. The Generalitat would therefore be unable to improve the minimal existing public services without increasing indirect taxation.[21]

Campaigning began at once for the election of the Catalan parliament on 20 November. The results were acclaimed by the Esquerra as its third successive triumph at the ballot-box. Its candidates won sixty-seven of the eighty-five seats in the regional parliament, leaving the Lliga a mere seventeen, and Acció Catalana one. But the figures for actual votes cast showed that the Esquerra had passed its zenith: its share of the poll fell from the record 68 per cent of the 1931 Cortes elections, to 46 per cent. The Lliga's share rose from 15 to 28 per cent.[22]

The parliament duly re-elected Macià president, and on 19 December he formed a so-called 'monocolour' government, the first to be composed exclusively from the Esquerra. To the resentment of the nationalist wing, Estat Català still had only one representative, while the other six councillors included no less than three members of the L'Opinió group. Since Terradelles, councillor for the interior, was increasingly identified with these, the Lluhins effectively held a majority in cabinet. Lluhí himself was appointed conseller delegat, a post apparently approximating to prime minister, though ill-defined in the statute.

Macià's advancement of the Lluhins caused surprise, since their social-democrat following in the party was small, but they had proved themselves in the Cortes to be the Esquerra's most capable parliamentarians. Lluhí was known to be highly regarded by Azaña and thus seemed a logical choice to pilot the Generalitat during the delicate transfer of powers.[23] Yet within a month the cabinet was in crisis, over an offer from Madrid to appoint Terradelles as civil governor of Barcelona. Lluhí welcomed the proposal, but Macià vetoed its acceptance. The Lluhins and Terradelles resigned on 18 January 1933. Macià chose a centrist, Pi Sunyer, as his new conseller delegat. To placate the nationalists, he also promoted to the cabinet the leading Estat Català demagogue, Dr Dencàs.

Although the January crisis was precipitated by a clash of personalities and factions, it reflected underlying divergences in appreciating the problems facing the Generalitat. These fell into three separate but connected categories: the CNT's espousal of revolutionary violence; the interminable delay in the transfer of powers from Madrid; and the growth of middle-class disillusion.

The division in Catalan syndicalism had dramatically deepened during the previous year. The old guard of treintista leaders, whether purists like Peiró or pragmatists like Pestaña, had not renounced the goal of social revolution, but saw it as culminating a process of consolidation of the CNT as a labour organization. Mindful of the union's near-annihilation under Primo, they valued the Republic's relative freedom of association. For their 'anarcho-bolshevik' rivals, the Faístas, the CNT was simply a tool to be used by a militant vanguard to overthrow the Republic by insurrection at the earliest opportunity. During

1932 the *Faístas* extended their hold from the regional committee (in April) to the big Barcelona unions (in autumn). They often achieved this by blatant abuse of union procedure,[24] though in general they were supported by unskilled workers, many of whom were politically naive immigrants from the South. Outside the city, however, many unions rejected *Faísta* leadership, ceased paying contributions to the regional federation, and disaffiliated or were expelled. The first to leave, in April, were the local unions of Lerida, Gerona and Tarragona, attracted to Maurín's autonomous communist Bloc Obrer i Camperol (BOC). In September the unions of Sabadell were expelled: this was the largest textile centre of provincial Barcelona, and henceforth the *treintistas'* main base.

On 8 January 1933 the *Faístas* launched a major insurrection, coordinated through the CNT's prisoners' defence committees. It extended throughout eastern Spain and Andalusia, where it provoked the Casas Viejas massacre. In Catalonia there were sixteen deaths, in various towns; *Faísta* groups attacked barracks in the hope of seizing arms, a town hall was captured, and there was much wild shooting and grenade-throwing, especially in central Barcelona. Though locally serious, the disturbances were soon suppressed by police. The *Faístas* called on workers to strike next day; response was poor, but the civil governor closed all Barcelona unions.

This fiasco brought the internal CNT dispute to a head. For the *treintistas* it was 'playing at revolution', alienating workers from syndicalism. They published figures indicating that defections had reduced the CNT's Barcelona membership, in eight months, from 162,000 to 72,000.[25] On 15 January thirty-two provincial unions joined those of Sabadell to sign a vitriolic anti-*Faísta* manifesto. They too were expelled from the CNT, and in May they founded a rival organization, the 'Opposition Unions', led by Pestaña.

These events illuminate the simultaneous Catalan cabinet crisis. The Lluhins were fascinated by the CNT's apparent decomposition. They were convinced that workers were now disenchanted with *Faísta* intuitive putschism, and that the Catalan unions must ultimately either come under communist direction, or – provided the Generalitat played its hand firmly – evolve towards reformist socialism. In their view, the time had come to exploit the schism by using the civil governor's powers to favour *treintistas* and similar 'better elements'.[26] Macià wanted to wait and see. If there had to be confrontation between authority and the CNT, he preferred central government to incur the odium.[27]

Macià's scepticism proved justified. Catalan workers were not so much divided, as demoralized, by the feud between syndicalist leaders. The Opposition Unions reached a total of only 35,000 members by August.[28] In Barcelona the unions remained in *Faísta* hands, but membership fell as a series of prolonged and bitter strikes – notably by the woodworkers (November–April), dockers (April–May) and construction workers (April–August) – failed to achieve their basic demands.[29] All were characterized by a proliferation of acts of violence. Throughout 1933 the Barcelona press reported arson in furniture factories, explosions in building sites, sabotage of vehicles, armed picketing, and the murder of several UGT strike-breakers. In midsummer there were two particularly ugly riots when several thousand striking bricklayers rampaged through central Barcelona, smashing shops and bars as they went. The new civil governor (Ametlla, of Acció Catalana) closed all Barcelona unions in July, but disorders continued.

Street lawlessness in successive labour conflicts contributed to a steady deterioration of the Esquerra's public standing. It coincided with a wave of hold-ups and payroll snatches by organized gangsters (and also by *Faístas*) that outraged middle-class opinion. The Lliga, regaining momentum as the party of law and order, organized protests against the authorities' inaction. There was a twenty-four hour closure of shops after raiders shot dead a prominent jeweller, and a crowd estimated at 20,000 booed the Generalitat's representatives in the funeral cortège.[30] The implication that the Esquerra connived at crime was preposterous: Barcelona's inadequate police force was still under state control.[31] But the Lliga blamed all ills, including the delay in implementing autonomy, on Esquerra ineptitude.

Indeed, twelve months after the statute's approval only three financially trivial services – hygiene, poor relief, and supervision of municipal government – had been transferred from Madrid, where treasury civil servants frustrated all advance.[32] The Generalitat, eager to inaugurate public works to mitigate unemployment, was consequently confined to the 45 million peseta income it had inherited from the former provincial councils, sufficient only for pre-existing (and largely rural) commitments. When anticipated transfers of services failed to materialize in April, it hurriedly had to issue loan stock for 15 million pesetas to avoid insolvency. The Catalan parliament languished similarly, having at times to suspend sessions for lack of legislation to handle.

The influence of Estat Català had grown rapidly within the Esquerra since the January crisis. This was partly a spontaneous expression of party frustration at the continued impotence of the Generalitat; it was also deliberately encouraged by Macià, for Estat Català's personal loyalty to him, its members' militancy, and their consequent disproportionate representation on the Barcelona area committee, allowed him to use it to counter other tendencies. He believed he could control its extremists, but the activities of its youth movement JEREC[33] became increasingly questionable during 1933. Led by Dencàs's secretary Badía, its 9000 members provided the *escamots* ('squads') that guarded Esquerra meetings against disruption by the *Faístas'* Juventudes Libertarias. In April, hundreds of them drove trams to break a transport strike called by the CNT to support the dockers. On occasions, *escamots* assaulted Lliga meetings, and vendors and printers of hostile periodicals. None of this was exceptional in the lamentably intolerant ethos of party youth movements of the time, but when they brought pistols into Esquerra centres to ensure election of Estat Català members as local committee officers, and their leader proclaimed 'the need, perhaps, to unfurl an anti-democratic flag', their excesses caused alarm within the party.[34] Yet Macià brooked no criticism of his 'lads', and when the Generalitat established a police college to train replacements for Castilians expected to request transfer to other regions, its 200 cadets were all selected from JEREC.

At the Esquerra's annual congress in July, Lluhí and Xirau warned that the party was becoming 'undemocratic and insufficiently leftist'. Delegates listened with displeasure, and passed overwhelmingly a motion of confidence in Macià. The Lluhins intensified, in *L'Opinió*, their comprehensive indictment of the Esquerra's failures: lack of labour policy, festering strikes, street disorder, inability to secure autonomous powers, scandal in the city council, and uncontrollable *escamots*. The inevitable denouement came in October: a special congress expelled the Lluhins, who founded a dissident party, the PNRE.[35] Simultaneously the important association of tenant-farmers, aggrieved by a ruling of Macià's agriculture councillor, withdrew support from the Esquerra.

Factional struggle in the Esquerra coincided with the disintegration of the republican coalition in Madrid. Two days after the Lluhins' expulsion, the Cortes were dissolved and general elections announced. Macià led the Esquerra into a stridently nationalistic electoral campaign. A parade by 8000 green-shirted *escamots* graced its major event, and half its Barcelona candidates were from Estat Català.[36]

There was also a last-minute appeal to the working class. In the last week of its life Azaña's government handed over competence in labour affairs to the Generalitat, and commenced transfer of the police forces. Macià remodelled his cabinet, appointing Barrera, a former CNT leader, as his labour councillor, and the newly acquired powers were ostentatiously used to detain a group of textile employers for thirty hours until they agreed to negotiate with a *treintista* strike committee.[37] Macià pledged himself to introduce 30 per cent retirement pension schemes by law in all industries after the elections.

Solidaridad Obrera and the CNT explicitly requested workers not to vote, but in Barcelona abstention on 19 November was only one per cent greater than in June 1931. Much more significant was the movement of the electorate to the Lliga: it won 40 per cent of the votes, and came first in three of the five Catalan constituencies, including Barcelona city, gaining twenty-eight seats in the Cortes. The Esquerra candidature won 41 per cent of the votes, but only twenty-six seats. The result effectively re-established a two-party system in Catalonia. It was the Esquerra's first electoral defeat, and if not a total disaster, it gave a stunning blow to the party.

The Generalitat now faced the latent threat of right-wing government in Madrid, which few doubted would seek pretexts to reduce the small measure of autonomy already won. Further blows befell it in the closing weeks of 1933. Public transport workers began an indefinite strike which proved to be, over the next nine months, the most destructively violent of all. On 8 December the third great *Faísta* uprising erupted in the working-class suburbs of Barcelona; the shooting, bombing and sabotage was less grave than in Aragón, but nevertheless took police in Catalonia four days to suppress. All CNT unions in Barcelona were once again closed. Finally, on Christmas Day, the waning charisma of Macià was abruptly extinguished by his sudden death from acute appendicitis.

Macià's disappearance made possible the formation of the broader alliance that he had so obstinately impeded and that was now plainly necessary. As in the rest of Spain, the right's victory in November forced the left to reunite; the difference was that in Catalonia it was done quickly, and from a position of at least nominal power. On the last day of 1933 the Catalan parliament elected Companys to the presidency of the Generalitat. His *bonhomie* and self-deprecation, even his faintly Chaplin-esque figure, contrasted unfavourably with his predecessor's elegant and inscrutable *gravitas*. Yet he was the inevitable choice, for no other Esquerra candidate could match his public popularity, his record of service to republicanism, and above all the promise of party reconciliation that he clearly represented. His occupations during 1933, as speaker of the parliament and later as an unlikely navy minister in Azaña's last government, had allowed him to stand aside from the factional feud in the Esquerra. He was clearly a republican more than he was a nationalist, and ideologically was presumed to sympathize with the Lluhíns, but Estat Català swallowed its objections to him as 'insufficiently Catalanist' in exchange for his undertaking to retain its two councillors in his cabinet.[38]

On 3 January Companys formed the expected four-party coalition government. Esteve, of Acció Catalana, became finance councillor, and Comorera, the new leader of Unió Socialista, took charge of agriculture and economy. Between these limits to right and left, the cabinet represented the traditional spectrum of the Esquerra. Lluhí was brought back, as justice councillor, and Companys reappointed four members of Macià's administration: Barrera continued as labour councillor, the centre-republican Selves handled the interior – which now entailed real command of the police – and Dencàs and Gassol kept the minor health and education posts.

Companys announced his government's immediate objectives as swift completion of pending transfers of powers from Madrid, firm enforcement of public order coupled with more agile intervention in labour disputes, and agrarian legislation to resolve tenant-farmers' grievances. 'Though grandiloquent posturing is not to my taste or proper to my position,' he added, 'we are ready to give our lives to defend Catalonia's rights, and the democratic parliamentary Republic.'[39]

An immediate opportunity to measure public response was provided by the thrice-postponed municipal elections which were finally held throughout Catalonia on 14 January. Companys invited to Barcelona the leaders of the Spanish republican left, now initiating their own *rapprochement*, and Azaña, Casares and Domingo came with Prieto to speak in support of the governmental coalition's joint municipal candidature at a mass rally. In a phrase that became a leitmotiv of 1934, Casares called Catalonia 'the bulwark of the Republic against the onslaught of the right'. Cambó, too, made the election a test of popular confidence beyond the municipal sphere, asserting that a Lliga victory would entitle it to demand early dissolution and new elections for the Catalan parliament. His optimism was however misplaced: the left won in all major towns. In Barcelona it gained 50 per cent of the votes, and the Lliga 41 per cent. Five days later, without giving explicit reasons, the Lliga began a boycott of the regional parliament that lasted until 1 October.[40]

The new government made determined efforts to put its programme into effect. Companys went to Madrid in February to urge greater expedition in transferring services. Lerroux appeared disposed to respect loyally the provisions of the statute, but his promises were vitiated by the usual treasury obstruction, and the Generalitat's assignments for transfers already authorized (particularly police, health, and the land tax) did not arrive on schedule, leaving it with mounting debts. In April and in June it had once more to resort to issuing loan stock, for a total 10.5 million pesetas.

Difficulties also arose with Madrid over the Generalitat's administration of labour affairs. Barrera and Selves intensified the policy of discriminating between unions in order to demonstrate to their rank and file the advantages of compliance with mandatory conciliation procedure, now that it was under Generalitat control. Barrera's nominees on arbitration boards accordingly handed down broadly favourable decisions to the non-CNT unions that presented claims. Employers baulked at these awards, and on 13 March Lerroux's labour minister signed an order empowering his delegate in Catalonia to hear individual employers' appeals.

As for the CNT, adamantly rejecting all arbitration, the Generalitat resorted to methods more draconian even than those of Anguera in 1931. Illegal strikes in the textile-finishing and rayon industries, and in the Llobregat potash mines, were forcibly terminated by mass detentions and dismissal of many employees. Selves kept the Barcelona CNT unions closed long after the lifting of the national state of emergency in March, and frequently banned publication of *Solidaridad Obrera*. Justification was provided by the incessant industrial sabotage, shootings and explosions. Each week nocturnal incendiaries destroyed tramcars in outer suburbs, trying to force the company to reinstate strikers dismissed in December. In March, when transfer of public order powers to the Generalitat was completed, Selves moved police onto the offensive against both illegal union activities and the criminal underworld, between which the Esquerra claimed – not entirely without reason – that Chicago-style connections existed. Badía was appointed secretary to the chief of police, and personally led regular forces and his own *escamot* cadets in repeated raids on *Faísta* haunts, breaking up illegal meetings and taking known 'extremists' into preventive detention. It became increasingly difficult for CNT unions to collect membership dues and to function even clandestinely: two attempts to organize protest strikes on 12 March and 7 May were only patchily supported, and on 9 May a CNT deputation visited Companys offering to moderate the unions' conduct if police persecution ended.[41]

Companys did not want to destroy syndicalism, but to draw or drive it into co-operation or at worst civilized opposition. He was not disposed to relax pressure at the moment when it appeared to be achieving results, and the Generalitat's note of reply said it found no ground to modify its 'impartial' application of the law. Companys had moreover further grounds for supposing that the tide of revolutionary syndicalism had finally turned, for Comorera's entry into his cabinet had split and largely neutralized in Catalonia a potentially threatening Marxist-led realignment of trade unions, the Alianza Obrera.

Alianza Obrera had originated notionally in March 1933, in a call for the creation of a 'Workers' Alliance against Fascism' published one week after the Nazi victory in the German elections. The initiative was promoted by Maurín's BOC, and was transparently a manoeuvre to extend communist influence among CNT unions, which pointedly ignored it. Even elsewhere it achieved only token adherence, until the CEDA landslide vote in November suddenly made an anti-fascist front appear relevant in Spain. In December an Alianza committee was constituted, incorporating the BOC, the *treintista* Opposition Unions, UGT, Unió Socialista, and the Unió de Rabassaires.[42]

These organizations totalled over 90,000 members, but their political and social disparity, and disagreement over relations with the Esquerra, prevented effective unity. In March 1934 Unió Socialista defected. Throughout the previous year Comorera had schemed to make it the single socialist party of Catalonia, by amalgamating it with the much smaller Catalan branch of the PSOE. Local negotiations ran smoothly, but the central PSOE executive committee rejected the proposed party statutes as excessively autonomous. When Largo finally came to Barcelona in February 1934 to resolve matters personally, he demanded that Comorera resign his seat in the Generalitat and sever connections with the 'bourgeois' Esquerra. The two leaders quarrelled acrimoniously in public, and merger negotiations were abandoned. Largo's strictures against Catalans also antagonized local PSOE leaders – who were *prietistas* – and most of them, and several of the UGT unions of Barcelona, affiliated to Unió Socialista, which by summer thus came to control some 20,000 workers.[43]

On 13 March, the day after the CNT's attempted protest strike, Alianza Obrera called its own twenty-four-hour regional stoppage as an intentionally competitive demonstration of strength. This strike was effective in hinterland towns, but in Barcelona it failed completely, and an Alianza communiqué accused Unió Socialista of sabotaging it there by countermanding its orders. Thus while Largo, attracted to the concept of an inter-union workers' front, extended Alianza Obrera through his UGT to other regions of Spain, in its original Catalan base it suffered a set-back. In April the *rabassaires* also withdrew, won back to the Esquerra by the passage of agrarian legislation. After these losses, Alianza Obrera in Catalonia comprised essentially only the BOC unions, the *treintistas*, and that part of the UGT still loyal to Largo, or approximately half the total it had reached in December.[44]

By late April there were two separate and mutually exclusive anti-fascist campaigns attitudinizing in Catalonia, as Alianza Obrera and the Esquerra jostled to occupy the verbal vanguard of the left.On the day CEDA Youth assembled in Castile at the Escorial to swear allegiance to its 'supreme leader' Gil Robles, Alianza Obrera in Barcelona issued a manifesto which denounced the Generalitat for an 'intimate sympathy with fascism' indistinguishable, in its provocation of the working class, from Lerroux's subservience to CEDA impositions. For its part, the Generalitat held its own spectacular anti-fascist demonstration: on

28 April Companys lit the first of seventy beacons on Catalan hilltops, and next day some 100,000 supporters of the coalition government filed past and heard him promise that Catalonia would come to the defence of the left in Spain, should reactionaries and fascists attack it.[45]

This demonstration was not simply a gesture of solidarity with anti-Radical republicans in Madrid, and with their attempts to induce Alcalá Zamora to dissolve rightist Cortes which – they contended – were 'mutilating' the Republic of 1931. It signalled also the opening of hostilities in the five-month conflict between central and regional governments, over the Cultivation Contracts Law, which was to lead ineluctably to the revolt of the Generalitat.

It was ironic that a crisis between Madrid and Barcelona should hinge upon an agrarian issue, for Catalonia was exempt from the perennial problems associated with the impoverished landless labourers of central and southern Spain. Catalan farms were small, but absentee landlordism was nevertheless common, in the form of complex sharecropping con-tracts with long-term tenants who worked their holdings as family units, often for successive generations, usually employing additional labour only at harvest time. These farmers (called 'rabassaires' when they grew vines, though other types of produce were also affected) had suffered from steadily falling market prices. As they were staunch Esquerra clientele, and numbered over 30,000, each summer from 1931 to 1933 Macià had negotiated temporary solutions involving reductions in the percentage of the harvest due to the landlords. The cultivation law of 12 April, passed by the Catalan parliament, gave rabassaires what they really wanted: the option to purchase the land they farmed – provided they had done so for eighteen years – by payments to the pro-prietors spread over fifteen years.

This was unacceptable to landowners, and on 17 April sixteen Catalan chambers of agriculture and commerce published a note indicat-ing their intention to challenge the law's constitutionality. On their behalf the Lliga requested the new Samper government, which de-pended on Lliga support, to lay the question before the Tribunal of Constitutional Guarantees, which was done (outside the legal time limit) on 4 May.

The government's juridical case impugned the cultivation law as an intromission into both social and contractual legislation, which were prerogatives of central power. The Generalitat argued that it was a matter of Catalan civil law and of agricultural legislation, in which the statute gave it full competence. The Tribunal's decision was largely predetermined by its political composition, and on 8 June it found against the Generalitat. The verdict went much further than strictly necessary, not merely declaring the law itself void, but providing ample basis for preventing the Generalitat from legislating at all in agriculture, and in practically any other area.

The Generalitat could not acquiesce in this judgement, so sweeping that it embarrassed central government itself. Nor was it to be supposed that the Esquerra, given its demagogic proclivity, would forgo exploiting the situation for party advantage, excoriating the Lliga for its treachery and striking heroic postures as the champion of outraged Catalan liberties. Samper was willing to negotiate a compromise, but Companys for the moment preferred to increase tension and orchestrate a repetition of the strident statute agitation of 1932.[46] Catalan deputies walked out of the Cortes, and on June 12 the parliament in Barcelona threw down the gauntlet to Samper by passing a second Cultivation Law identical to the one declared null. Adopting the role of a surrogate Macià, Companys publicly radiated confidence and called on the people to await serenely the watchword for action, but at the same time the Generalitat tacitly encouraged ultra-nationalist associations to inflame Catalanist susceptibilities through press, parades and meetings.[47] As a further signal to Madrid of his obduracy, Companys moved his Estat Català councillor Dencàs to take charge of the department of the interior – fallen vacant through Selves's illness – and Badía was formally appointed chief of police. It was rumoured that Dencàs had orders to prepare for armed resistance to Madrid; this was indeed the case, but Companys took care to allow him no funds to purchase arms, and all he could do was begin to collect in rifles from the rural *Sometent*, the special constabulary composed mainly of small landowners.[48]

The Generalitat's display of belligerence was, *at this point*, largely a pretence. It was the well-worn tactic of arousing sentimental Catalanist solidarity, and the attendant spectre of separatism, to wring concessions from Madrid. There was no need for this – except to save face – because Samper was actually ready to accept the substance of the cultivation law, and during June Alcalá Zamora and Hurtado outlined a compromise capable of satisfying both sides. Gil Robles, however, made it clear before the Cortes rose for the three-month summer recess, on 4 July, that his party expected Samper to enforce the Tribunal's sentence in its full rigour.

Free from the pressure of daily scrutiny in the Cortes, the cultivation law conflict became the subject of unofficial negotiations between the two governments, and by early August the Radicals let it be known that they would not object to the compromise formula, under which the text of the law would stand unchanged while important modifications would be introduced in the appended enforcing regulations.[49] The Esquerra's press jubilantly claimed that the Generalitat had won its struggle with Madrid, but the sense of victory was short-lived, for in mid-August Gil Robles returned from vacation in Germany and made plain his displeasure with Samper's appeasement. On 8 September he was guest of honour at an assembly of some 5000 Catalan landowners who came to Madrid by special trains to demand the invalidation of the cultivation law. It was now an open secret that the CEDA and the Agrarian Party had agreed to bring down Samper at the opening session of the Cortes on 1 October and seek power for themselves. In any case, Gil Robles made it absolutely clear that the CEDA's conditions for supporting any new government would include the abolition of the cultivation law and the removal of all police powers from the Generalitat.[50]

Therefore the suggestion that the Esquerra continued *unnecessarily* to mouth threats in defence of a law that had already been accepted by central government is a fundamental misapprehension. The Generalitat had gained only a temporary reprieve. Not merely the law, but any realistic interpretation of Catalan autonomy, would be forfeit if the CEDA entered the government. The Esquerra was thus drawn inevitably into September's machinations by Spanish republicans and socialists to exclude the right from power.

Companys was impelled along this course by the conjunction of three forces. First, for the reasons we have seen, the Generalitat committed itself to join ranks with the Spanish left to bar the door to what it saw as the Dollfuss-style fascism of the CEDA. For nine months the republicans, and latterly the socialists, had flattered Catalonia as 'all that is left standing of the Republic', 'the only place where the Republic has struck roots'.[51] Some close observers were convinced that the ascendancy over Companys of Lluhí and Comorera (with their close personal links with Azana and Prieto) were decisive in this respect during the weeks immediately preceding the final débâcle.[52]

Secondly, Companys was subjected to unremitting pressure from the ultra-nationalist agitation that he himself had unleashed in June. Then, it had proved convenient; now, it had run out of control, provoking incidents (with Spanish judges in Barcelona courts) that caused in mid-September a fresh crisis between the Generalitat and Samper. Estat Català's object was to worsen relations with Madrid to such a point that the only alternatives would be abject submission or an explicitly separatist rupture.

The third force was Alianza Obrera. A manifesto from its Catalan committee in late May gave full backing to the *rabassaires* and rallied to support the Generalitat which only a month earlier it had castigated as quasi-fascist. Maurín's analysis of the conflict between central and regional powers was that it was capable of development into a revolutionary situation, and that the Alianza should precipitate this by forcing the Generalitat towards the proclamation of a Catalan republic that would thereafter be appropriated by the workers. Maurín's immediate goal was thus identical to that of the ultra-nationalists, and on 8 September representatives from Alianza Obrera and the separatist parties and youth movements met in Barcelona to appoint a joint action Committee.[53]

It is a matter of controversy which of these three factors most influenced Companys during the crucial days of early October, or whether indeed he actually ceased to be a free agent.[54] Until 4 October, at least, he retained the initiative, exerting upon Alcalá Zamora the political blackmail of threatened rebellion, in unison with the Spanish left. If he appeared to be bowing to intolerable ultra-nationalist and proletarian pressure, that was a necessary part of his bluff.[55]

On 1 October, as expected, Gil Robles forced Samper's resignation in the Cortes. To the dismay of the Spanish opposition, and the consternation of the Generalitat, Alcalá Zamora disregarded their threats and entrusted the formation of a coalition government to Lerroux. Announced on the evening of 4 October, it included three CEDA ministers, amongst whom – holding the labour portfolio – was the Esquerra's arch-enemy Anguera de Sojo, who had recently joined

Acción Popular. The CEDA's accession to power, even as minority partner in the coalition, called the opposition's bluff. The anti-Radical republican parties in Madrid merely issued statements 'breaking off relations' with the regime. Alianza Obrera declared a national general strike, but poor organization rendered it largely ineffective except in Asturias and Catalonia.

In Barcelona the CNT rejected an appeal to join Alianza's action. Nevertheless, by the afternoon of Friday 5 October the city and all Catalan industrial towns were at a complete standstill. Armed Alianza militants and *escamots* had toured the factories, and it was impossible to say whether workers went home from solidarity or from fear. It was the first non-CNT strike to succeed in Barcelona.[56] Unofficially protected by the regional government, it continued next day. The Generalitat was now in a grave situation: its real objective of keeping the CEDA from power had failed, and Companys saw too late that he had left himself no dignified route of retreat. Conflicting reports were received of fighting in various Spanish cities, especially in Asturias. Swept along by the momentum of his own past rhetoric, during that Saturday morning he took the decision to imitate the Spanish republicans' rupture of relations with the regime. Unlike them, he did so from a position of regional power, and thereby converted a political threat into an act of rebellion.

At 8 p.m. on 6 October Companys spoke to the people by radio from the balcony of the Generalitat. He stated that monarchists and fascists had taken control of the Republic, and henceforth Catalonia 'broke off all relations with its falsified institutions'. He did not proclaim the independent Catalan Republic demanded by Alianza Obrera and Dencàs, but 'the Catalan State of the Federal Spanish Republic', whose provisional government he invited to constitute itself in Barcelona.

The rebellion of the Generalitat was a half-hearted affair. Companys was aware that he had miscalculated, and went through with it in a fatalistic spirit, out of loyalty to the Spanish left and to avoid accusations of betrayal within his own party. He and Lluhí apparently still believed – in spite of Azaña's warnings – that everything might end in secret negotiations, as in April 1931 and July 1934, to allow the Generalitat to submit with grudging grace. He refused requests from Alianza Obrera to arm the people, and Dencàs' *escamots* were simply put on stand-by in their places of assembly.

Martial law had been instituted throughout Spain several hours earlier, and within minutes of Company's proclamation Lerroux ordered the commander of the Barcelona garrison, General Batet, to put an end to the rebellion. Companys' last hope was that Batet – a Catalan and a personal friend – would not act, but at 10.30 p.m. a company of machine-gunners with a light artillery battery made its way through the deserted streets to the Generalitat, defended by its own small autonomous police force, and began shelling both it and the adjacent town hall. Dencàs, in his interior department headquarters half a mile away, promised to send reinforcements, but the regular police officers refused to accept his orders and the *escamots* – who were to be used as reserves – melted away. In the skirmishes of the night, in the city and throughout Catalonia, some forty men died. At dawn Companys and his government (except Dencàs, who fled abroad) surrendered to the army.

The October rebellion brought a hiatus in Catalan autonomy. The offices of president of the Generalitat, mayor of Barcelona, and chief of police, were respectively filled by Colonels Jiménez, Martínez and Ibáñez. The parliament was closed, the statute was suspended, and control of public order and labour affairs reverted formally to the central power. The cultivation law was annulled, and 1400 *rabassaires* were subsequently evicted from their farms. Many of the wage increases awarded by the Generalitat's *jurados mixtos* were revoked. The governing body of Barcelona University was dismissed, and Catalan-language newspapers suppressed. Over 3000 Catalans were still held in prison at the end of the year for their role in the rebellion. Companys and his councillors stood trial in June 1935 before the Tribunal of Constitutional Guarantees, and received thirty-year sentences. Martial law lasted in Catalonia until May. Thereafter, under Governors-General appointed by Madrid, the activity of various departments of the Generalitat was allowed to resume slowly, under CEDA, Radical and Lliga councillors.

The treatment of Catalonia by the right during the suspension of the statute ensured the victory of the Popular Front throughout the region in the general elections of 16 February 1936. The left won 60 per cent of the votes. The statute was hastily restored, and Companys and his councillors (except Dencàs) resumed their posts in the Generalitat in

March. The Lliga returned to the Catalan parliament and performed the functions of a loyal opposition during the four months until the military rising of 18 July, in which it had no part.

The immediate origins of the Civil War had nothing to do with Catalonia, where the almost complete absence of political violence and social unrest during the spring of 1936 contrasted strikingly with the deteriorating situation elsewhere in Spain. Nevertheless the rebellion of the Generalitat – which was universally perceived by the Spanish right, and the army, as a salutary unmasking of separatism – was possibly of even more significance than the Asturian uprising in hardening their resolve to destroy the Republic. The material causes of a working-class revolution were comprehensible, but Catalanism implied a threat to the essential moral unity of the fatherland, that required not remedy but extirpation.

It would be difficult to argue that the experiment in autonomy was a success even within Catalonia. For all the panoply of statute, president and parliament, the Generalitat's real powers were not markedly greater than those of an English county council. It was established in conditions of gathering economic recession which the Republic tried to meet by classic deflationary measures, and central government often yielded to the temptation to manipulate the long period of transfer of powers to reduce public expenditure in Catalonia to an unacceptable minimum. The Generalitat was always starved of finance. Without adequate authority or resources, the regional government found itself at the centre of a triangle of forces – Madrid, the Lliga, and the CNT – each of which was eager to exploit difficulties with the others. Largo's desire to expand the UGT in Catalonia embroiled it with the mass of workers. The Lliga – which, having created political Catalanism, felt cheated of the opportunity to govern – challenged its power to legislate. The CNT preferred to discredit it by forcing it into policies of repression.

Alcalá Zamora believed that 'the greatest difficulty of the Catalan problem lies in the fact that the region that demands the widest autonomy is the one least fitted to exercise it.'[57] By this *boutade* he referred to the ease with which Catalan parties – the Lliga and the Esquerra successively – were able to mobilize mass movements of sentimental solidarity devoid of social or political consistency. The Esquerra certainly resorted to such tactics, but only when autonomy was under attack from central power, and not simply to manufacture support for purely party purposes. As to its social basis, the Esquerra was indeed a conglomerate. This was the result of the CNT's abstention from institutional politics, and of the fine gradation of the transitional zone between the Catalan working and middle classes.[58] In its pragmatism and undoctrinaire social welfare programme, the Esquerra was almost a Labour Party, and it won and retained the electoral support of a large sector of the Catalan working class. Like all left-wing parties in the region, it aspired to direct Catalan syndicalism; and eventually Lluhí's prediction that the Catalan masses would abandon anarchism and opt for either reformist socialism or communism was realized. That resolution took place, however, only during and after the Civil War.

Notes

1 *L'Opinió*, 5 September 1930.

2 *L'Opinió*, 3 August 1929.

3 Unpublished memoirs of Casanelles, cited in J. B. Culla, *El catalanisme d'esquerra (1928–1936)* (Barcelona, 1977), 59.

4 C. Ametlla, *Memòries polítiques* (2 vols., Barcelona, 1979), II, 78; A. Hurtado, *Quaranta anys d'avocat* (2 vols., Barcelona, 1969), II, 23.

5 *El Combate Sindicalista*, 6 September 1935, quoted in John Brademas, *Anarcosindicalismo y revolución en España 1930–1937* (Barcelona, 1974), 57.

6 Francesc Soldevila, *Història de la proclamació de la República a Catalunya*, ed Pere Gabriel (Barcelona, 1977), 26.

7 Prieto urged in cabinet the use of force against Macià. Mañuel Azana, *Obras completas* (4 vols., Mexico D.F., 1966–8), IV, 154.

8 For a comparison of the draft statutes of 1919 and 1931, see J. A. González Casanova, *Federalismo y autonomía: Cataluña y el Estado español 1868–1938* (Barcelona, 1979), 280–5.

9 By one decree alone, Maura appointed 70 Castilians as town clerks. *L'Opinió*, 12 August 1931. He preferred independent republicans and members of Acció Catalana as civil governors. Companys' appointment was forced on him in the confused events of 14 April. Soldevila, *Història*, 41–4; Miguel Maura, *Así cayó Alfonso XIII* (Mexico, 1966), 182–3, 237.

10 Albert Balcells, *Crisis económica y agitación social en Cataluña 1930–1936* (Barcelona, 1971), 74–6.

11 Niceto Alcalá Zamora, *Memorias* (Barcelona, 1977), 45, 216, 265; Hurtado, *Quaranta anys*, II, 43.

12 Macià claimed that he had been promised real power by the three ministers. *L'Opinió*, 11 June 1931.

13 L'Opinió, 31 July 1931; Maura, Así cayó, 288.
14 La Publicitat, 6 May 1931.
15 La Publicitat, 10, 16 May 1931. Companys retorted that by his intervention he had averted fifty strikes in one week.
16 L'Opinió, 25 September 1931.
17 L'Opinió, 14 February 1932.
18 Madrid's view of Macià as a hothead is best expressed by Maximiano García Venero, Historia del nacionalismo catalán (2 vols., Madrid, 1967), II, 305.
19 J. M. Roig, L'Estatut de Catalunya a les Corts Constituents (Barcelona, 1978), passim.
20 Right-wing newspapers, such as La Nación, featured reports of 'paramilitary training' (pistol practice) at Estat Català and Nosaltres Sols summer camps. L'Opinió, 12 June 1932.
21 L'Opinió, 1 October 1932.
22 L'Opinió, 23 November 1932.
23 Azaña, Obras, III, 19, 151.
24 Eulàlia Vega, El trentisme a Catalunya (1930–1933) (Barcelona, 1980), 266–9.
25 Cultura Libertaria, 1 December 1932. According to Salvador Seguí's son, by November 1932 the Barcelona federation had only 23,800 fully paid-up members. L'Opinió, 13 January 1933.
26 L'Opinió, 27 May 1933.
27 E. Udina, Josep Tarradellas, l'aventura d'una fidelitat (Barcelona, 1978), 94–8; Culla, El catalanisme, 111–27.
28 L'Opinió, 17 August 1933.
29 The main demand was for a shorter working week to combat unemployment. Average unemployment in Barcelona was 10 per cent, but among CNT woodworkers it was 42 per cent. Over half of the CNT dockers and builders were out of work. Balcells, Crisis, 36–7.
30 L'Opinió, 25 March 1933.
31 The police establishment of Barcelona numbered 650 but its actual strength was only 400. L'Opinió, 19 July 1933.
32 Carlos Pi Sunyer, La República y la guerra civil (Mexico, 1975), 132.
33 Joventuts d'Esquerra Republicana Estat Català.
34 L'Opinió, 12 August, 30 September, 7 October, 17 November 1933.
35 The Partit Nacionalista Republicà d'Esquerra had 1500 members. It allied with Acció Catalana in the November elections. Culla, El catalanisme, 351–7.
36 L'Opinió, 11 November 1933.
37 L'Opinió, 21 October 1933.
38 Ametlla, Memòries, II, 269.
39 L'Opinió, 6 January 1934.
40 Pi Sunyer, La República, 183–208.

41 *L'Opinió*, 10, 11 May 1934.
42 *L'Opinió*, 15 December 1933.
43 *L'Opinió*, 27 February, 10 March, 17 April 1934. The PSOE's Catalan Federation had only 1000 members. Unió Socialista had 4000 and controlled mainly white-collar unions with nearly 19,000 members. See J. L. Martín Ramos, *El origen del PSUC* (Barcelona, 1977), 118–29.
44 *L'Opinió*, 18 March, 28 April 1934.
45 *L'Opinió*, 22 April, 1 May 1934.
46 Hurtado, *Quaranta anys*, II, 281, 288.
47 *L'Opinió*, 31 May 1934.
48 *L'Opinió*, 11, 20 June, 10 July 1934; Josep Dencàs, *El 6 d'octubre des del Palau de Governació* (Barcelona, 1935), 37–48.
49 Statements by Guerra del Río to *ABC* quoted in *L'Opinió*, 3 August 1934.
50 *L'Opinió*, 16 August, 9, 26 September 1934; José María Gil Robles, *No fue posible la paz* (Barcelona, 1968), 132.
51 Azaña, *Diario de sesiones de Cortes*, 25 June 1934; Jiménez de Asúa, *L'Opinió*, 15 September 1934.
52 Ametlla, *Memòries*, 249, 268–9; Pi Sunyer, *La República*, 280; Azaña, *Obras*, IV, 657; Alcalá Zamora, *Memorias*, 299.
53 *L'Opinió*, 26 May, 10 September 1934; Martín Ramos, *PSUC*, 166–9.
54 Culla, *El catalanisme*, 298–303.
55 Pi Sunyer, *La República*, 243; Hurtado, *Quaranta anys*, II, 312.
56 *L'Opinió*, 1, 5 October 1934; Brademas, *Anarcosindicalismo*, 142–4.
57 Alcalá Zamora, *Memorias*, p. 298.
58 See Enric Ucelay da Cal, *La Catalunya populista* (Barcelona, 1982), *passim*.

5
The epic failure: the Asturian revolution of October 1934

Adrian Shubert

The working class of Spain greeted the Second Republic with exceptional enthusiasm. For them it did not mean a mere change of political organization. The Republic carried with it the promise of major social change. In September 1931 one coal-miner in Asturias wrote to the local Socialist newspaper that 'the workers saw the creation of the Republic as their saviour. If these thoughts had not existed the workers of this town would now be caught up in the whirlwind of a new struggle.'[1] Social reform or social conflict, this was the choice which the Republic faced from the moment of its birth. With the first lay the continued support of millions of working-class Spaniards, with the second failure and ultimately civil war.

Until the First World War the Restoration monarchy and its corrupt parliamentary democracy was able to withstand without difficulty the forces of protest in the country. Even the disaster of 1898 and the much heralded Regenerationist movement it spawned did not seriously threaten the system. It was the war and more specifically Spain's neutrality which eventually proved as fatal for the country's monarchy as did participation for the Russian and Austro-Hungarian monarchies.

Neutrality favoured economic growth but it also spurred an inflation which far outran the substantial wage increases the war brought to the working class. Labour organization and labour protest increased dramatically. At the same time the traditional parties of the Restoration system, Liberals and Conservatives, were splintering into numerous bickering cliques, regionalists and reformists were demanding substantial political changes and discontented peninsula-based military officers were forming *juntas de defensa*, essentially unions, to demand better conditions although they also made vague noises about reform. In 1917 these three streams of protest: social, political and military, almost converged to overturn the Restoration system.[2]

A replay of the February Revolution in Russia was avoided only because the unnatural and fragile alliance of unionists, politicians and soldiers broke down under the pressure of the general strike of August 1917. Terrified by an authentic mobilization of the masses (although it was peaceful and unarmed) the officers and socially conservative regionalist politicians rallied to the monarchy. However, the defeat of the movement of 1917 did not bring an end to social protest. An outbreak of peasant rebellion, the *trienio bolchevique*, rocked Andalucía between 1918 and 1920 and Barcelona endured years of street warfare between anarchists and gangs of gunmen working for the employers.

These conflicts reached their peak in 1920–1 but it took an event outside the peninsula, the annihilation of the Spanish army in Morocco at Annual in 1922, to bring down the Restoration system. In September 1923 General Miguel Primo de Rivera staged a *coup* and took power, closing the Cortes and banning political parties. The country was ruled by a military dictatorship until the elections of April 1931 although Primo himself fell from power in February 1930. Violent social protest was suppressed but its causes remained.

Thus when the dictatorship gave way to the Republic, demands for change were once again made. The region where such demands were made most frequently and most forcefully was the northern coal-mining province of Asturias. In both 1932 and 1933 it led all Spanish provinces in the number of strikes. In number of strikers it was first in 1932 and second the next year.[3] But most impressively – and most violently – in October 1934 it was the site of a major armed insurrection which during the two weeks of its existence abolished the political authority of the state and the economic and social authority of the bourgeoisie. As the first major outbreak of class war in Spain it also foreshadowed the Civil War.

In order to appreciate the degree of working-class militancy which made the Asturian revolution of October 1934 possible it is essential to review the major developments in the region from the First World War on. The major economic activity in Asturias is coal-mining. Large-scale exploitation of the deposits began in the 1850s but the industry was beset by chronic crisis until the war.[4] The European conflict provided an undreamed-of bonanza for mine owners as the termination of British coal exports left Spain dependent on domestic coal production. Profits reached unprecedented levels as prices soared, from a base of 100 in 1913 to 563 five years later.[5]

While the boom lasted the mineworkers did well. The owners preferred to meet almost any wage demand than to interrupt production. The Socialist mineworkers' union, the Sindicato de Obreros Mineros Asturianos (SMA), negotiated a series of collective agreements which included a minimum wage and per ton payments to the union itself. In 1919 it successfully struck for a seven-hour day 'from pithead to pithead', the shortest working day in Europe.[6]

The boom did not last long. The industry's prosperity was completely artificial, dependent as it was upon the disruption of the normal patterns of European trade. Production increases were achieved through the opening of new mines, not through technical improvement and the intensification of production. The necessary increase in the workforce – 17,796 in 1913 and 33,020 in 1918 – could only be realized by hiring inexperienced hands, usually poor farmers from Galicia and northern Castile. In 1919 one economic journal remarked that 'it is a fiction to work uneconomic mines with unskilled labour to produce unburnable coal'.[7]

This situation came to an abrupt end with the armistice. British coal once again began to reach Spain and the industry relapsed into its chronic crisis condition, but now in an exacerbated state. Prices plummeted and most of the marginal mines opened during the war were closed. In 1919 there were 1426 mines, in 1921 1232 and in 1923 only 1130. At those mines which stayed in production owners and managers sought to improve their competitive position and protect profits through the intensification of production: reducing the number of oncost workers, cutting wage rates and mechanizing production; in short, to produce more coal with fewer workers earning less pay.[8]

The mine-owners succeeded in their objective of cutting costs and increasing efficiency. In 1920 the index of wages was 298 (taking 1914 as the base). In 1923 and 1924 it was down to 223. At the same time productivity rose from 121 in 1920, to 153 in 1923 and 162 in 1924. Wages remained fairly steady thereafter, dropping to 219 in 1929, but productivity continued to rise and reached 193 at the end of the decade. Over the 1920s as a whole wages fell by a third, from an average of 78.12 pesetas per week to an average of 53.75. The workforce was reduced from 39,093 in 1920 to 30,759 in 1924 and only 25,803 in 1928.[9]

The miners responded to these developments with a vigour which forced the moderate leadership of the SMA into calling a number of general strikes it did not want. The mine-owners' announcement in December 1921 of planned sweeping changes in the organization of labour led to spontaneous local strikes which the union later made official. In April 1922 an announced twenty-per-cent pay cut triggered 'a spontaneous movement of protest' which again forced the SMA into a general strike, this one lasting two and a half months.[10]

The drastic reconversion of the industry in the early 1920s did not succeed in pulling the coal industry out of its crisis, basically because it did not address itself to the major cause of the high price of Asturian coal: transportation costs. The industry struggled through the decade only to have its problems compounded by the onset of the depression which severely affected the iron and steel industry, the largest consumer of Asturian coal.[11] Strikes were more difficult under the Primo de Rivera dictatorship but the SMA called a third general strike in 1924. The union's strategy was to rely on the state to defend the workers against the owners and for a while this was successful. However, the greater political influence of the mine-owners eventually won out and in 1927 they achieved what they had been after for eight years, the extension of the working day to eight hours.

At a congress called in October 1927 to debate this issue the SMA executive succeeded in having its anti-strike motion approved but only 'in a bitter vote' and with a majority of only 787. Even so the disapproval of much of the membership (the union had to cancel a series of propaganda meetings due to 'the excitement, fervour and passion' in the valleys)[12] and the intransigence of the owners once again compelled the union into a general strike which it lost. The weakness of the SMA and its inability to shield its members from the worst effects of the crisis led to a massive drop in its membership, from 24,557 (62.8 per cent of the workforce) in 1920 to 8870 (32 per cent) in 1929.[13]

The Socialist union was also engaged in an unending struggle with anarcho-syndicalists and Communists for the allegiance of the mine-workers. The general strike of May to August 1922 had seen a great deal of inter-union fighting due to the recent schism between Socialists and Communists.[14] Although the rival Sindicato Unico Minero (SU) – supported by both anarcho-syndicalists and Communists – was banned by the dictatorship it was able to operate underground with considerable success, so much so that in the spring of 1928 the SMA had to undertake a propaganda campaign to counter the 'disorientation' of the workers. The struggle heated up again in 1929 and by the time the SU was legalized in May 1930 there was 'a battle between the unions . . . in the coalfields'. In May 1931, just after the declaration of the Republic, it had 9000 members in forty-two sections.[15]

Thus, on the eve of the declaration of the Republic, the outlook for social peace in the Asturian coalfield was not bright. The coal industry continued to be afflicted by a crisis which only went from bad to worse and those miners who held on to their jobs were being made to work longer and produce more for less pay. The Socialist SMA, badly weakened but still the largest union, had a new, initially more militant leadership under Amador Fernández who succeeded Manuel Llaneza following the latter's death in January 1931, and was engaged in a fierce struggle with the rival SU. The only hope was the initial enthusiasm of the Asturian working class for the Republic as a reforming regime.[16]

For Socialists in Asturias, as in the country as a whole, the potential for reform inherent in the Republic was unlimited. So was Socialist support for the regime. The SMA recovered much of its support between 1931 and 1933 largely through the role played by its leaders in the Republic's creation. Membership rose from 11,022 (38.7 per cent of the workforce) in 1930 to 20,892 (68.7 per cent) in 1932 and 19,155 (69 per cent) in 1933 and throughout this period the union's policy was to avoid strikes whenever possible and rely on the government to satisfy its demands.

At the SMA congress in May 1931 Ramón González Peña spoke of the necessity of 'trusting the present government to include the workers' fundamental aspirations in the laws to be presented to the forthcoming parliament'. On the second anniversary of the Republic, 14 April 1933, Amador Fernández told a rally in Oviedo that 'the working class will always be ready to defend the Republic because it is the appropriate means of establishing the society for which we Socialists have struggled.'[17]

Following Hitler's coming to power in Germany the Republic took on the added dimension of the Spanish workers' only defence against fascism. The elections of November 1933 were presented as a clear choice between fascism and Socialism. 'Acción Popular offers a fascist regime . . . and fascism means war. Europe is on the verge of war because of German provocation and within Spain fascism will mean civil war.'[18]

Unquestioning in its support of the Republic, the SMA refused to blame it for the continuing – and worsening – crisis of the coal industry. In 1932–3 wage-cuts, layoffs and shutdowns once again became daily events and by 1934 a number of major companies were up to four months behind in paying their wage bill. One, Fábrica de Mieres, was forced to declare bankruptcy in February 1934. Socialists called the crisis an inheritance from the monarchy and labelled mine closures 'monarchist sabotage of the new regime'. Union criticism of the government was 'what the owners want'.[19]

It followed from this that the union was reluctant to strike. Strikes were denounced as 'attacks on the Republic [which] affect the money market, contribute to the flight of capital and stimulate the thousand other tricks which capital uses to try and undermine our achievements'.

At the union congress in May 1931 the executive had the article of the constitution governing the calling of strikes revised to give it total control and the following year a motion was passed further restricting the ability of local and regional committees to call strikes.[20]

The union's alternative to the strike was reliance on a supposedly sympathetic government which included Socialist leader Francisco Largo Caballero as the Minister of Labour. The best statement of the SMA's position in this period is the following definition of the class struggle offered by the union-financed daily *Avance* in August 1932:

> By respecting the existing work norms we will create a system of civility and mutual understanding and limit social conflict to that natural area defined by the logical antagonism of interests. It should not be a war between slavers and Africans, a struggle between slaves and tyrants, but simply the disagreement between the worker who aspires to a more humane and better life and the employer who understandably desires to obtain a reasonable return on his investment. From a struggle imbued with this spirit it is always easy to reach an understanding which harms the interests of neither party. This is how we understand the class struggle and this is how we will practise it.[21]

Consistent with this declaration the union used the general strike only as a last resort. In August 1932, in the face of an announced shutdown at Industrial Asturiana, the introduction of a four-day week at Hulleras del Turón and the lowering of piece-work rates at a number of other mines, the SMA decided to call a general strike, but only after studying 'the spirit of the workers' and finding them eager for it. The strike had a purely defensive aim, 'the job security of 50,000 proletarians employed in the coalfields'; and the union's demands were a steady six-day week and government measures to increase the consumption of Asturian coal.[22]

The strike was called off when Hulleras del Turón offered to reorganize its working week but, following the refusal of the government to accept the union's proposals, it was scheduled once again. It was cancelled a second time when the government changed its mind and promised to assure a six-day working week. The strike was called a third time in mid-November following announcements of indefinite closures by three of the four largest companies and this time it was held. 25,000 men struck for six days until the government agreed to a union proposal based on control of iron imports, tariff protection for the coke industry and state acquisition of coal.[23]

In January 1933 a national coal conference was held but resolved nothing. Mine-owners insisted on raising prices, lowering wages and firing more miners. The union announced a referendum on 'whether the men prefer a strike to dismissals and wage cuts'. Seventy per cent of the membership took part, voting 15,128 to 113 in favour of a strike.[24]

The walkout lasted a month, from 6 February to 4 March, and drew 27,500 workers according to government sources. It was highlighted by a considerable amount of violence. On the night of the 15th five bombs exploded in La Felguera and there was a shoot-out between police and anarchists.[25] Finally the union called a referendum to decide on a government proposal to have a team of accountants and technicians go over the companies' books to check their claims and that during the three months the investigation was to last the government would lend them 2.4 million pesetas. In addition sixty centimos per ton would be paid into a retirement fund – to which the miners would also contribute – to relieve unemployment by allowing early retirement. This package was approved 15,105 to 410.[26]

In September the companies cancelled their payments to this fund and the union responded with a general strike, this time supported by both Communists and anarcho-syndicalists. After two weeks it spread from Asturias to the rest of the country, the first nationwide miners' strike in Spanish history. 50,000 workers were out, demanding that subsidies to mines be made available to companies outside Asturias and that payments to the retirement fund be resumed. When the strike ended on 28 September the National Miners' Federation claimed a complete victory.[27]

The moderation of the Socialists was in direct contrast to the behaviour of their Communists and anarcho-syndicalist rivals for whom the Republic was essentially the same as the monarchy. The struggle between the SMA and the SU continued, and escalated into all-out war during the general strike called by the latter in June 1931. The SU demanded the restoration of the seven-hour day, unemployment pay, the elimination of piece-work and an across-the-board wage increase of two pesetas. The strike was supported by between 20 per cent (according to the employers association) and half (according to government sources) of the miners. Its centre of gravity was Turón and Sama although there were some stoppages in Aller and Mieres.[28]

The strike was unusually bitter and violent. On 2 June there was a shoot-out between groups from the two unions and in Mieres many miners stayed away from work 'for fear of disagreeable encounters with those who want the strike to continue'. On the 11th there was an armed attack on a train carrying workers to Turón. Sabotage emerged for the first time as a part of mining strikes in the province. The power lines to Hulleras del Turón and Fábrica de Mieres were blown up and there was an attempt to disable the generator at the Barredos mine.[29]

The SMA reacted strongly to attacks by SU members. Armed militants protected Socialist miners at the Corujas mine, one of the 'compact guards organized by the Sindicato Minero to guarantee the right to work as the authorities have done nothing in this regard'. At the same time Amador Fernández and González Peña joined the Chamber of Commerce in sending a telegram to the Minister of the Interior. 'Urgent measures to guarantee life of men and security of mines, continually threatened by minority audacious troublemakers. . . . Vast majority of men want to work.'[30]

The general strike of June 1931 was the high point of SU activity during the first two years of the Republic. Other strikes it organized received much less support. Only 3000 of 26,000 miners took part in a strike in December 1931 and a general strike a year later in support of metalworkers in La Felguera was poorly supported by the miners. Some mines were shut down but this was due more to the dynamiting of power lines – quickly becoming a local speciality – than to anything else. The general strike of May 1933 which *Avance* called a 'reactionary offensive against the Republic' was supported only in Langreo.[31]

Following of the restoration of the seven-hour day by Largo Caballero in August 1931 the SU split as the Communists left to form their own union, the Sindicato Unico de Mineros Asturianos. The SU was left with only 1168 members in February 1933. However, not all the rest (and there had been 9000 in May 1931) had gone with the Communists. The 'deception' and 'disorganization' caused by the schism led many workers to go 'with neither one group nor the other'.[32]

At the National Conference for Syndical Unity organized by the Communists in September 1932 the SUMA claimed to have 5000 members, all in Turón. This was clearly wishful thinking. The situation of the Communist Party in Asturias was the object of strong criticism at the party congress in Seville. It was said to be split by sectarianism and isolated from the masses. At the regional party congress held in Mieres in April 1933 the political secretary's report criticized the union's failure to take the initiative in strike movements and one delegate described its deterioration following the forty-eight-hour general strike of 1–2 May 1932 as 'a real disaster, especially in Turón where the best militants have been left in the street due to the lack of organization'.[33]

Under these circumstances the collapse of anarcho-syndicalist and Communist support among the miners in 1932–3 and the increasing dominance of the SMA and its policy of restraint, the Asturian coalfields should have been relatively untroubled by conflict. But this was not the case. As we have mentioned, Asturias led the country in strikes in both 1932 and 1933. Thus, the miners present us with a contradiction. Unlike the years of the dictatorship when mass militancy resulted in the decline of the SMA, in the first two and a half years of the Republic militant miners remained within the union even though they found themselves in conflict with the policy of its leadership.

The general strikes the union called in 1932–3 were purely defensive, a reaction to the deteriorating condition of the industry which was leading, as it had ten years before, to layoffs, wage-cuts and short weeks. The miners responded with spontaneous strikes and the union's repeated warnings of their danger reveal the degree to which it was losing control of its membership. As the SMA stumbled toward the November 1932 general strike the Civil Governor expressed his doubts about the union's ability to maintain control. His fears were later verified by Amador Fernández when he admitted that the union had not actually organized the strike which brought out 25,000 workers.[34]

The Socialist press reported the miners' growing restiveness with great concern. On 3 January 1933 El Socialista described the social climate in the coalfields as 'charged with passion and madness; only our comrades are holding the lid on'. Avance had numerous reports of the rising social temperature. The depression was 'increasing the restlessness of the workers', 'adding to the miners' anguish' and 'creating an extraordinary enthusiasm for a strike to defend the hundreds of comrades the capitalists want to sacrifice altogether'. At Hullera Española, where the workers were owed two months' wages 2000 struck in March over the disciplining of a worker, while in November 'unrest and disgust reigned'.[35]

The victory of the right in the November 1933 election marked the beginning of a new period. The Socialist press declared the death of the 'republican Republic'. Ten days after the election came the first outright rejection of the regime by Asturian Socialists. 'The working classes have nothing to do with democracy', *Avance* declared.[36] The suspension of the CNT following its attempted insurrection in December 1933 was taken as proof of the fascist nature of the new government. Comparisons were drawn between Spain and Russia on the eve of the November revolution and Amador Fernández was calling on Spanish workers to 'echo the shout that Lenin gave and that brought victory, "Now or never" '.[37]

By the summer of 1934 the radicalization of the Socialist leadership was complete. In August *Avance* proclaimed that 'the working class is not interested in the Republic in its original state . . . it wants only to finish with it.' At the same time as they were talking of revolution union leaders continued to warn the membership against going on strike without orders although the reason now given was that frequent strikes would dissipate the strength of the working class before the final struggle.[38]

The civil war rhetoric of the Socialist press was given credibility by the increasing repression directed at the labour movement by the Lerroux and Samper governments. Police began to search the *casas del pueblo* (union halls) for arms in February following the approval of a law requiring all privately owned guns to be turned in to the authorities. These searches reached a peak in September when the *casas del pueblo*, workers' cultural centres, the offices of *Avance* and the Teatro Llaneza in Sama were all searched. The *casa del pueblo* in Sama was searched three times in seven months. Despite all these efforts, no guns were found.[39] In March the government announced an anti-strike bill and the police were increasingly used to break up strikes and demonstrations. The Civil Guard were called in during strikes at Duro-Felguera in May and September and on 1 September police attacked a rally of Socialist women's organizations in Sama, killing six people.[40]

Avance was a special target of this repression. In the course of 186 days beginning in March 1934 the paper was banned ninety-four times, fined 25,000 pesetas and its editor, Javier Bueno, jailed three times. Its presses were attacked and its street vendors harassed. The union kept the paper going despite the great financial drain this represented. The money to pay the fines was raised by public subscription and mass visits of thousands of people to Javier Bueno while he was in prison became a regular feature of Sunday life in Oviedo.[41]

The swing to the left of the Socialist leadership in Asturias formed part of the radicalization of Spanish socialism as a whole following the election of November 1933. As early as 26 November the executive of the Socialist Party was discussing an armed insurrection against the government.[42] But the radicalization of the Asturian Socialists was less a direct response to the political course the country was taking than to the growing militancy of their own rank and file. The SMA had had difficulty in controlling its members before the November elections and it had even more trouble afterwards. The beginning of direct repression by the state shattered the Republican illusion held by the working class. The regime had been greeted as the saviour of the workers but that saviour had clearly failed. Not only failed but turned from saviour to scourge. Yet it was clearer than ever that the miners' well-being was dependent on the state and this gave their economic demands a revolutionary edge.

The course of the strike movement after November 1933 illustrates the miners' rejection of republican legitimacy and the increasing politicization of their actions. In the first *bienio* of the Republic there was only one strike which could be called political, but in the first nine months of 1934, of thirty-two strikes mentioned in the press, there were eight which were political and of these three were general strikes.

The first came in February and was a twenty-four-hour strike in solidarity with the Austrian Socialists defeated in the civil war of that month, and it effectively closed down mining operations in the province. With the exception of the construction workers of Oviedo and 'some isolated instances in other towns' it was exclusively a miners' strike and one which the SMA did not call.[43]

Five of these strikes were in protest against police actions. In March miners in Langreo, San Martín del Rey Aurelio, Tudela-Veguin,

Laviana and Siero staged a spontaneous general strike to protest against arms searches in the *casas del pueblo* and the frisking of the men as they left the mines. On 2 April 1500 men at the Mariana mine struck to protest against the arrest of five militants and the next day there were 15,000 on strike in Mieres, Aller and Lena. The five men were freed when a crowd of 3000 demanding their release surrounded the Mieres jail.[44] In July all the men at the Barredos mine struck to protest against the confiscation of *Avance* and in September there was a general strike in Langreo, Laviana and San Martín del Rey Aurelio to protest against the attack by police on a rally in which six people were killed. 'The stores did not open, nor did the bars, the cafes, the banks or the bakeries. Everything was shut tight as a drum.' Finally, on 27 September miners in Boo stayed away from work in order to be present while police searched their homes for arms.[45]

The two remaining political strikes were to protest against rallies organized by the right wing CEDA party. In April the Communists called a twenty-four-hour general strike against the rally scheduled at El Escorial. Despite Socialist opposition 4000 miners came out, in Aller, 1000 in Sama, 250 in Quirós and 'plenty' in Mieres, Moreda and Turón. The most impressive of all these strikes was that of 8–9 September against the CEDA rally to be held at Covadonga, the shrine of the Reconquest, in Asturias itself. The entire central zone of the province was shut down; stores closed, train services stopped, telephone lines were cut and groups of armed workers patrolled the highways to turn back cars.[46]

September 1934 was the 'climax of social tension' in the Asturian coalfield. In addition to the two general strikes already mentioned there was at the Fondón mine a strike which was on the verge of becoming general at the end of the month. In this last month before the revolution the Asturian miners were openly contesting the legitimacy of the Republic and Socialist leaders found themselves caught in a dilemma.

On the one hand to maintain the pressure and respond to government provocation; on the other to rein in the movement and try to avoid the revolutionary crisis breaking before the arrival of the word from Madrid which would start the insurrection. This tactic had to be applied to an ever more irritable and touchy mass movement which was increasingly opting for the street, the strike and often for guns.[47]

The young miners were crucial to this process of radicalization. One of the outstanding features of Asturian labour militancy in the period before the revolution and during the revolution itself was the protagonism of the younger workers in the Socialist Youth. 'The youth were the real base of the armed movement, the vanguard. Their role was so decisive that it is difficult to imagine the ''Asturian commune'' without them.'[48]

Although it is not possible to assess the influence of the younger miners within the workforce as a whole, it does appear that much of the growth in the UGT and the SMA in particular came from this sector. At the beginning of October 1934 the Socialist Youth had 153 sections and almost 18,000 members. At this time the Asturian UGT had 40,000 members and the SMA claimed 25,000.[49] Yet it was precisely these younger miners who were least susceptible to the authority of the union hierarchy. In March 1932 the SMA claimed that an unauthorized strike at Fabrica de Mieres was 'the work of the youth element . . . comic opera radicalism'. An article in July 1934 by Graciano Antuña, a member of the executive, called on the young not to be pushed into premature action by the stimulus of political and social events. 'We need not only enthusiasm, strength and determination from our youth, but also something much more important, absolutely indispensable in difficult times: discipline.' That same month González Peña had to warn against the revolutionary enthusiasm of the youth. 'We cannot allow . . . our young comrades to monopolize the revolution.'[50]

This growing militancy among the mineworkers was the basic component of the October revolution, but although the insurrection was never fully under the control of the Socialist leadership it was not entirely spontaneous or unplanned. As early as 26 November 1933 the Socialist Party executive began to discuss an armed insurrection against the Republic. On 12 January 1934 Indalecio Prieto presented a 'possible programme for a united action against the forces of the right' which Largo Caballero described as 'simply a programme to be realized the day after the revolution has triumphed . . . the bourgeois elements will not be able to accept its contents.'[51]

Prieto's proposal was eventually accepted although it was not made public until January 1936. It called for educational reform, the collectivization of the large estates, dissolution of the religious orders, the reorganization of the armed forces and the purge of all officers hostile to the Republic, dissolution of the Civil Guard and its replacement by a popular militia, more advanced labour legislation, fiscal reform and the destitution of the president, Alcalá Zamora. A liaison committee between the PSOE, UGT and Socialist Youth was set up to handle the preparations. In Asturias the Socialists were able to secure a considerable supply of arms, none of which were discovered during the numerous searches by the police in 1934. Some came from Eibar smuggled in crates of sewing machines, others were secreted piece by piece from the state small-arms factory in Oviedo. The committee authorized its provincial and regional branches to form *alianzas obreras* (workers' alliances) with other working-class organizations, but only if they could guarantee that 'the Party never lost control of the insurrectionary movement'.[52]

Asturias was the only place in Spain where the Alianza Obrera became a reality. This was due in large part to the more moderate attitude of the regional committee of the CNT which was the only one in the anarcho-syndicalist organization prepared to co-operate with the Socialists. Despite the bitterness with which *cenetistas* and Socialists had fought each other over the years, the regional CNT leadership, and especially José María Martínez, realized that a revolutionary situation was developing and that it could only be taken advantage of in co-operation with the UGT, which was the most important labour organization in the province. On 9 March 1934 the CNT regional committee agreed to make contact with the UGT in order to begin negotiations. The first meeting was held on the 13th and negotiations began, although marked by great suspicion on both sides.[53]

At the CNT regional plenum held in May the La Felguera delegation demanded that the committee be censured for having made the alliance without consulting the local organizations. However, had the Alianza Obrera merely been a pact between the two union organizations made behind the backs of the workers, as was charged, it would have been worthless. No treaty was going to create overnight camaraderie between two such long-standing enemies. But, as José María Martínez said in defending the alliance, 'the openly pro-alliance attitude which exists among the workers means that the *Alianza* will exist anyway for it is what the workers want.'[54]

Co-operation had begun in a slow and piecemeal manner more than a year before the creation of the alliance. Socialists and anarcho-syndicalists ran a number of local strikes together in 1933–4 and in January 1934 the Langreo Committee for the United Front, composed of Socialists, Communists and 'libertarian groups', sent a note to *Avance* urging 'the various workers' parties to establish liaison committees to make the desired united front a reality.'[55] Amador Fernández's criticism of two meetings which had been jointly addressed by Communist and Socialist speakers were answered the following week by a miner who described the support among Socialist miners in Figaredo for an alliance. There was certainly considerable sympathy in Sama where the meeting drew more people than could be squeezed into the Teatro Llaneza.[56]

On the other hand, in La Felguera where the struggle between Socialists and anarcho-syndicalists was unrelenting there was little support for the Alianza Obrera. The CNT was dominant in this area and in 1932 had staged a general strike lasting nine months against Duro-Felguera. The SMA was not directly involved but the length of the strike led to mine closures which began to cause hardship for Socialist mineworkers. The SMA then began to distribute relief money, but only to Socialist workers. This created an ineradicable fund of bitterness which helps explain the opposition of the *cenetistas* in La Felguera to the Alianza Obrera.[57]

By the end of September the Asturian coalfields were a powder-keg ready to explode at any moment. The ministerial crisis which ended on 3 October with the entry of three members of the CEDA into the cabinet provided the spark and the Socialist revolutionary committee in Madrid gave the word for the insurrection. Teodomiro Menéndez, the most moderate of Socialists, unhappily did his duty and arrived in Oviedo late on the 4th with the watchword in his hatband. When the signal was given late that night Asturias exploded with the full force of the miners' anger and frustration.

The Socialist leadership had prepared a very precise military plan which called for the miners quickly to take control of the coalfields and launch a surprise attack on Oviedo, the provincial capital. The first step was an assault on the Civil Guard posts in the coalfields. This was a success but took longer than had been anticipated. In Sama the battle lasted a full thirty-six hours and thirty-eight Civil Guard were killed.

After having eliminated the police presence in the coalfields the miners were to march on Oviedo in three columns: from Ablaña, Mieres and Langreo. However the delay and poor co-ordination among the columns removed the element of surprise and allowed the forces in the city to prepare their defences. The group from Ablaña, under the command of González Peña, spent all of the 5th on the outskirts of the capital waiting for the provincial committee inside the city to give the order to attack. The order was not given until the 6th and, to make matters worse, the workers of Oviedo did not rise. When the siege finally began some 1400 soldiers and 300 Civil Guard were defending the city from about 1200 workers.[58]

Although after the first day of fighting the revolutionaries controlled a large part of Oviedo they had to endure four days of street fighting before being able to take the central core and reduce the defenders to a few isolated pockets: the barracks, the jail, the civil government building and the cathedral. At the same time the workers scored three other important victories around the capital. On the 6th a small group staged a surprise attack on the cannon factory during which the workers inside were able to disarm the soldiers on guard. Twenty-seven cannon were captured. The next day the explosives factory at La Manjoya was captured. Finally, the revolutionaries captured the state small-arms factory in Oviedo itself after a three-day battle.

The obsession with Oviedo meant that the other major city in the province, Gijón, with its large and combative working class composed mainly of anarcho-syndicalist metalworkers, dockers and fishermen, was neglected. Oviedo was, of course, politically symbolic but Gijón and its port were strategically much more significant. The workers of the city were left short of arms and were unable to hold the port and prevent Colonel Yagüe's troops from landing.

Meanwhile, at the southern end of the coalfield, on what was known as the southern front, General Bosch and his column advancing along the main highway from León were encircled at Vega del Rey by between two and three thousand miners. The amateurs made skilful use of the mountainous terrain to trap a professional soldier who had badly underestimated his opponent. The miners organized field-kitchens, medical assistance and even telephone links to the local committees in Pola de Lena and Mieres. Bosch's troops were trapped for six days before the arrival of reinforcements allowed them to break out and retreat. On the 15th, almost totally out of ammunition, the miners began to withdraw but the efforts of a small guerrilla force and the concern of the new commander, General Balmes, not to fall into another trap meant that the troops advanced very cautiously and never reached Mieres.

The military achievement of the revolutionaries was considerable for they were facing a well-armed, professional force of some 26,000 men: General López Ochoa advancing on Oviedo from Galicia, Colonel Yagüe's African troops joining the attack after landing at Gijón and General Solchaga's force marching on the Nalón valley from the east, in addition to the Bosch-Balmes column trapped on the southern front. The real interest of the Asturian revolution, however, lies not in its military aspects but in the social organization which began to emerge in the zones controlled by the workers.

The insurrection was theoretically under the control of the provincial revolutionary committee in Oviedo composed of five Socialists, two Communists[59] and an anarcho-syndicalist, but it did not provide any effective direction. In contrast to the precisely planned military operation there was no predetermined revolutionary blueprint 'In which the goals of the revolution were set out. . . . There was only a programme for taking the *physical centres of power* by military action.'[60] When we recall that the Asturian insurrection was part of a nationwide movement to allow the Socialists to take power and make a number of not terribly radical reforms it is fair to assume that the objectives of the provincial committee in Asturias did not go much beyond subduing the military forces of the state and replacing the existing political authorities.

However, the writ of the provincial committee did not run into the coalfields, where the revolutionary impetus of the miners far exceeded the limited official objectives of the rising. During the two weeks of the Asturian revolution the workers controlled about one-third of the province and 80 per cent of its population. Within this zone, with the coalfields at its heart, all established authority vanished with the subjugation of the Civil Guard. It was replaced by local revolutionary committees composed of the relevant working-class organizations – although not necessarily in direct relation to the local balance of forces. The Sama committee included the PSOE, CNT and Communists while in Turón there were only Socialists and Communists represented. In Mieres Manuel Grossi, a member of the Alianza Obrera executive, appointed the local committee 'with two Socialists, two anarchists, two Communists from the official party and myself, representing the Alianza Obrera and the Bloque Obrero y Campesino'.[61] In La Felguera the anarchists of the FAI (Federación Anarquista Ibérica) were in control on their own.

These local committees took control of all aspects of social organization incumbent on a government. As well as military affairs they were active in food supply and rationing, health, labour, communications, propaganda, public order and justice. Money was abolished and replaced by vouchers issued to each family and valid for an amount of food determined after a thorough census. In Sama the supply committee dealt with local farmers to assure quantities of milk, eggs and meat. In Oviedo, Sama and Mieres hospitals were organized and the wounded of both sides treated. Nuns and doctors staffed these hospitals although the latter often had to be forcibly recruited. Works committees organized the conservation of mines and the operation of essential public services such as water and electricity. Explosives were produced in Mieres and armoured vehicles in Turón. In La Felguera the FAI kept the Duro-Felguera foundry going, turning out armoured cars in three eight-hour shifts per day.

A central motor pool of 600 vehicles was created in Sama with smaller ones in Mieres and Turón. Trains were used to move troops and supplies, especially between Sama and Noreña. Telephone connections were extended to allow more effective communications and there was even a radio transmitter in Turón which broadcast to France and Belgium although most of these broadcasts were blocked. Public order was maintained by armed police forces, in Sama called the Red Guard, composed of workers not involved in the fighting at Oviedo or on the southern front. In the capital, where the workers controlled the bourgeois residential and business districts, special efforts were made to prevent looting by what one participant called the 'canaille'.[62]

Jails were improvised where necessary – there were 200 prisoners in Oviedo – and in general the prisoners were well treated. There were some killings, mostly in the latter stages of the revolution when defeat was imminent and word of the brutal repression began to spread. Eight monks and a priest were shot on the orders of the Turón committee and later Rafael de Riego, the manager of Hulleras del Turón, was also killed although this was probably an act of personal vengeance. The revolution had its excesses but it was far less bloodthirsty than the 'forces of order'. At least sixty-one innocent civilians were shot in the outer districts of Oviedo as the army occupied the city and between twenty-five and fifty prisoners summarily executed in the Pelayo barracks shortly afterwards.

The Socialist-dominated provincial committee began to consider abandoning the movement as early as the 9th, when it was clear that Asturias had risen alone. On the 11th, with López Ochoa's troops entering the capital, the committee fled. González Peña, the so-called '*generalísimo*' of the revolution was not seen again until he was arrested, long after the insurrection was over. The precipitous unannounced flight of the committee caused a brief panic – in Sama the Red Guard abandoned their weapons in the street – but the local committees stayed put, determined to resist. The next day a second committee composed of five Communists, an anarcho-syndicalist and two members of the Socialist Youth was elected at a meeting in the main square of Oviedo. The committee lasted only a day, launching a counter-attack on the troops entering the city. The most interesting feature of this brief period of Communist dominance was the attempt to replace the existing workers' militias by a 'Red Army' based on the conscription of all workers between eighteen and thirty-five.

On the 12th some of the Socialist members of the first committee returned and a third, and final, committee was formed. This one had six Socialists and three Communists. Representatives from the CNT attended but refused to serve as members. The next day the committee moved to Sama although the Communist delegates stayed in Oviedo to mount a last defence. The Socialists' main concern was to find a way of winding up the struggle but they had trouble convincing the local committees that further resistance was useless. On the 17th Belarmino Tomás, the Socialist president of the provincial committee, negotiated a surrender with General López Ochoa. All arms were to be handed in in return for the general's promise that the Moorish troops would not be allowed into the coalfields, a promise which was not kept. The next day the committee issued its final communiqué: 'Everyone back to work and to continue fighting for our victory.' The Asturian revolution was over.

The Asturian revolution of October 1934 clearly foreshadowed the Spanish Civil War which lay less than two years in the future. At one level the military aspects of the war in Asturias resembled those of the revolution. In 1934 the workers concentrated all their efforts on taking Oviedo ignoring other, more important objectives, especially Gijón. During the Civil War the value of the Asturian working class to the Republican cause was seriously undercut by the deceitful seizure of Oviedo by Colonel Aranda which made necessary another siege of the city, this time lasting until the northern front fell to Franco in November 1937.

At another level the political and social aspects of the two conflicts have important resemblances. The Alianza Obrera of 1934 presaged the close wartime co-operation of the UGT and CNT in Asturias. Likewise, the reluctance of the Communists to participate in the alliance and their attempt to convert the workers' militias into a regular army anticipate one of the central conflicts in the Republican camp during the Civil War. During the revolution there was a pronounced tendency towards the disintegration of all central authority symbolized in the predominance of the local committees over the provincial committee. During the war, mines and factories were run by individual councils but political authority was retained by the Republican government as represented by the Council of Asturias. However, the fracturing of political authority did take place but at the level of regions, not of towns. In 1934 the first act of the revolution was to destroy the power of the state while in 1936–7 this was not the case. Yet while the Council of Asturias theoretically represented the central government, in fact it acted as an independent entity.

Finally, the Asturian revolution signalled the Republic's failure to resolve its central dilemma: the promise of social conflict if it did not provide meaningful social reform. In Asturias, as elsewhere in Spain, the Second Republic was received by the working class as its salvation but it only took five years to realize that this was a mistake and that if social reform were to come it would have to be fought for. In Asturias, where the coal-miners had been fighting a defensive battle against the mine-owners since 1919, this realization came earlier than in other regions. So too did the violent conflict it engendered. Both the Asturian revolution and the Spanish Civil War were social conflicts fed by the disappointment of the hopes for a better life that the Republic had kindled in the Spanish working class. They were also both failures, but failures of heroic and epic proportions.

Notes

1 *Aurora Social (AS)*, 11 September 1931.
2 On the crisis of 1917 see J. A. Lacomba, *La Crisis Española de 1917* (Madrid, 1970).
3 M. Tuñón de Lara, *El Movimiento Obrero en la Historia de España* (Madrid, 1972), 903.
4 For a detailed discussion of the problems of the industry see my dissertation, 'The social origins of labour militancy: Asturias, 1860–1934' (Department of History, Queen Mary College, London, 1982), 26–43.
5 *Estadística Minera y Metalúrgica de España* (1913–18); M. Aldecoa, *Dictamen oficial sobre la minería carbonera de Asturias* (Madrid, 1926), 34; Ministerio del Trabajo, *Estadística de salarios y jornadas de trabajo 1919–1930* (Madrid, 1931), LXII.
6 *El Noroeste (NO)*, 24 September to 13 October 1919.
7 *Revista Nacional de Economía* (January 1919), 161.
8 For details see Shubert, 'Social origins', 105–21.
9 R. Perpiñá Grau, *Memorándum sobre la política de carbón* (Valencia, 1935), 30; *El Socialista (ES)*, 7, 12 March, 24 September 1921.
10 The plan announced by the owners would have turned the clock back to before the war. Instituto de Reformas Sociales, *Crónica acerca de los conflictos en las minas de carbón de Asturias desde diciembre de 1921* (Madrid, 1922), 100–1. For details of the strikes see Shubert, 'Social origins', 247–54.
11 Iron and steel production fell from 1,793,500 tons in 1929 to 832,800 tons in 1934. J. Vicens Vives, 'Movimientos obreros en tiempos de depresion economica', *Obra Dispersa* (Barcelona, 1965), 151.
12 *ES*, 15 March 1928.
13 Shubert, 'Social origins', 260–75.
14 On the schism see G. Meaker, *The Revolutionary Left in Spain, 1917–1923* (Stanford, 1973), 225–312.
15 *AS*, 9 March 1928; *ES*, 9 October 1928; *NO*, 24 May, 11, 16 November, 1930, 5 May 1931; M. Villar, *El anarquismo en la insurrección de Asturias* (Barcelona, 1935), 48–9.

16 In Asturias the Republic was received with 'unprecedented enthusiasm
    . . . something extraordinary which exceeds even the possibility of describ-
    ing it'. *NO*, 15, 16, 19 April 1931.
17 *ES*, 28 May 1931; *Avance (AV)*, 15 April 1'33.
18 *AV*, 24 October, 18 November 1933.
19 *AV*, 13 May 1932, 6 January, 2, 7 February 1933.
20 *NO*, 26 May 1931; *AV*, 8 December 1931, 21 March, 24 September 1932.
21 *AV*, 2 August 1932.
22 *ES*, 3, 6, 13 September 1932; *AV* 6–13 September 1932.
23 *ES*, 15, 20 November 1932; *AV*, 14–22 November 1932. The strike was
    widely supported everywhere but Turón, where the Communists held
    back. According to the Civil Governor only 30 per cent of the miners in
    Turón struck.
24 *AV* 26–31 January 1933; *ES*, 31 January 1933.
25 *ES*, 7 February–1 March 1933; *AV*, 7 February–1 March 1933.
26 *ES*, 1–5 March 1933; *AV*, 1–9 March 1933.
27 *AV*, 2–30 September 1933; *ES*, 2–7, 23, 30 September 1933.
28 *NO*, 2–6 May 1931; *ES*, 2 June 1931; *AS*, 12, 19 June 1931; *EMME*
    (1931), 11, 303.
29 *NO*, 3–12 June 1931; *ES*, 11 June 1931; Civil Governor to Minister of the
    Interior, 6 June 1931, Archivo Histórico Nacional, Madrid, Gobernación,
    legajo 7A, expediente 8.
30 *NO*, 4 June, 3 July 1931; *ES*, 11 June 1931; Civil Governor to Interior, 11
    June 1931, AHN Gob., leg. 7A, exp. 8. Even before the strike Fernández
    and González Peña had complained of the 'passivity' of the authorities' in
    the face of attacks on SMA members. On 1 June they sent a telegram to the
    Minister of the Interior denouncing the Civil Governor as soft on Commu-
    nists and anarcho-syndicalists. *NO*, 31 May 1931; Fernández and González
    Peña to Interior, 1 June 1931, AHN Gob., leg. 7A, exp. 8.
31 Civil Governor to Interior, 15 December 1931, AHN, Gob., leg. 7A,
    exp. 8; *ES*, 15, 18 December 1932, 10–11 May 1933; *AV*, 16 December
    1931, 10–13 December 1932; 9, 10 May 1933.
32 A. Oliveros, *Asturias en el resurgimiento español* (Madrid, 1935), 320; Villar,
    El anarquismo, 51–2.
33 Fundación de Investigaciones Marxistas (Madrid), microfilm 5, section
    81; Actas de las Sesiones de la Conferencia Regional, microfilm 6, section
    88.
34 Civil Governor to Interior, 4 September 1932, AHN, Gob., leg. 6A,
    exp. 50; *AV*, 15 November 1932.
35 *ES*, 3 January 1933; *AV*, 11, 19 January, 4 February, 28 March, 12 Aug-
    ust, 26, 28 September, 7 November 1933.
36 *AV*, 29 November, 9 December 1933.
37 *AV*, 26 December 1933, 28 January 1934.
38 *AV*, 19 August 1934.

39 *AV*, 13 February, 28–31 March, 16, 22 September, 2 October 1934; *ES*, 23, 25 September 1934; *NO*, 30 September 1934.
40 *AV*, 17 May, 2, 4, 8 September 1934.
41 *Historia General de Asturias* (Gijón, 1979), VII, 33–41; *AV*, 19, 23 May, 29 June, 11, 17, 18, 29 July, 11 August 1934.
42 Actas de la Reunión del Comité Nacional, 26 November 1933, Archivo del PSOE, 24–1, Fundación Pablo Iglesias (FPI), Madrid.
43 *AV*, 14, 20 February 1934; *NO*, 20 February 1934.
44 *AV*, 25 March, 3, 4 April 1934; *Historia General de Asturias*, VII, 29. On 15 March 3000 people had gathered outside the jail where two Socialists were being held on charges of burning packets of the Catholic paper *El Debate*.
45 *AV*, 11 July, 2, 4, 28 September 1934.
46 *NO*, 30 September 1934; *Historia General de Asturias*, VII, 28; *ES*, 9 September 1934; B. Díaz Nosty, *La Comuna Asturiana* (Bilbao, 1975), 123.
47 *Historia General de Asturias*, VII, 97.
48 Díaz Nosty, *La Comuna*, 151.
49 *Historia General de Asturias*, VII, 61.
50 *AV*, 7 May 1932, 11, 29 July 1934.
51 Actas de las Reuniones del Comité Ejecutivo, 12 January 1934, Archivo del PSOE, 20–3, FPI.
52 J. S. Vidarte, *El Bienio Negro y la Insurrección en Asturias* (Barcelona, 1979), 186; *Historia General de Asturias*, VII, 17–20.
53 For a first-hand account of the negotiations see 'Gestiones para la Alianza Obrera Revolucionaria en Asturias,' a 74-folio document in the Archivo de la Guerra Civil, Salamanca, Gijón, serie J, carpeta 12. The programme for the alliance, 'to fight openly against fascism' and 'to oppose any hint of war', was published in *Avance* on 1 April 1934.
54 FIM, microfilm 10, section 131.
55 *ES*, 10 February 1933; *AV*, 17 August 1933, 26, 28 January 1934.
56 *AV*, 6, 7, 15 February, 9 March 1934.
57 *Historia de Asturias* (Salinas, 1982), VIII, 225–9.
58 This description of the revolution is taken from the accounts in M. Grossi, *La insurrección de Asturias* (Gijón, 1977), N. Molins i Fabrega, *UHP. La insurrección proletaria de Asturias* (Gijón, 1979) and Díaz Nosty, *La Comuna*.
59 The Communists had not joined the Alianza Obrera, urging instead a 'popular front from below'. They finally did join on the eve of the insurrection.
60 Díaz Nosty, *La Comuna*, 159.
61 Grossi, *La insurrección*, 27.
62 ibid., 40.

6
Economic crisis, social conflict and the Popular Front: Madrid 1931–6

Santos Juliá

On 1 June 1936, there began in Madrid the fourth and longest construction strike during the Republic, involving 80,000 workers. Those in heating, elevators and sanitation had already been on strike for a few weeks and the brewing, ice and soft-drinks workers had been idle for some days. In the very important union of waiters, great confusion reigned, for while the Sindicato Unico de la Industria Gastronómica (CNT) had given the order for a general strike on 21 May, the Agrupación General de Camareros (UGT) gave the order to go to work.

When the construction workers had already been on strike for two weeks, the 6000 furniture workers and all 1500 tailoring workers also came out. In addition to the multitude of workers from small and middle-sized businesses, the strikers were also to be joined by the workers of Euskalduna, the glovers, the leather-workers, and the women from the factories of Gal and Floralia. Madrid, in the months of May and June 1936, was really on strike.[1]

This was not the first time during the Republic that a wave of strikes shook the main industries of the city. From October 1933 to June 1934 an all-out strike had also been declared three times by the construction workers and, once each, by the hotel, printing and metal workers. There had also been threats of a strike of shop assistants, and of railwaymen. In the first fortnight in March 1934, with more than half of the city's workers on strike, Madrid experienced a very similar situation to that of June 1936.[2] Then, all these industrial strikes, fuelled by growing expectations, shared by both Socialists and anarcho-syndicalists, that a general strike would immediately provoke the social revolution, turned into the insurrectional strike of October 1934, which completely paralysed the city for ten days. Now, in June 1936, believing less in the miraculous effects of the general strike, the workers were hesitant about launching a revolution, but that did not keep them from going out into the streets. And there, in the streets, they were caught by the military uprising which was to transform the wave of strikes into armed resistance against a *coup d'état*.

Armed resistance to a military uprising was perhaps the last scenario imaginable for those who, in those same streets of Madrid, had proclaimed and celebrated the Republic five years earlier. After all, if the people of Madrid and, of course, of many other cities had not interpreted, felt and celebrated the electoral triumph of the Republican-Socialist candidates at the ballot box as the decisive political victory over the monarchy, then very possibly the monarchy might have been able to ignore its electoral rejection. The popular celebration, however, eliminated the possibility of any political initiative other than the proclamation of the Republic. Thus, to general surprise, the Republic was established as an immediate result of a popular movement.[3]

It was a movement of the people in the sense that it consisted of an alliance of working-class trade unions, petty bourgeois democrats, urban middle-class radicals and the moderate bourgeois reformists. Those elements, which came together in the last months of the dictatorship, demonstrated in the streets as a celebration of the triumph of national sovereignty over a monarchy which had tied its destiny to the dictatorial regime. The old regime was incapable of resistance. The army joined in the celebrations; the Church of Madrid sent its emissaries to congratulate the new ministers and even the civil guards stopped on street corners to share cigarettes with the crowds of revellers. The monarch left Madrid to the accompaniment of popular songs and the Republic was born out of the people's celebration of their regained sovereignty.[4] The composition of the provisional government clearly reflected this origin. Moreover, its programme consisted of old working-class aspirations, some bourgeois reforms and, naturally, rhetorical appeals to the urban middle sectors. With such a government and such a project, the Republican-Socialist coalition was resoundingly successful in the first general elections.[5] Problems were to arise by the score, however, once the lights went out on that initial great popular fiesta in Madrid.

In fact, the immediate problems were the corollary of the emergence of that powerful popular movement. Behind that movement lay the existence of an old, popular, integrated, and proto-industrial city in the heart of the Madrid of the 1930s. Around that city, by mere cumulative growth, another city had been created, which broke the continuity of its traditional urban structure without yet creating a modern and industrial structure. Madrid, at the beginning of the 1930s, had within it a popular city; but Madrid was then no longer a popular city nor was it yet an industrial one. This situation explains the obduracy of class confrontations as well as the type of tensions which quickly accumulated and the collapse of the institutional channels which might have given them an outlet.

Madrid had experienced since the turn of the century, and especially from 1910 onwards, a swift growth that practically doubled its population. In 1930, there were more inhabitants who had been born outside the city than in it.[6] That growth, notable especially in the areas of the *Ensanche* (expansion) and the *Extrarradio* (outskirts), involved some neighbouring municipalities which in only twenty years increased their population three- or four-fold. Those municipalities – Chamartín,

Carabanchel, Vallecas – grew to meet the outskirts of Madrid to form large proletarian conglomerates which surrounded on the north, south and south-east the bourgeois or petty bourgeois zones of the *Ensanche*. The previously integrated social pattern of the inner city was thus shattered by these new divisions.[7]

The enormous flood of new arrivals in the capital – mostly young people – usually lacked professional qualifications. Many were illiterate and almost all came to Madrid attracted by the construction boom of the 1910s and 1920s. The capital, becoming increasingly the headquarters for banks and private companies and already the main centre of communications and transport, had expanded its building industry more than any other, filling in the empty spaces of the *Ensanche* and overflowing into the *Extrarradio*. Accordingly, many came to work in the new services – offices, banks, transport, communications. Many more came to work on the building of the new commercial centres and houses. Others entered service therein. It is, doubtless, a crude simplification to say that in Madrid there were only bricklayers, clerks and maids. Nonetheless, it is true that Madrid lived on services and the building industries.[8]

In the 1930s, this growth had not yet obliterated old popular Madrid. However, it had transformed its character, but not yet spawned a new industrial city. The old ecological balance had disappeared and a new one had yet to take its place. There had been a merely cumulative growth. The industrial life of Madrid, except in some traditional industries like printing or the manufacture of furniture and luxury items, depended almost entirely on the construction of buildings and the public works made necessary by the demographic growth of the city. This dependence was in some cases very direct, as in the woodworking industry and in small metallurgy. In others, such as commerce, it was indirect but no less noticeable because the purchasing power of much of the population of Madrid depended on the health of the building industry.[9]

A rapid demographic growth and an extraordinary expansion of the urban space, both based on a very weak industrial and mercantile structure: that was the Madrid of the 1930s. The growth of the city was chaotic. Successive plans were ignored and space was filled in a spontaneous and haphazard way, usually without even the most basic facilities.

Unprotected rubbish dumps, septic tanks and sewage ditches ensured that infection and disease were rife. Misery was palpable. These huge working-class slums began to cause alarm because of the threatening character of their poverty.[10]

As regards class relations, it is not surprising that there should still be a great abundance of a pre-capitalist type of relationship with piecework and cottage industry, low wages, non-fulfilment of the eight-hour day, uncertainty in employment, living-in, the almost complete lack of social security or of the right to holidays, the absence of retirement pensions, all still common. In contrast, the more established industries, in which old workers' societies functioned, had already achieved substantial improvements, but the new wave of immigrants rarely found work in those industrial islands.[11]

Problems were hidden while there was still the 'construction orgy' of the fat years. As long as there was near full employment, the signs that the end of the boom was approaching could be covered up. However, as soon as the rhythm of building began to slow, and then when the whole construction sector began a rapid decline, the social crisis was dramatically apparent.[12]

The workers who lost their jobs, apart from swelling the legions of the unemployed who lacked all subsidies, returned to poverty-stricken neighbourhoods. The city was unable to raise funds to employ them in any productive activity. Both municipal welfare schemes and public subscriptions to assist the unemployed proved insufficient and ruinous, given the magnitude of the problem.[13]

To make matters worse, the crisis of the Madrid economy was not only in the building industry. The chaotic growth of the city brought wider problems. The diminution of new building works produced rampant unemployment, which affected a considerable proportion of the population of Madrid and, in addition, reduced activity in sectors such as woodworking and small metallurgy. Finally, by reducing the purchasing power of great masses of the population, it spread panic among shopkeepers who found themselves trapped both by the decrease of their own trade and the appearance of big department stores and merchandising companies.[14]

This panic reflected vividly the kind of crisis Madrid was going through at the time of the coming of the Republic. In fact, the norm in industry and commerce in Madrid was the small employer – perhaps himself a one-time worker made good – who had fewer than a dozen workers, with whom he established relations of a guild-like character, living from day to day, responding to a stable demand with which he could survive and, during the best times, slowly extending his business. The drop in that demand provoked by the decrease in building made him vulnerable, for he lacked the resources to subsist with the same labour costs but without the capital to increase productivity by other means. Inevitably, he faced a ruinous competition with his peers and a clear inferiority to the large private companies which started to dominate industry and commerce.[15]

Thus, at a time of rapid and meaningful access to politics by all groups and sectors of society, the building crisis generated serious tensions. On the one hand there was conflict between the masses of unskilled wage-earners, employed mainly by private companies on big public works, and their firms; and on the other, between skilled workers, traditionally organized in craft trade unions, and their employers, who prepared to confront new demands by reviving their dormant employers' associations. The confluence of these tensions in a single and generalized confrontation came about because of the type of political decisions and institutional mechanisms with which each sector tried to defend its interests in a time of crisis and in a fragmented urban space.

While this crisis was brewing, a coalition of Republicans and Socialists took control of both the national and the city governments. Several decisions were taken which were to have major repercussions on social relations within Madrid. The coalition was obsessed above all by the need to balance the budget. As regards Madrid, it tried to promote big public works, assigning special credits to the capital city and creating technical organizations to promote access highways and works in the outskirts. At the same time, encouraged by the coalition's programme, the trade unions of Madrid presented new labour terms to the *comités paritarios* and mixed juries pushing for wage improvements and cuts in working hours, as well as a gradual extension of social insurance and assistance.[16]

The impact of these measures of economic and social policy on an already crisis-torn Madrid led to workers and employers adopting tactics which were eventually to destroy that popular movement from which the Republic had emerged. Austerity budgets made credits for construction more difficult. Suddenly, the great number of contractors of Madrid, who previously had financed their buildings with money obtained from the mortgage or second mortgage of plots, found themselves either with very expensive money – hence their constant denunciation of the 'usurers' – or else with no money at all. To make matters worse, there was a drastic reduction in demand for rented property. Building became dearer and its profits more random. It came to a virtual standstill. The licences for new construction fell steeply and many of those applied for were only for small houses. With the purpose of halting as far as possible the decline in building activity, the state encouraged the undertaking of some public works: the underground, railway junctions, new ministerial buildings, the extension of the Castellana Avenue, the University City and the Isabel II canal.[17]

The increase in public works and the simultaneous collapse of construction produced a radical change in the composition of the main sector of the industry in Madrid. The small or medium-sized contractor, who employed a few gangs of workers led by master craftsmen, who were themselves midway within the trade hierarchy, gave way to the large private company, which employed thousands of labourers simultaneously on the same site and on the same job. These workers had no security and could be sacked and find themselves out of a job any Saturday afternoon. The trade-union organization which traditionally represented working-class interests in Madrid found itself completely impotent in dealing with the main problems affecting this new mass of wage-earners: dismissal and unemployment. A growing dissatisfaction was felt on Madrid building-sites as the months went by and the pace of the works did not increase sufficiently to meet the demands for employment. Those workers who lived on the outskirts of the city and were in the outer margins of its labour market, found themselves without any effective trade-union representation. The UGT's traditional organization of the workers of Madrid by craft societies effectively excluded these new unskilled labourers from the protection of the unions and their social policies.[18]

UGT policy centred on the arbitration committees or mixed juries. Considering the almost exclusive power of the UGT of Madrid in the channelling of workers' claims at the beginning of the Republic, the rapid growth of the CNT in the capital is astonishing. The anarcho-syndicalist success can be explained only with reference to these lesser skilled masses of day-labourers. Threatened with unemployment, and with no possibility of social welfare benefits in case of unemployment, they found no solutions to their problems in the social policy of the UGT. The UGT had come to control nearly all the workers' representative posts in the mixed juries. This, together with the powerful support of the Ministry of Labour headed by Largo Caballero, its leader, enabled the UGT to impose improvements in the labour contracts of all trades and industries. There was a general increase in wages, the working day was reduced, and existing legislation was enforced. It is probable that these were the only policies open to the UGT given its traditions, its craft society structure and the expectations that the arrival of Socialists in the government had awakened among many *Madrileños*.[19] Such essentially moderate social reformist policies, when adopted at a time of crisis, with the building industry at a standstill and commerce in difficulties, met with insuperable obstacles.

During the first two years in government, the Socialists' policies managed to satisfy workers' claims and to isolate threatened conflicts in the telephone, railway and retail commerce sectors. From the beginning of 1933, however, there was an increasingly perceptible *malaise* in two of the main industrial and service sectors. Construction workers, excluded from the benefits obtained by their fellow-workers, began to force violent entry on to building-sites in an attempt to impose a demand which was about to become the Madrid battle-cry: work sharing. Similarly, waiters set out to get a new labour contract which would establish them as wage-earners rather than social pariahs. They were bitterly disappointed when the new work contract prepared by the mixed jury accepted their salaries as a minimal part of their total income, the rest to be made up by gratuities. These two failures of the mixed juries, in one case to provide work and in the other to improve the status of the workers, led to the main institutional instruments of Socialist policy being the object of serious hostility by mid-1933 among two important sections of the Madrid working class.[20]

Accordingly, the summer of 1933 saw an intensification of a smear campaign against UGT leaders who were denounced as racketeers and traitors to the workers. On occasions, there were clashes between unemployed workers and those coming out of work; harassment on building-sites, shooting incidents and beatings. The reason was basically that if some levels of the working classes had benefited from the action of the UGT and now enjoyed better wages and more dignified-contracts, many others lost what little work they had. Indeed, the workers' dissatisfaction and consequent agitation began among the unskilled constantly threatened by unemployment and unable to turn to other jobs.

The CNT grew precisely in these sectors and used them as a base from which to launch an offensive against its rival union, the UGT, whose hegemony it had tried to overthrow ever since the beginning of the Republic. The first all-out strike in the building trades was declared by the CNT contrary to the instructions of the UGT. The first total strike of waiters, and ultimately of the entire hotel industry was also to be encouraged and then called by the CNT in the face of the indecision of the UGT waiters who only joined the strike when the CNT had already given the order not to go to work.[21]

At the same time, the UGT policy of wage increases and of the re-definition of workers' rights and status provoked a violent reaction among the employers. This was especially bitter in small and medium-sized concerns, such as retail businesses, involved in a long dispute with the shop assistants, and jobbing builders and contractors who found themselves dragged into hard-fought all-out strikes just at the moment when they thought they had bought off danger by conceding wage increases and a reduction of working hours. Two employers' organizations, the Defensa Mercantil Patronal, for retail business employers, and the Federación Patronal Madrileña, representing building trades employers, launched a major offensive against the mixed juries and against Socialist participation in government at precisely the same time as the CNT was beginning to attack. The employers blamed all their problems on the continued presence in power of the Republican-Socialist coalition and on the activities of the mixed juries.[22]

Thus, the worst moment of the economic crisis and of unemployment coincided in Madrid with the peak of political agitation by the employers and by the CNT. Although the policies of the UGT managed to avoid in Madrid the great class conflicts seen in other Spanish cities from the first days of the Republic, the accumulated tensions of two years erupted simultaneously in the autumn of 1933. When the Socialists had left the government and were about to start their electoral campaign, the anarcho-syndicalists declared in Madrid the first all-out industrial strike. Thereafter, there were to be constant general strikes as the most frequent form of working-class protest.

The departure of the Socialists from government and the breakdown of their coalition with the Republicans allowed the local leaders of UGT federations to regain the freedom of action which had been restricted by the presence of their comrades in government. In Madrid, the first all-out building strike had been called and led by the CNT against UGT opposition to anarcho-syndicalist violence. The waiters' strike similarly had been called by the CNT trade union in the face of UGT hesitation. However, strikes in the first three months of 1934 were to be the joint work of both unions. Despite the disapproval of the UGT's national executive committee, local UGT and CNT committees acted together to call workers' assemblies, to issue leaflets, to direct strikes through joint committees, and to negotiate directly with employers. They joined in describing as useless the efforts of the mixed juries.[23]

This united front of the two great unions appeared in Madrid at a moment of tremendous political confusion. The government of Alejandro Lerroux, according to a Radical deputy, 'depends on the pity of the Right' and was under constant rightist pressure. The fears provoked in the Radical ranks by rightist threats of withdrawing parliamentary support led to continual government crises which did nothing to abate tension in the streets. Since these were the worst moments of unemployment and economic crisis, with price increases or proposed increases on necessities, assaults on shops increased. Not a day went by without a robbery and the victims were not the rich bourgeois, but rather rent-collectors or else small shopkeepers. Not long before, the anarcho-syndicalists had launched an uprising which had left several dead after bomb incidents in Madrid. The Falange had also recently been founded and the fascists were coming onto the streets, raiding union offices, noisily peddling their newspapers and working hard at provoking disorder with constant street clashes, chases and shooting incidents with serious casualties on both sides.

In this atmosphere, the emergence of a united trade-union front had a serious two-fold impact within the Madrid Socialist movement. On the one hand, the old trade-union bureaucracy of the UGT which had lost direction after the collapse of the mixed juries dramatically altered its line and argued as if the only viable policy was the final seizure of power by means of a decisive action of the entire working class. These old UGT leaders came to believe that a general strike in reply to right-wing efforts to enter the government would not only finish off the right but also put an end to the bourgeois Republic and replace it with a socialist Republic. Madrid UGT leaders were convinced that the future would be theirs provided they were prepared when the moment came. Accordingly, UGT directives after April 1934 aimed to block strikes in the capital to prevent a gradual dissipation of proletarian strength. Joint actions with the CNT were rejected. For its own part, after the great exertions of the autumn and winter of 1933–4, the CNT returned to its usual stance of distrust towards what it saw as the political manoeuvres of the 'bourgeois' Marxists aimed at seizing power and subjugating the real working classes.[24]

While talk of the seizure of power through a general strike gripped UGT leaders and the gap widened between the UGT and the CNT in Madrid, a further, and equally important, development took place. This was the eruption onto the scene of the Socialist and Communist Youth movements both by the revitalization of their own organizations and by the infiltration of trade unions hitherto not especially combative, such as that of bank and stock-exchange employees. The young militants quickly took up in simplified form the new vision of the future preached by union leaders and they elaborated a theory of class conflict in Madrid as the final struggle between the bourgeoisie and the proletariat. The experience of the bourgeois Republic was seen as being in the past and the only possible future was full-blown socialism. However, while the union bureaucrats believed that socialism could be established via a general strike, the young militants were convinced that the only means validated by history was armed insurrection. The older generation let things happen rather than control events. The offices and cellars of the *Casa del Pueblo* started to store a ludicrous collection of small-arms, machine-guns and ammunition.[25]

The occasionally spontaneous coming together of worker activities and youth initiatives under the expectant gaze of the union leadership created the mirage of an inevitable socialist victory. This required, above all, the conservation of working-class energies, the avoidance of partial or single-industry strikes. Responsibility for this was undertaken by the leaders of the various worker unions. The second requirement was the encouragement of a spirit of insurrection, the preparation of armed actions and the putting of the final touches to a theory of revolution. This task fell to the youth and the intellectuals. The last thing to be done was simply to await the opportune moment and then to decide on tactics. This was the responsibility of the political leadership of the Madrid Socialist movement which, in 1934, had the same personnel as the UGT leadership.[26]

The conviction that an opportunely timed insurrection backed by a general strike would be sufficient to establish socialism dominated the entire panorama of the social conflicts of the capital in 1934 from the end of the wave of industrial strikes in March until the outbreak of the general strike in October. The events of October constituted in Madrid the fusion of accumulated social tensions with the political line which interpreted such tensions as the prelude to proletarian revolution. Inspired by the more politicized sections of the youth movement, an already militant working class came to see the establishment of socialism as imminent. Current militant practice and the new revolutionary ideology fitted well into the confused strategy declared by the Socialist leadership after the loss of power in late 1933 based as it was on rhetorical threats of revolution.

Madrid, ever since the emergence of a workers' united front, and especially since the end of the spring strike wave, was living in the shadow of the revolution. It was on everyone's lips. Among self-declared Marxists, there was a conviction that if the right pushed for inclusion in the government, then it would be met by a movement of working-class resistance. Nobody knew, however, how far such a movement would go. Those who knew least were its own leaders. So much had been said about the inevitability of the revolution, victory had been so taken for granted that, in fact, except for some groups of youths, no one had taken any steps to organize it.[27]

The general strike was called only when the Socialist and UGT leadership had no other alternative. It ended without achieving any of the expected results. The workers went on strike, certainly, but contrary to their practice on previous occasions, they stayed at home rather than going onto the streets. There was sporadic shooting between snipers and police for a few days. In what was presumably conceived of as insurrectional action, some members of the Socialist Youth barricaded themselves into their headquarters to fight the forces of order who surrounded them. The executive committees of the UGT and the PSOE, as well as the administrative board of the *Casa del Pueblo* went into hiding and lost contact with the strikers and with the youth movement who were left without knowing the objectives of the movement. In fact, the only thing made abundantly clear by Socialist propaganda throughout the year was that the workers would oppose the entry of the CEDA into the cabinet. The workers' action, therefore, was intended to prevent that entry, but the strike call came only after the leaders were sure that the threat of insurrection had prevented what they feared. The CEDA was already in government.[28]

The strike in Madrid ended in the worst possible way. The workers simply drifted back to work, in the conditions of defencelessness which can be imagined. The young Socialists and the strike leaders went to jail, some of them having first gone home where they awaited the police with that passive tranquillity sometimes mistaken for courage. While the workers were returning to work, the Communist and Socialist youths had plenty of time in prison to exchange experiences and prepare future strategies with the leaders of the failed revolution, the old UGT bureaucracy. That lengthy contact was to be of fundamental importance in the elaboration of the new strategy which distinguished the Socialist left after October from the centre under Prieto and, naturally, from the reformists associated with Besteiro.

As regards the class struggle in Madrid, October had a two-fold consequence. The government closed the *Casa del Pueblo*, dissolved all workers' societies and jailed all the main trade-union and political leaders of the Socialist movement. Furthermore, it gave employers, in practice, *carte blanche* to conduct relations with the workers as they thought best. The strike had been illegal and therefore the strikers had lost all their rights. The employers, when they readmitted workers, wanted to start from scratch in their contracts with them and so interpreted the readmission as nullifying previous agreements.

In real terms, the employers used the opportunity in many cases to reduce the labour force and to eliminate militants. Those not allowed back to work were effectively sacked. Even the fortunate ones were forced to sign unfavourable contracts which ignored the agreements made with the mixed juries.

Accordingly, the 'new' workers found themselves deprived of the rights to which their years on the job entitled them, forced to accept lower status than before and to take lower wages or longer hours than those stipulated in the official work conditions. The small and medium-sized employers, therefore, brought their offensive against the mixed juries to a successful conclusion, removing their relations with the workers from trade-union or government interference. After October 1934 they did as they pleased.[29]

Against the abuses of employers delighting in their revenge, the government offered only words and a decree rendered useless by the fact that, with the unions closed down, the workers could not get it enforced. 1935 did not see the restructuring of class relations on new terms, but simply the deepening of working-class hatred towards the employers who tried to sweep away their historic rights. That dumb anger now inexpressible through trade-union activity was the basis of the re-emergence of a political formula thought to have been buried forever. In fact, the elimination of the trade unions, the closure of the *Casa del Pueblo* and the 'privatization' of worker-employer relations opened the way for efforts to rebuild the Republican-Socialist coalition as the only legal way of regaining the lost rights and obtaining a general amnesty for the October insurrection.[30]

The terms on which the new Republican-Socialist coalition was created were established partly in the model prison in Madrid where Socialist and Communist Youth, UGT and PSOE leaders involved in October were incarcerated. There they were subjected to a double pressure. On the one hand, the centrist tendency of the PSOE was anxious to reconstruct the historic alliance with the Republicans now that the ruling right-wing coalition was falling apart. On the other hand, many local Socialist leaders were asking for guidance as to whether or not to encourage the creation of working-class alliances with the Communists or other workers' parties. Neither hindering the efforts of the centrists and even showing agreement with some of their initiatives, nor answering decisively the question about the working-class alliance, the Socialist left showed plainly that its only policy during the first half of 1935 was to wait and see.[31]

The left was pulled out of its hesitations by the clinching of agreement between the Socialist centre and the Republicans, by the clear decomposition of the government and by the enthusiasm stimulated among the workers of Madrid by Manuel Azaña's speech at Comillas in the south of the city. That meeting put an end to the doubts remaining on the left about the convenience of a new agreement with the Republicans and even convinced those who were hostile that, in any case, Azaña could make a good Kerenski. Largo Caballero exploited his well-known opposition to the pact to demand that it should be extended to the left and include Communists and anarcho-syndicalists.[32] He believed that, in this way, the unity of the working classes would be maintained under Socialist leadership. Support for the coalition with the Republicans would thus seem to be merely circumstantial. The Communists, who had already given up the demand they had made after October 1934 for an exclusively working-class alliance and had been pushing for popular front committees, naturally hastened to join the new pact and managed to change its name, if not its substance. The Republican-Socialist coalition would henceforth be called the Popular Front.[33]

In Madrid, the expectations aroused by the announcement of the pact were enormous. Again it was believed that the establishment of a more just and egalitarian society was within reach. More immediately it was expected that, after the coalition's victory, prisoners would be released; the labour conditions suppressed after October 1934 would be re-established; the workers sacked would be readmitted to the same jobs they had before and compensated for wages lost since then; employers should employ an identical number of workers as before October and, lastly, that labour contracts would be reviewed.

In the celebrations for the electoral victory of February 1936, the distances separating the popular movement of April 1931 from this popular front were starkly clear. There were no longer small and middle-sized employers nor well-dressed ladies with the Republican tricolour to be seen along the streets. The bourgeois hoped only that perhaps Azaña would impose order on all the confusion. The streets no longer belonged to all the people of Madrid, but only to its workers and employees whose immediate demand was the release of all imprisoned strikers. The government hurried to decree what would have occurred anyway, giving that release a veneer of legality. However, it was a worrying precedent for an isolated government since the workers were ready to take by coming onto the streets what they believed to be their due.[34]

The employers, after October, ruined any opportunity of re-establishing equilibrium in their relations with the workers. The workers, now appearing at the doors of the workshops, shops and sites, imposing their readmission and constantly pressurizing government for a decree on compensation, also destroyed any possibility of offering the small and middle-sized employers the class pact which was implicit in the very concept of the Popular Front. The decree that again set off the tensions between workers and employers was that of readmission and compensation for the victims of the post-October reprisals. Once again, the workers themselves enforced it directly, imposing the expulsion of the non-unionized workers who had replaced those sacked after October. Workers obliged employers to pay them for the jobs they had had before. This settling of accounts overflowed all institutional mechanisms and was not the object of any negotiation. The workers imposed it with their physical presence at the workplace.[35]

When this first phase of regaining lost ground was barely over, the workers began to press new demands when the labour contracts were being prepared to substitute those agreed in 1932 and 1933. The traditional mechanisms for channelling these demands had not functioned in Madrid since early 1934. Now, the widespread trade-union practice of convoking massive assemblies of all the workers of an industry, rather than just those of one craft union, to approve the terms worked out by the committees, led to even greater working-class mobilization in the capital at a moment of high tension provoked by the series of political assassinations being perpetrated in its streets. Thus, one after another, the workers of the main industries of Madrid went on all-out strike. At the beginning of June, the city avoided a general strike only because UGT leaders resisted it, as they had done in March 1934. UGT recommendations now reopened the old distances between members of the CNT and the UGT. Confrontations between workers of the two unions, beginning at the time of the waiters' strike, caused further assassinations among workers as a result of the construction strike.[36]

The scale of the workers' demands, the growing hegemony of the CNT in trade-union struggles, disturbances in the streets, the general climate of unease, rumours of military subversion, the weakness the government showed in the face of these problems, all obliged many Socialists to wonder if the moment had not come to put an end to internal divisions and give full support to the government even to the extent of PSOE participation therein. There was not time, however, to put an end to the internal fragmentation of the Socialist Party. The military *coup* reduced all the conflicts present in Madrid during the spring of 1936 – workers against employers, UGT against CNT, Socialists of the centre against Socialists of the left, fascists against Marxists – to one very simple one: those who supported the Republic against those who wanted to destroy it.

The strikes and the class conflicts which took place during the Republic have been repeatedly attributed to political causes. Thus, it has become the norm, and even a cliché, to attribute the strikes to political passion. The thesis is then inserted in a general conception of the Republic as a bipolar confrontation of the two Spains, inevitably bent on a fratricidal struggle. Some timid social reforms provoked a united and disproportionately offensive reaction by the right and the employers. They, in revenge, destroyed the reforms introduced by the left and the working classes. A comfortable appearance of chronological clarity – two balancing two-year periods and a tragic four-month addition – reinforces this impression: the right lost in 1931 and it and the employers' classes organized the great offensive which culminated with their victory in 1933. The left lost in 1933 and the working classes in their turn organized the great offensive which culminated in 1934 and, after a forced parenthesis, started again in 1936. Workers' strikes and employers' lock-outs are no more than a convenient piece of the argument.

As regards Madrid, things do not seem to have been so simple. There, what broke the original civic or popular conscience on which the Republic was founded was the economic crisis and rampant unemployment, which introduced an intense awareness of class interests. This process took place in an urban space characterized by a rapid and chaotic growth, with a massive immigration of unskilled workers. At the same time, the only possible way to palliate the effects of the crisis in a city without a solid industrial structure was to promote public works financed by the state. This brought about a rapid transformation of the main industry of Madrid. All this took place at a time when great masses were participating in politics through class organizations, which were struggling not to lose ground in a labour market reduced by the crisis. Strikes in Madrid were a result of the fact that the workers of the least skilled sectors, kept in the outskirts of the city, unemployed or destined to be so, did not receive the benefits of reformist policies and were mobilized by a trade union which was disputing territory with the traditional representative of Madrid working-class interests.

Naturally, the social conflicts themselves, given their magnitude, had political results. Worker mobilizations, the constant assemblies, the occupation of the streets by striking workers ended up destroying the ownership of the city by all its people and put an end to the concept of the city as the scene of the people's sovereignty. That break-up of the popular space leads directly to the main political consequence of the class struggles of Madrid: the complex corporative organism which served to conciliate the interests of workers and employers was smashed, and thus the traditional political representation of both workers' and employers' interests disappeared. In the case of the workers, neither the UGT nor the CNT knew what to do when they had all the workers of Madrid on strike. As far as the employers were concerned, their societies were incapable, apart from complaining about politics and politicians, of anything other than petty private revenge, believing that as long as the employers regained control of their businesses, everything would once more function in peace and order.

The collapse of the representative channels of traditional class interests produced that impression of disorder and confusion which is so often blamed on the loss of direction suffered by the trade-unionist and working-class party leaders. In fact, what seems to have occurred is the opposite: that the obvious loss of direction was rather a consequence of movements – very common in the crises of all the proto-industrial cities of Europe – for whose leadership neither the workers' parties nor trade unions had the necessary organizational instruments. All of a sudden, trade unions and working-class parties perceived that the magnitude of proletarian mobilization overflowed the capacity of existing institutions to represent it. Simply, they did not know what to do with it and lacked adequate mechanisms for channelling it because its magnitude and development depended not on the parties or trade unions, but on the collapse both of a process of urban growth based on chaos and marginalization and of a structure of industrial and class relations based on crafts and guilds with islands of great concentrations of unskilled workers. The momentum of growth hid its tensions, but when the growth stopped and the strong contradictions on which it was based became manifest, all the tensions came to the surface and swept away mechanisms for the conciliation of interests patiently created for another city, another industry and another class relationship. In these conditions, no political formula produced by the same parties and trade unions that had lost their footing after the great strike wave could put the city back on its feet. The Socialists, traditional representatives of working-class interests in Madrid, tried out the corporative-reformist, the insurrectional and the Popular Front formulae. None of them provided the results hoped for because the fundamental need was not for a political formula, but for a new structure of class relations for a new city. There was no time to build that structure.

Notes

1 The best sources for the strikes of 1936 are *El Sol*, May–July, and *Boletín del Ministerio de Trabajo* (May–August 1936).
2 *The Times*, 12 March 1933; cf. telegrams from British Ambassador to Sir John Simon, 12, 16 March 1934, *FO* 371/18595.
3 Raymond Carr, *Spain 1808–1939* (Oxford, 1966), 603.
4 On the composition of the Republican-Socialist alliance, see the propaganda leaflet, *Al pueblo de Madrid* (March 1931). On the attitudes of the armed forces, see *El Sol* and *ABC*, 15, 16 April 1931 and Fernando de los Ríos, Political Report to PSOE Executive Commission, 'Actas de la CE del PSOE', Fundación Pablo Iglesias, Archivo Histórico (henceforth FPIAH), 20–1, fol. 33.
5 Javier Tusell, *La segunda República en Madrid: elecciones y partidos políticos* (Madrid, 1970), 47.
6 See Ayuntamiento de Madrid, *Información sobre la ciudad. Año 1929 Memoria* and Fernando de Terán, *Planeamiento urbano en la España contemporánea* (Barcelona, 1978).
7 The city of Madrid grew from 539,835 inhabitants in 1900 to 952,832 in 1930. In the same period, greater Madrid and its adjacent municipalities grew from 585,587 to 1,153,546 inhabitants. The fastest growing municipalities were Vallecas (10,100 to 151,800), Chamartín de la Rosa (4,500 to 38,800)

and Carabanchel Alto/Carabanchel Bajo (7900 to 41,100), *Censo de la Población 1900/1930.*

8   30 per cent of Madrid's population in 1930 was aged between 15 and 30. 40 per cent was illiterate in the most densely populated *barrios* and nearly 20 per cent in the capital proper. *Censo de la Población 1930.* On Madrid's growth as the headquarters of capitalism, see Tomás Jiménez-Araya, 'Formación del capital y fluctuaciones económicas', *Hacienda Pública Española*, 27 (1974), 169–70.

9   *Estadística de los salarios y jornadas de trabajo referidas al período 1914–1925* (Madrid, 1927) CLXXII–CXCIII; *Apuntes para el momento de la industria española en 1930* (Madrid, n.d.), vol. 2, 515–601; *Memoria-Anuario industrial de la Provincia de Madrid*, published annually by the Camera de la Industria.

10 Ayuntamiento, *Información*, 28 and *Plan general de extensión. Memoria* (Madrid, 1929), 35.

11 On the minimal extent of social security, see 'Memoria', published each year in *Anales del Instituto Nacional de Previsión.*

12 Licences granted by the *Ayuntamiento* for new building starts averaged 1107 in the years between 1924 and 1930. By 1934, they had dropped to 276; López Baeza, 'El crecimiento de Madrid', *El Sol*, 28 July 1931, and *Boletín del Ayuntamiento de Madrid*, 29 May 1935.

13 On the penury of housing, see José Bravo Ramírez and Alberto León Peral, *Escasez, carestía e higiene de la vivienda en Madrid* (Madrid, 1926). On the *Ayuntamiento*'s social and welfare policies, see Ramiro Gómez Fernández, *Lo que fue, lo que es y lo que debe ser la Asistencia Social en el Ayuntamiento de Madrid* (Madrid, 1935).

14 In January 1934, 30,000 of the 90,000 workers included in the union census were unemployed as follows: construction – 18,500; transport – 2500; small-scale metallurgy – 2200; food – 1700; commerce, woodworking and printing – 1200. *Boletín de Información de la Oficina Central de Colocación Obrera y Defensa contra el Paro* (1933–4), 1046–8. These figures differ from those given in other official publications but they seem to be the least unreliable ones. Needless to say, the union census far from covered the entire Madrid working class. Some authors, notably A. and I. Aviv, 'The Madrid working class 1934–1936', *Journal of Contemporary History*, XVI (1981), 247, go so far as to take the social electoral census as a comprehensive working-class census and confuse provincial data with figures relating only to Madrid city, thereby elaborating entirely invalid unemployment percentages.

15 For private companies with Madrid headquarters, see *Anuario Financiero y de Sociedades Anónimas* (1935). Cf. *Boletín del Ministerio de Trabajo* (December 1932), supplement.

16 Jordi Palafox, 'La gran depresión de los años treinta y la crisis industrial española', *Investigaciones Económicas* (January–April 1980), 32 ff.

17 Ministerio de Obras Públicas, *Cómo coperará el Estado a la transición y*

engrandecimiento de Madrid. Enlace y Electrificación de Ferrocarriles. Accesos y Extrarradio (Madrid, n.d. [1933]) and *Ayuntamiento de Madrid, Memoria sobre la labor realizada por el primer Ayuntamiento de la segunda República española* (Madrid, 1933).

18 *El Sol*, 12 January 1932; *La Edificación*, 15 January 1932; *CNT*, 5 September 1933.

19 Labour contracts were published by González Rothvoss in *Anuario Español de Política Social 1933–1934* (Madrid, 1934).

20 *La Edificación*, 15 September 1933; 'Actas de la Agrupación General de Camareros, 1933', Archivo Histórico Nacional, Salamanca, sección Madrid (henceforth AHNS), folder 1667.

21 I deal with strikes in detail in *Madrid 1931–1934. De la fiesta popular a la lucha de clases* (Madrid, 1984).

22 *El Mercantil Patronal*, July 1933; *Labor*, 15 and 20 July 1933.

23 *La Edificación*, 15 November 1933; *CNT*, 28 November 1933; 'Actas del Comité Ejecutivo' of the Local and National Building Federation, AHNS, 788, 789, 822. Cf. 'Circulares' of the Local Federation to section committees, AHNS, 952, 1614, 2394; *Luz*, 24 February 1934; 'A todas las Federaciones', *Boletín de la UGT* (March 1934).

24 Cf. speeches by Largo Caballero in 'El Arte de Imprimir', *El Socialista*, 2 and 23 January 1934. See also the declaration approved on 15 March 1934 by the PSOE executive, 'Actas de la CE del PSOE', EPIAH, 20–3, fol. 26; 'Reunión ordinaria del Comité Nacional', *Boletín de la UGT* (June–July 1934), 115; 'Circular No. 13' of the Local Building Federation, 3 March 1934, AHNS, 2394. Carlos Hernández, secretary of the *Casa del Pueblo*, rejected a general strike in support of the metalworkers in 'Carta a la Federación Local de Sindicatos Únicos', 2 May 1934, AHNS, 960. For the CNT's distrust, see *CNT*, 21 August 1934.

25 The Socialist Youth's first major intervention was during the strike called in protest at the CEDA's rally in El Escorial, *El Socialista*, 22, 24 April 1934, a strike considered by the UGT Executive to be 'undue' and unlikely to be effective. AHNS, 2174. The Supreme Court sentence on the arms cache was published in *Memoria de la Junta Administrativa de la Casa del Pueblo, octubre de 1934 a junio de 1936* (Madrid, 1936).

26 Cf. *El Socialista*, 12 July 1934.

27 *El Socialista*, 21 December 1933; *Luz*, 8, 12 February 1934; 'Actas de la CE del PSOE', FPIAH, 20–3, fol. 4.

28 *ABC*, 5–12 October; *El Sol*, 14 October 1934. Cf. Consuelo Berges, *Explicación de octubre. Historia comprimida de cuatro años de República en España* (Madrid, 1936).

29 *Labor*, 16 October 1934; *Trabajo*, 2 January, 20 April 1935.

30 On the rebuilding of the Republican-Socialist coalition, see Paul Preston, *The Coming of the Spanish Civil War* (London, 1978), 131–50; Santos Juliá, *La izquierda del PSOE 1935–1936* (Madrid, 1977), 5–52.

31 The Communist aim to submerge the PSOE in front organizations was resisted by both the PSOE and UGT executives, 'Actas del CE del PSOE', 4, 7 December 1934, 13 February 1935, FPIAH, 20–3; 'Actas de las reuniones de la Junta Administrativa de la Casa del Pueblo de Madrid', 4 April, 23, 30 May, 7 June 1935, AHNS, folder 833. The circular inviting the Republicans to join an alliance was approved by the entire executive, including Largo Caballero. 'Actas de la CE del PSOE', 9 April 1935, FPIAH, 20–3.

32 See previously unpublished correspondence between Manuel Azaña and Enrique de Francisco, *Revista de Derecho Político*, vol. 12 (1982), 271–5.

33 The negotiation of Madrid candidacies can be reconstructed from the correspondence and minutes of meetings between the Agrupación Socialista Madrileña and the representatives of the Izquierda Republicana, FPIAH, 17–1.

34 Trade-union concern about worker presence on the streets is evident in a *Casa del Pueblo* leaflet of 17 February 1936 appealing for no strikes, AHNS, folder 833. Cf. *El Sol*, 18, 25 February 1936.

35 'La incomprensible actitud del Poder público', *Labor*, 7 March 1936.

36 The Madrid building strike of June–July 1936 was a microcosm of CNT-UGT relations. It was started and led jointly until the UGT accepted government recommendations and convoked a referendum among its members. See leaflets from 1, 5, 11 June 1936, AHNS, folder 1558; and strike manifestos, AHNS, folder 1559; *El Sol*, July 1936.

7
The agrarian war in the south
Paul Preston

It is the central theme of this book that the Spanish Civil War was not one but many wars. The contention underlying this chapter is that the agrarian conflict which had been endemic for centuries and which became chronic during the Second Republic should be seen as the most crucial of those several component confrontations within the civil war which broke out in 1936. This is not to dismiss other areas of conflict between Catholics and anti-clericals, regionalists and centralists, especially military ones, or between industrial workers and employers. Even less does it imply that the complex interactions between religion, ideology and economic interest which are discussed in other chapters can be reduced to one single motive force. Clearly, Navarrese Carlists or Basque Nationalists were impelled to take up the positions that they did by causes other than the social antagonisms of Andalusia and Extremadura. However, no single area of social or ideological confrontation during the 1930s matched in scope or impact the agrarian problem.

The two largest mass parties of the Second Republic, the Partido Socialista Obrero Español and the Catholic authoritarian Confederación Española de Derechas Autónomas each found substantial parts of their electoral support among the peasantry; the PSOE amidst the landless *braceros* of the south; the CEDA among the smallholding farmers of the centre and north. The agrarian conflicts of these areas were then channelled into national politics through the two parties and thereby had a polarizing effect far beyond their own local confines. More particularly, the social distress suffered by the southern *braceros* affected the wider political scene in two principal ways. The intransigence of the landlords drove the local peasantry to a state of desperation which in the case of anarchists found its expression in disorder and agitation. For those *braceros* who owed allegiance to the Socialist movement, and maintained their discipline, frustration at right-wing obstruction of agrarian change was translated into disillusion with the moderate reformism of the PSOE. Accordingly, pressure from the southern grassroots militants gave a mass impetus to the drive to radicalize the party which was being spearheaded by the Madrid Socialists. Both the spontaneous explosions of despair by the anarchists and the undermining of Socialist moderation had far-reaching effects on Republican politics; the one in consolidating rightist belligerence against a regime which permitted such outbursts, the other in depriving the Republic of the support of its most loyal pillar.

Apart from generalized propagandistic exploitation of social disorder in the south in order to inflame middle-class fear of the Republic, the agrarian conflicts of Andalusia and Extremadura were specifically reflected in a greater militancy on the part of the CEDA and its component organizations. This was not because the aspirations of landless labourers challenged the interests of smallholders directly, although claims to decent wages hit small, occasional employers as much as big landlords. It was rather that the big landowners, whether Castilian or Andalusian, who dominated the CEDA ensured that its political role was not to defend the interests of its electorate but those of its most powerful backers. Since the greatest challenge came largely, although far from exclusively, in the south, the political deployment of the CEDA was primarily directed at blocking the impulse to agrarian change emanating from the area. Between 1931 and 1933, that involved the creation and instrumentalization of a mass base among the Catholic smallholding peasantry, the obstruction in parliament of efforts to introduce agrarian reform and the defence of the violence employed by big landowners at a local level. After 1933, it meant the legal destruction of the agrarian social legislation of the Republican-Socialist coalition and the effective annihilation of rural trades unions.[1] After the elections of 1936, and their challenge to the legal defence of right-wing agrarian interests, the dominant landlords of the CEDA abandoned legalism and turned to the military for their defence. Individual landlords participated in the repression of the southern peasantry during the civil war and the agrarian policies of the CEDA became those of the Franco regime thereafter.[2]

The process whereby the Catholic farmers of Castile were mobilized in defence of big landholding interests began during the second decade of the century. With left-wing ideologies capturing the urban working classes, the more far-sighted landowners realized that efforts had to be made to prevent the poison spreading to the countryside. Counter-revolutionary agrarian syndicates sponsored by landlords began to appear from 1906 but the process was systematized by a group of dynamic social Catholics led by Angel Herrera, and formed in 1909 into the Asociación Católica Nacional de Propagandistas. By 1912, Herrera and the Palencian landowner, Antonio Monedero Martín, were making efforts to block socialism and anarchism in the countryside by the implementation of the encyclicals of Pope Leo XIII. In the next five years, there spread across León, Salamanca and Castile a series of Catholic Agrarian Federations which tried to prevent impoverished farmers turning to the left by offering them credit facilities, agronomic expertise, warehousing and machinery. Access to such assistance was made openly dependent on adherence to a virulent anti-socialism. Ultimately, the rhetoric of the federations implied a challenge to the economic interests of big landowners but, in the north at least, an uneasy balance was maintained between the mitigation of poverty and acceptance of the socio-economic status quo. By 1917, the various local federations were united as the Confederación Nacional Católico-Agraria but their implantation outside León-Castile was sporadic. This was understandable since, in the south, the only palliative that landowners could offer the *braceros*, possession of the land, involved an unacceptable transfer of wealth.[3]

The CNCA would almost certainly have remained confined to the smallholding areas of central and northern Spain had it not been for the massive upsurge in the revolutionary militancy of the rural proletariat of the south after 1917. The fear provoked by the peasant insurrections of the *'trienio bolchevique'* ensured widespread interest in the CNCA from big landowners. That was hardly surprising since, as one observer of the revolutionary agitation of the spring of 1919, the distinguished agronomist Pascual Carrión, noted, 'we cannot forget the extension and intensity of the workers' movement; the strike in Cordoba, among others, was truly general and impressive, managing to frighten the landowners to such a degree that they were ready to hand over their estates.'[4] The CNCA began a huge propaganda campaign in Andalusia in January 1919, denouncing the blind egoism of the landowners who were 'loud in their charity, then paid wages so low and exacted rents so high that they would not dare admit to their confessor'. Teams of CNCA representatives toured the southern provinces and were greeted by the ACNP newspaper, *El Correo de Andalucía* with the declaration that 'If the landowners of Andalusia follow you, they will be saved; if they repudiate you, they will be drowned in their own blood.' In the first months of the year, the CNCA campaign was extremely successful. In their panic, a number of *latifundistas* were prepared to put up money and make available a few plots of waste land for settlement by suitably deferential labourers. However, not all landowners were prepared to make concessions and many more preferred to employ the unrestrained violence of their retainers backed by the Civil Guard in order to intimidate strikers. The CNCA continued to preach the gospel of class collaboration but its real position was starkly exposed as conflict grew more acute.

On 18 April 1919, Antonio Monedero Martín was made Director-General of Agriculture and soon found himself making calls for the closure of working-class organizations and for the deportation and imprisonment of strike leaders. In May, the government intensified the scale of repression by sending in General La Barrera with cavalry units to reinforce the Civil Guard. With the area under virtual military occupation, the revolutionary movement was gradually brought under control.[5] Landowners' interest in palliatives to take the edge off popular militancy declined until the Second Republic revived the spectre of land reform. In fact, the repression of 1919–20 and the dictatorship of Primo de Rivera between 1923 and 1930 did nothing but silence an agitation which continued to smoulder. The consequences of the *trienio bolchevique* were not to become visible until the passing of the dictatorship. Above all, the conflicts of those years ended the uneasy *modus vivendi* of the agrarian south. The repression intensified the hatred of the *braceros* for the big landowners and their estate managers. Similarly, the elements of paternalism which mitigated the daily brutality of the *braceros'* lives came to an abrupt end. The gathering of windfall crops, the watering of beasts, the collection of firewood were subject to the vigilance of armed guards.

The failure of the spontaneous actions of 1918–20 was to have another, unexpected, effect. The anarcho-syndicalist Confederación Nacional del Trabajo was largely behind the strikes, especially in Cordoba, Seville, Cádiz, Huelva and Malaga. The Socialist Unión General de Trabajadores, whose strength in the rural south was to be found in the Extremaduran provinces of Badajoz and Cáceres, and in Granada, Jaén and Almería, was also involved in the strikes but was much more legalist in its attitudes.[6] Inevitably, the CNT suffered more in the repression and was eventually banned by General Primo de Rivera. The UGT also lost rural members during the dictatorship because, despite the privileges bestowed by its collaboration with the regime, the repression in the countryside continued and sixty-five of its rural sections were closed down. Moreover, landowners took advantage of the situation to maintain wages at a low level despite rising food prices and, in consequence, many *braceros* simply could not afford to pay their union dues. None the less, the Socialists exploited their relatively privileged position to step up their propaganda in the south. In contrast to the CNT's commitment to *reparto*, or the division of the land among individual peasants, the UGT began to push for the expropriation and collectivization of the big estates. That, together with their advocacy of the introduction of rural *comités paritarios*, arbitration committees to negotiate wages and working conditions, gave them an unprecedented impact in the south.[7]

In contrast, the CNCA, which had greeted the dictator within days of his seizure of power with a fulsome commitment to his 'great work of cleansing and regenerating Spain' and whose local leadership had played an enthusiastic role in building up his single party, the Unión Patriótica, was vehemently opposed to the extension of the *comités paritarios* to the countryside. Indeed, the dictatorship's feeble and inconclusive efforts to introduce them were to be instrumental in uniting southern landowners against the regime.[8] One by one, the dictator alienated his supporters throughout the 1920s. In doing so, he temporarily discredited authoritarian solutions to the problems of an increasingly beleaguered Spanish right. That situation was to change rapidly and the dictatorship was soon remembered nostalgically by industrialists and landowners alike as a golden age. However, the mood lasted long enough to facilitate the coming of the Second Republic. In general, the hope in right-wing circles was that a symbolic sacrifice, the substitution of the disgraced Alfonso XIII by a president, would be sufficient to pacify the masses. The landowners of the south, however, began to look for other means to defend their interests. With the prospect of a Socialist Minister of Labour, landless labourers began to flood into the Socialist landworkers' union, the Federación Nacional de Trabajadores de la Tierra. Many landowners were happy to put funds up for organizations committed to the defence of the old order by violence. Many more, however, were sufficiently flexible and farsighted to seek political solutions. For some, this meant a renewed interest in the CNCA and the various political offshoots which were to grow from it in the early 1930s and eventually culminate in the Confederación Española de Derechas Autónomas. Others, more liberal, or perhaps more cynical, threw in their lot with conservative Republican parties, especially the Radicals.

Whatever the political vehicle chosen, the goal of landowners was the defence of their property. Given the legacy of the *trienio bolchevique*, and as their reaction to Primo de Rivera's reforming ambitions had shown, they were in no mood for concessions. That was made starkly clear in the transitional period between the dictatorship and the Republic.

Persistent drought prevented the planting of winter vegetable crops in October 1931 thereby depriving landless labourers of a valuable month's employment. The year's olive harvest was also wrecked in December and into January 1931. The three worst-hit provinces were Jaén, Córdoba and Seville where olive trees occupied respectively 55 per cent, 47 per cent and 34 per cent of cultivated land. With the yield reduced to seven-eighths of the previous year's harvest, the landowners were anxious to recoup their losses by slashing wages. The *braceros* were plunged into the direst misery. The olive harvest, which permitted work for the entire family, constituted the two best-paid months of the year without which the most abject subsistence was impossible. Now there was no more than two weeks' work anywhere in the olive belt. The system whereby the authorities tried to mop up labour by mounting public works could not cope with the scale of unemployment. Big landowners naturally resisted the device of *alojamiento* by which numbers of workers were 'placed' on an estate to be given any tasks that could be invented for them. Disorder soon followed. Bakeries were assaulted in villages in the province of Cádiz. There was looting of shops in Jaén. In Antequera, in the province of Malaga, over 1800 workers virtually took over the town for two weeks in November 1930 until their action was suppressed by the arrival of troops from Spanish North Africa.[9]

Natural disaster merely exacerbated class hatred. The coming of the Republic, and at its head a Republican-Socialist coalition government containing a Socialist Minister of Labour, intensified it further. The new regime inevitably inflamed the expectations of the landless peasantry and consolidated the intransigence of the landowners. The *latifundistas* had good reason to regard with trepidation the arrival at the Ministry of Labour of the UGT leader, Francisco Largo Caballero. It was not just that he was anxious to apply in rural Spain the machinery of wage arbitration which had been operated in the cities during the 1920s. Rather they feared that the power of the state would now be put behind the basic aspirations of the rural proletariat. Largo Caballero was notoriously sensitive to the shifts in mood of the UGT rank and file. Since the foundation of the Federación Nacional de Trabajadores de la Tierra in April 1930, an ever-increasing proportion of the UGT grassroots was made up of landless labourers. Founded with 157 sections of over

27,000 members, by June 1930 the FNTT had grown to 275 sections of 36,639 members. It soon overtook the UGT's pre-dictatorship agrarian section's strength of 65,405 despite the enormous difficulties posed by the collection of subscriptions at a time of great economic hardship. UGT membership grew from 277,011 in December 1930 to 1,041,539 in June 1932. The FNTT component rocketed from its June 1930 figure to 392,953 two years later. In 1930, 13 per cent of the UGT membership was made up by rural labourers. Two years later, the proportion had grown to nearly 38 per cent.[10] In the south, the CNT was being pushed into the bigger towns as the *braceros* looked to the Socialists for legal solutions to their problems. The impact on the UGT and the Socialist movement in general was considerable. From a union of skilled craftsmen, the UGT was being turned into the political representative of the unsophisticated labourers who were in the forefront of the southern class war. Once the FNTT became the largest section of the UGT, its reactions to rural conflicts came to have an immediate repercussion at a national level. A similar process ensured that the views of the southern landowners were transmitted into Madrid politics via various local organizations affiliated to the rightist Acción Popular, which became the CEDA in early 1933.

The fears of the landowners were rapidly justified. The new government was determined to alleviate the distress of the southern masses. Although ministers' intentions were to do no more than mitigate the immediate misery of the *braceros*, their measures had an unexpectedly revolutionary implication. Given that the inefficient *latifundio* system relied on the existence of a reserve army of landless labourers paid a pittance for fleeting periods of the year, legislation to guarantee better wages and protection against dismissal inevitably constituted a challenge to the entire system. Moreover, the context of world depression rendered the administrative palliatives introduced by the Republican-Socialist coalition even more far-reachingly conflictive. With agricultural exports declining, landowners could not absorb higher wage costs by increasing prices, so better wages implied a redistribution of wealth. Government efforts to find employment for large numbers of workers were rendered difficult by the return of emigrants from France and Latin America. Moreover, many unskilled labourers who had been tempted to the towns in the 1920s by Primo de Rivera's building projects now returned to their villages.[11]

The measures which had the greatest effect in the south emanated from the Ministry of Labour in the spring of 1931. The most dramatic was the decree of municipal boundaries (*términos municipales*) issued on 28 April. By preventing the hiring of outside labour while local labour in a given municipality remained unemployed, the decree struck at one of the main repressive weapons of the landowners, the power to break strikes and keep down wages by the import of cheap blackleg labour. On 7 May, Largo Caballero did what Primo de Rivera had been unable to do, he introduced arbitration committees now known as *jurados mixtos*. Previously, working conditions and wages were subject only to the whim of the owners. The new decree recognized that the *braceros* had rights and created a machinery for their defence. One of the rights that would have to be protected, the eight-hour day, was established by a decree of 1 July. Since the day wage or *jornal* usually involved sun-up to sun-down working, the new decree implied that owners would either have to pay overtime or else employ more men to do the same work. Finally, in the hope of forestalling the sabotage of these measures by lock-outs, an additional decree of obligatory cultivation (*laboreo forzoso*) prevented the owners merely ceasing to work the land. The limitation by the state of the owners' right to use their land as they willed and the blunting of a crucial device of social control especially outraged the *latifundistas*.[12] They were even more alarmed by the fact that in May a Technical Commission began work on a projected law of agrarian reform.

The response of the big landowners to these measures was rapid and varied. Various employers' federations – the Agrupación de Propietarios de Fincas Rústicas, the Confederación Española Patronal Agraria, stock-breeders' associations, olive-growers' associations, wheat-growers' associations – were either founded or revitalized. They began to flood the local and national press with doom-laden propaganda about how the government was destroying Spanish agriculture, as if the endemic misery were the result of Largo Caballero's decrees. Reports were commissioned and published ingenuously denying the existence of excessive *latifundios*, absenteeism and the deficient exploitation of the land. Real dangers that the municipal boundaries decree was too rigid in areas of crops requiring special skills or that obligatory cultivation might be an incitement to occupations of pasture were inflated beyond all bounds into a threat to 'the economic interests of the entire nation'. Appeals were made to make war on 'the enemy' responsible for such disasters, the Socialists. In parliament, a wide range of filibustering tactics was used to block attempts at agrarian reform. Across the country, a massive propaganda campaign equating Socialist reforms with the 'worst excesses of bolshevism' was made to turn the ACNP electoral organization, Acción Nacional, into a mass party to defend landowners' interests.[13]

What the vituperative outbursts of the landowners' organizations failed to stress was the extent to which Socialist measures remained little more than hopes on paper. There was little machinery to enforce the new decrees. The social power consequent on being the exclusive providers of work remained with the owners. The Civil Guard was skilfully cultivated by, and remained loyal to, the rural upper classes. When Socialist and anarchist *alcaldes* (mayors) tried to impose the government's social legislation, they often found that the obstruction of the big landowners was supported both by the Civil Guard and by provincial officials. The landed middle classes who had joined the Radical Party and other conservative Republican groupings in 1930 and early 1931 now found their tactics paying off. Moreover, concerted efforts were made by the rural bourgeoisie to seduce the loyalty of government officials. Socialist deputies from the south regularly complained in the Cortes about the way in which the civil governors of their provinces displayed little energy in preventing the local *caciques* (political bosses) from simply ignoring legislation and even less in ensuring that the Civil Guard did not continue to side with landowners in defiance of the new laws.[14] Most of the officials concerned had been appointed when the conservative Republicans, Niceto Alcalá Zamora and Miguel Maura, were respectively prime minister and Minister of the Interior, and were far from being progressive. Maura himself complained of the need to use Radicals and Radical-Socialists who were most unsuitable in terms of their ideological leanings or honesty.[15] Civil governors who tried to apply the law found themselves obstructed by the local middle classes' deployment of subtle, as well as the most obvious, devices.[16]

The way in which the rural middle classes used Republicanism to defend their position provoked the frustration of the workers who had expected so much from the new regime. At a national level, this was reflected in a growing Socialist disillusion with the efficacy of collaboration with the left Republicans. In the south itself, the landowners' successes led to spontaneous outburts of popular rage. The intransigence of the *caciques* was often deliberately designed to push disputes into violence. In August 1931, owners in Cádiz, Malaga, Seville and Jaén banded together in a refusal to plant winter crops, hoping to smash the *jurados mixtos* by means of a virtual lock-out.[17] In Jaén, the already desperate day-labourers destroyed farm machinery and set fire to farm buildings, thereby permitting the owners to unleash the forces of repression, the Civil Guard and their own armed retainers, as well as intensifying propaganda associating the Republic with disorder.[18] The FNTT, which tried to restrain its members from reacting to provocation, was in a thankless position since the intransigence of the owners was matched by the opposition of the CNT to both the *jurados mixtos* and the law on municipal boundaries. Anarcho-syndicalist hostility was grounded on the belief that both measures tended to give a monopoly in labour relations to the UGT.[19]

Expectations that agrarian reform was imminent prevented violence from getting out of control. However, in December, the limits of piecemeal reform were starkly exposed. In Badajoz, the FNTT called a strike in protest at the way in which the civil governor was conniving with local landowners and the Civil Guard to prevent the application of social legislation. The strike of 30 and 31 December was a peaceful one in most of the province. However, in the depressed village of Castilblanco, a crowd of peasants was fired on by the local four-man Civil Guard unit, one man was killed and two others wounded. Crazed with anger and panic, the villagers set upon the four guards and beat them to death. The consequent uproar illustrated graphically the way in which the fate of the Republic was linked to the resolution of the conflicts of the south. The right, both locally and nationally, accused the Socialists of turning the 'mob' against the Civil Guard. A virulent press campaign set out to prove that Socialist reforms in the countryside were really an attack on 'the essence of Spain'. It was the first step towards appealing to the army to save the existing structure of landed property. For the FNTT, the incident and the rightist response to it were indications of the futility of moderate reformism in the face of *latifundista* intransigence.[20]

Throughout 1932, however, the FNTT worked hard to contain the growing desperation of its southern rank and file. At the beginning of the year, with widespread unemployment the norm after the end of the olive harvest, confrontation between owners and *braceros* intensified. With agrarian reform imminent, the landowners did not feel disposed to invest in their land. The law of *laboreo forzoso* was effectively ignored and labour was not hired to do the tasks essential for the spring planting. Weeding, hoeing, stone-clearing and other preparatory jobs, which usually provided scant enough work between the major harvests, were not being undertaken. In Socialist-controlled *ayuntamientos* (town councils), *alojamientos* were decreed but the owners then refused to pay the wages of the 'placed' workers. Elsewhere, labourers simply did the necessary jobs and then demanded payment, their success depending on the goodwill or lack of armed guards of the particular landlord.[21] The FNTT received complaints from all over the south that many men were being refused work because they belonged to the landworkers' union. Nevertheless, under moderate leadership, the FNTT confined itself to formal protests to the relevant ministries about infractions of social legislation. At the Congress of FNTT members from Andalucía and Extremadura, which began on 7 February at Montilla (Cordoba), it was decided to follow the reformist line being established nationally by the UGT. Appeals were made to the grassroots militants to refrain from extremism and not to expect too much from the forthcoming agrarian reform.[22] After a summer of parliamentary obstruction by the right, the reform bill was finally passed on 9 September in the wave of Republican euphoria provoked by the defeat of the military *coup* of General Sanjurjo. The consequent wave of disappointment was eventually to sweep away the FNTT's reformist leaders.

Although the reformists were correct in their analysis that extremism merely played into the hands of the right, the situation in 1932 was hardly propitious for moderation. Emboldened by the success of the parliamentary right in emasculating the agrarian reform bill and by the extent to which the local forces of order continued to defend their interests, landowners became more provocative. In addition to the refusal to pay wages, incidents were staged to bring about clashes between workers and the Civil Guard. The CNT fell into such traps more often than did the FNTT but the restraint of the Socialists also had its limits. With labour relations punctuated by increasing numbers of lock-outs in the countryside and with the emergence of the slogan ¡Comed República! (literally, 'Eat Republic', but 'Let the Republic feed you'), it was inevitable that conflict would become more violent. Pilfering of crops, especially olives, acorns and chick-peas, and of fire-wood became common. Traditionally, the workers were allowed to collect olives left on the ground after the harvest, in a process of scavenging known as the *rebusca*. Now, permission was not given, denunciations were made to the Civil Guard and the rightist press complained of the 'collective kleptomania' that the peasants had been led to by the Republic. Workers arrested were the subject of frantic rescue attempts by fellow *braceros*. Clashes with the Civil Guard fed the rightist propaganda to the effect that the Republic meant anarchy and plunder.[23]

In fact, the improvements in wages and working conditions which in theory, and often in fact, the *jurados mixtos* were able to implement constituted far more of a threat to the owners than did spontaneous disorder. Against the Civil Guard and the *caciques'* retainers, badly-fed strikers could do little damage, whereas the Republic's social legislation implied real shifts in rural wealth. Rightist protests that the wages established by the *bases de trabajo*, the working conditions laid down by the *jurados*, made it uneconomic for the land to be worked were taken by the FNTT as a definitive denunciation of *latifundismo* and proof that the land should be collectivized.[24] The right was much happier dealing with disorder by traditional repressive methods than coping with government efforts to alter the economic balance of rural labour relations. Accordingly, the insurrectionism of the CNT between 1931 and 1934 played into the hands of the right. When disorder took place, the rightist press did not make subtle distinctions. Although the CNT regarded the Republic as being 'as repugnant as the Monarchy', its strikes and uprisings were blamed on the Republican-Socialist coalition which was working hard to control them. Because of the relative success of the *jurados mixtos*, the CNT's Federación de Trabajadores Agrícolas denounced them as a sordid racket based on deals between 'bosses and marxists, blacklegs and reds'. The notion that the problems of the countryside might be solved by other than revolutionary means drove the anarcho-syndicalists to denounce the UGT as 'social-fascist'. While the extreme right in the *pueblos* was content to condemn the disorder of the anarchists, the more far-sighted members of the rural bourgeoisie, who had found a home in the Radical Party, were able to use the CNT's hostility towards the Socialists in order to drive wedges between the different working-class organizations.[25]

The most dramatic example of this process took place as a result of a nationwide revolutionary strike called by the CNT for 8 January 1933 and of its bloody repercussions in the village of Casas Viejas in the province of Cádiz. In an area of the largest estates and the poorest *braceros* in southern Spain, the local landlords and the Civil Guard had long worked together to counter the threat of the land-hungry peasantry. In the 1880s, they had fabricated the notorious Black Hand conspiracy to justify the arrest of 5000 workers. A similar plot in 1915 led, in addition to the usual quota of arrests and beatings, to the suicide of the president of the Casas Viejas workers' society. In the lock-out conditions of 1932, four out of five of all workers in Casas Viejas were unemployed for most of the year, dependent on charity, occasional roadmending and scouring the countryside for wild asparagus and rabbits. The desperation of the *braceros*, inflamed by an increase of bread prices, ensured a ready response on 11 January to the earlier CNT call for revolution. Their hesitant declaration of libertarian communism led to a savage repression in which twenty-four people died.[26] At first, the rightist press was as delighted as it had earlier been appalled by the events of Castilblanco.[27] However, as soon as it was realized that advantage could be taken of the situation, howls of indignation were heard.

The subsequent smear campaign ate into the time and morale of the Republican-Socialist coalition to such an extent that, to the joy of the right, the work of government was virtually paralysed. The Socialists loyally stood by Azaña who bore the brunt of rightist abuse for Casas Viejas.[28] However, the incident heralded the death of the coalition, symbolizing as it did the government's failure to resolve the agrarian problem. If the CNT's insurrectionism had over-estimated the revolutionary capacity of the depressed *braceros*, the FNTT's moderation had over-estimated their patience. Henceforth, at a local level, the FNTT was to become more belligerent and its attitude filtered through into the Socialist Party in the form of a rejection of collaboration with the Republicans. With both the olive and wheat harvests of 1933 down by half on the previous year, unemployment oscillated between 13 per cent and 60 per cent throughout the south. The owners were increasingly ignoring the *bases de trabajo*, trying to impose piece-work, flouting the eight-hour day and using harvesting machinery. Assaults on bakeries and food stores became common again. In the CNT-dominated provinces of Seville and Cádiz, there were outbreaks of burnings of harvested crops, hay-ricks, machines and occasionally of estate buildings. There were sporadic strikes in CNT strongholds in May 1933. Then in June the provincial federation of Cordoba of the FNTT called a harvest strike. Its objectives were moderate and aimed at combating unemployment. They called for the elimination of piece-work, a limitation on the use of machinery to half of the area to be harvested and strict rotation of workers to be hired, starting with heads of families. The strike was belatedly settled in favour of the workers by a delegate from the Ministry of Labour.[29]

The Cordoba strike marked a watershed in the attitude of the FNTT. As one of its leaders remarked indignantly, 'for two years we have been putting the brakes on the impulses of the suffering masses . . . and when our sacrifice reaches the maximum, we are faced with the manoeuvres of the bosses and their Republican cronies.' After firmly defending the Republican-Socialist coalition, imposing discipline yet being accused by the right of fomenting anarchy, important elements of the FNTT began to call for an exclusively Socialist government. Mounting outrage at the way landowners simply ignored social legislation and openly provoked workers found an echo in the increasingly revolutionary rhetoric of Largo Caballero. The national leadership of the UGT was becoming worried that its efforts to prevent strikes were likely to stimulate a drift of members to the CNT or the Communist Party. The post-Casas Viejas campaign against the government carried out by the Radicals and the right bore fruit in the fall of Azaña's cabinet. On the formation of a Radical administration on 11 September, the Socialist executive committee decided to put an end to the agreement with the left Republicans. Considerable debate ensued as to whether, in the consequent elections, local pacts between Socialists and Republicans should be permitted. It was decided that each case would be considered on its merits and should be submitted to the executive. Although a considerable number of provincial federations opted to make local electoral alliances, it was significant that the firmest rejections of collaboration came from

Extremadura and Andalusia.[30] It was a recognition of the success of the southern rural bourgeoisie in infiltrating the Radicals and other conservative Republican parties. It was also a major step on the road to the radicalization of the PSOE.

Even before the elections of November 1933, the rural right was quick to take advantage of the Socialists' departure from the cabinet. A determination to return to the pre-1931 socio-economic situation was sharpened by a desire for reprisals against those who had inflicted the 'humiliations' of *jurados mixtos*, *términos municipales* and *laboreo forzoso*. The social laws of the Republican-Socialist coalition were totally ignored, wages were slashed and acts of violence against union members became common. During the election campaign, the Civil Guard and the *caciques* collaborated to impede the Socialists. Threats and bribery were used to diminish the leftist vote. Promises of work, gifts of food or blankets could sway any workless *bracero*. In addition, there was a complex social network of people dependent on the *caciques* whose vote could be easily manipulated. Household servants, permanent estate workers (*fijos*), armed guards, or the casual labourers who were given preference at harvest time because of their proven loyalty (*pegaos*) were all defenceless against the pressure of their employers. The fact that the Radicals lined up with the right in the south and the abstention of anarchist voters in the aftermath of Casas Viejas clearly contributed to Socialist defeat. None the less, in the light of the FNTT's spirited defence of working-class interests in the rural south between 1931 and 1933, the Socialists were understandably dismayed when their parliamentary representation in Andalusia and Extremadura dropped from fifty to nineteen deputies. The sense that they had been swindled electorally accelerated the trend to radicalism among the southern Socialists. In particular, in the provinces of Badajoz, Malaga and Cordoba, the margin of rightist victory was sufficiently narrow for electoral pressures to have been effective.[31]

Bereft of official support, the southern peasantry was once again at the mercy of a vengeful landed class. The difficulties of the *braceros* were intensified in December 1933 when the CNT held a re-run of the nationwide insurrection which had given rise to Casas Viejas. The tragedy of eleven months earlier was nearly repeated at Bujalance in the province of Cordoba. Armed peasants took over parts of the town and tried to capture the *ayuntamiento*. In thirty-six hours of fierce fighting, five civilians, including a child and an old man, and one Civil Guard were killed. Only two of the alleged leaders of the movement were captured and both were shot by the Civil Guard 'while trying to escape'. Both nationally and locally, the right called enthusiastically for firm measures to deal with such subversion.[32] Throughout the early part of 1934, with owners blatantly ignoring the *bases de trabajo* in most southern provinces and wages plunging, there were increasing reports of assaults on workers' societies and *casas del pueblo* by the Civil Guard and the retainers of the *caciques*. Union members were singled out for beatings. The owners relished the return to semi-feudal relations of dependence which had prevailed before 1931. Seasonal unemployment was no longer officially countered by the application of the decree of *laboreo forzoso*, but the owners loudly dispensed meagre charity in the form of soup kitchens for the starving.[33]

In the atmosphere of frustrated rage which pervaded the workers' movement, the moderate leadership of the FNTT under Lucio Martínez Gil was overturned at the end of January 1934 by followers of Largo Caballero led by Ricardo Zabalza. Despite a more combative rhetoric in its newspaper, *El Obrero de la Tierra*, in practical terms the FNTT could do little beyond making official complaints to the relevant ministries about infractions of social legislation. In Badajoz, where the landowners were especially aggressive, a congress of the provincial sections of the PSOE, the UGT and the FNTT held in the first week of March concluded that the partisan nature of the authorities made it pointless to make protests about the excesses of the *caciques*.[34] Finally, against the advice of the UGT leadership, the FNTT decided to call a national strike despite the problems inherent in the different timing of the harvest in various areas. The procedures for calling a strike legally were scrupulously observed. The objectives of the strike were above all to secure the application of the law throughout the rural south where it was flouted daily. However, it was treated by the Minister of the Interior, the reactionary Radical Rafael Salazar Alonso, as a revolutionary threat. The representative of the landowners of Badajoz and a close collaborator of the CEDA leader, José María Gil Robles, Salazar Alonso anxiously seized the opportunity to smash the FNTT. Sweeping arrests were made and, with Civil Guard protection, the harvest was brought in by cheap Portuguese and Galician labour and the extensive use of machinery. *Casas del pueblo* were closed down. Together with the arrests which followed the Asturian insurrection in October 1934, the repression of the harvest strike effectively crippled the FNTT until 1936.[35]

Throughout 1935, the rural unions in the south were reduced to a clandestine existence. Socialist town councils were overthrown and replaced by nominees of the local *caciques*. Union leaders were subject to frequent searches of their homes by the Civil Guard or else obliged to appear at the barracks at regular intervals. Prominent trade unionists were beaten up by the *caciques'* retainers or by the Civil Guard, on occasions with fatal consequences. Estate security was tightened to prevent the *rebusca* of olives or the illicit collection of firewood. Since much of Andalusia was affected by drought in 1935, unemployment rose. Beggars thronged the streets of southern towns to the indignation of the rightist press. Palliatives in the form of hunting or poaching were restricted by the fact that the Civil Guard had seized all shotguns. There were few strikes in 1935, although probably more than a closely censored press reported. That was hardly surprising given the weakness of the workers' movement after the defeats of 1934.[36] None the less, hatred smouldered on both sides of the social divide. Living in close proximity, near-starving *braceros* and the comfortably-off rural middle classes regarded one another with fear and resentment. Just as the *trienio bolchevique* had worn away the paternalism and patronage which mitigated the brutality of daily life, so now too the advances made between 1931 and 1933 had intensified the belligerence of the owners.

The accumulated bitterness of the *bienio negro*, or the two black years of 1933–5, was reflected both in a growing apprehension on the part of the landowners and in rank-and-file pressure for a more radical stance by the Socialist movement. Inevitably, when the Radical-CEDA coalition finally fell, the subsequent elections took on, in the south at least, the character of a life or death struggle. Votes were bought with money, food, blankets or promises of jobs. Intimidation of individuals ranged from threats that they would never work again to beatings. The use of glass voting urns supervised by the *caciques'* retainers constituted a check on how the *braceros* voted. Armed gangs prevented the candidates of the Popular Front from carrying out their election campaign in many villages. On voting day, many *braceros* were physically prevented from voting by early closure of the polls. After the elections, the ballot-boxes were tampered with, quite blatantly in the case of Granada. Rightist propaganda terrified the southern bourgeoisie with apocalyptic warnings that leftist victory would mean 'the arming of the rabble; the burning of private houses and banks; the division of private property and land; uncontrolled looting and the common ownership of women'. Inevitably, when the Popular Front won, this inflammatory campaign increased the polarization of the southern towns during the spring of 1936. As far as the left was concerned, the main consequence of the *bienio negro* in the south during the election campaign was the shift of support towards more radical elements in the PSOE. Candidacies were not monolithically pro-Largo Caballero but the tendency towards maximalism was most marked in the provinces, such as Badajoz and Jaén, where the local Socialists had been subjected to persecution.[37]

Even without the conflict generated by the election campaign and right-wing horror at the subsequent left-wing victory, natural disaster would have ensured social tension in the south in early 1936. After the prolonged drought of the previous year, heavy rainstorms across much of Andalusia ruined the olive harvest and then persisted into the spring to damage the wheat and barley crops. Thus, the election results coincided with acute unemployment. The local middle classes were deeply alarmed by triumphant demonstrations of popular joy, dancing in the streets, marches of out-of-work *braceros*, the flying of red flags from municipal buildings, assults on landowners' *casinos* and other signs that peasant submissiveness was at an end. The *caciques'* men were removed from the town councils and replaced by the legitimately elected Socialists who had been bundled out in 1934. Emergency *jurados mixtos* were set up. *Alojamientos*, began again with large numbers of the unemployed 'placed' on the bigger estates. All this infuriated the southern landowners but what enraged them most was the determination and assertiveness which characterized those whom they expected to be servile. The rank and file of the workers' movement was not to be cheated out of reform as it had been in the first *bienio*. The FNTT encouraged its members to take at its word the new government's proclaimed commitment to rapid reform. In Badajoz, there were large-scale land seizures. Elsewhere, especially in Cordoba and Jaén, there were fewer take-overs but frequent invasions of estates by peasants who stole olives or cut down trees.[38]

The shift in the balance of local power provoked the anger, and often also the fear, of the landowners. The really big *latifundistas* were absentees, living in Seville or Madrid or even Biarritz or Paris. Now many owners of medium-sized estates closed their houses in the country and removed to the provincial capitals or to Madrid. There, many of them enthusiastically joined, financed or merely awaited news of, the ultra-rightist plots against the Republic. Those who stayed, dug in for outright conflict. Throughout April and May, there was a virtual lock-out in many southern provinces. In Badajoz, harvesting was done by machinery at night. Landowners abandoned the last vestiges of their faith in legalist organizations and turned their hopes to the military. The agrarian pressure groups gathered together under a liaison committee known as the Comité de Enlace de Entidades Agropecuarias which declared that the time had come for defenders of agrarian interests to stand up and be counted. At about the same time, the CEDA, which had previously been the principal vehicle of right-wing agrarian aspirations, began a drift away from legalism and many of its middle-rank members acted as links between military and civilian elements in the preparations for the July 1936 uprising.[39]

Even before 18 July, the situation in the south had reached breaking point. The Republic's reforms applied with determination meant the end of the *latifundio* system and the *latifundistas* were not disposed to see themselves reformed out of existence. The outbreak of civil war, to which the conflicts of the south had contributed so much, unleashed the latent belligerence of both sides. In towns and villages where the Republic held sway, cruel reprisals were often taken against landowners and the priests who had legitimized their tyranny. Then, with varying degrees of success, the local branches of the FNTT and the CNT went about collectivizing the big estates. However, retribution was not long in following. In an offensive of little military importance, but which clearly underlined the socio-economic motives of the Nationalist war effort, troops advanced eastwards from Seville. As villages were captured, massive acts of revenge took place often supervised by the very *latifundistas* who had fled in the spring and taken part in the conspiracy.[40] The *braceros* who survived were subjected to strict military regimentation. Wages were slashed; strikes were treated as sabotage and made punishable by long prison sentences.[41] In the decade following the war, the central plank of Francoist social and economic policy became the maintenance of the rural property structure which had been threatened by the Republic. In that sense, the war was fought and won for the *latifundistas*.

Notes

1 On the instrumentalization of the smallholding peasantry, see Paul Preston, *The Coming of the Spanish Civil War: Reform, Reaction and Revolution in the Second Republic* (henceforth *CSCW*), 2nd edn (London, 1983), chs. 2, 4 and 6; José Montero, *La CEDA: el catolicismo social y político en la II República* (2 vols., Madrid, 1977) 2, pp. 109 ff.; Eduardo Sevilla Guzmán and Paul Preston, 'Dominación de clase y modos de cooptación política del campesinado en España' in *Agricultura y Sociedad*, no. 3 (1977).

2 Eduardo Sevilla Guzmán, *La evolución del campesinado en España* (Barcelona, 1979), 133–76.

3 Juan José Castillo, 'Notas sobre los orígenes y primeros años de la Confederación Nacional Católico-Agraria' in José Luis García Delgado (ed.), *La cuestión agraria en la España contemporánea* (Madrid, 1976), 203–48; Josefina Cuesta, *Sindicalismo católico-agrario en España (1917–1919)* (Madrid, 1978), *passim*.

4 Pascual Carrión, *Los latifundios en España* (Madrid, 1932), 415.

5 Juan José Castillo, *Propietarios muy pobres: sobre la subordinación política del pequeño campesino* (Madrid, 1979), 202–20; Juan Díaz del Moral, *Historia de las agitaciones campesinas andaluzas*, 3rd edn (Madrid, 1977), 361–76.

6 Díaz del Moral, *Historia*, 305–6; Constancio Bernaldo de Quiros, *El espartaquismo agrario y otros ensayos sobre la estructura económica y social de Andalucía* (Madrid, 1973), 183–92.

7 *El Socialista*, 15 May 1924, 21 May 1929; Enrique de Santiago, *La UGT ante la revolución* (Madrid, 1932), 44–5; *Boletín de la UGT*, February 1929; Partido Socialista Obrero Español, *Convocatoria y orden del día para el XII Congreso ordinario* (Madrid, 1927), 11–12.

8 Castillo, *Propietarios*, 337–59; Eduardo Aunós, *Itinerario histórico de la España contemporánea* (Barcelona, 1940), 377–9.

9 Constancio Bernaldo de Quiros, *Informe acerca del paro de los jornaleros del campo de Andalucía durante el otoño de 1931*, reprinted in *El espartaquismo*, 99–126; *El Socialista*, 14, 29 January, 18 March 1931; Ray Steele, 'The Andalusian Agrarian Crisis of 1930–1931', unpublished paper, University of Lancaster; Jacques Maurice, *La reforma agraria en España en el siglo XX* (Madrid, 1975), 22–4.

10 *El Obrero de la Tierra*, 10, 17 September 1932; *Boletín de la UGT*, November 1931. The PSOE also grew dramatically in the south. See Actas de la Comisión Ejecutiva del PSOE, Fundación Pablo Iglesias (henceforth Actas), AH-20-1, 26 May, 4, 10 September 1931, 14, 28 January, 11 February 1932.

11 *Boletín de la UGT*, December 1931; Ramón Tamames, *La República, la era de Franco* (Madrid, 1973), 56–66; Mercedes Cabrera, *La patronal ante la II República: organizaciones y estrategia 1931–1936* (Madrid, 1983), 115–31.

12 *Boletín de la UGT*, May, June 1931; Edward E. Malefakis, *Agrarian Reform and Peasant Revolution in Spain* (New Haven, 1970), 166–71; *Acción Española*, 15 December 1931.

13 Cabrera, *La patronal*, 152–91. For a fuller discussion of the rightist distortion of the implications of these reforms, see Preston, *CSCW*, 32–40, 56–9.

14 *Diario de sesiones de las Cortes Constituyentes*, 11, 24 September, 1, 23 October, 4 November 1931; *El Obrero de la Tierra*, 14, 28 January, 25 February 1933; Actas, AH-20-1, 18 February 1932.

15 *El Debate*, 25 August 1931; *El Socialista*, 5 March 1932; *El Pueblo Católico*, 4 May 1933; Miguel Maura, *Así cayó Alfonso XIII* (Barcelona, 1966), 265–72; Manuel Pérez Yruela, *La conflictividad campesina en la provincia de Córdoba (1931–1936)* (Madrid, 1979), 102, 117–18.

16 José Aparicio Albiñana, *Para qué sirve un gobernador* (Valencia, 1936), 21–39; Alicio Garcitoral, *El crimen de Cuenca* (Madrid, 1932), 59–64, 93–4, 117–18.

17 *Diario de sesiones de las Cortes Constituyentes*, 5 August 1931; *El Pueblo Católico*, 18 July, 21 August 1931.

18 *El Pueblo Católico*, 10, 15, 16, 17 September 1931.

19 Pérez Yruela, *Córdoba*, 111–2, 124–7; Sevilla Guzmán, *Campesinado*, p. 95; José Manuel Macarro Vera, 'La autovaloración anarquista: un principio de análisis y acción (Sevilla, 1931–1936)' in *Estudios de Historia de España: homenage a Manuel Tuñón de Lara* (3 vols., Madrid, 1981), vol. 2, 136–7.

20 Luis Jiménez de Asúa et al., *Castilblanco* (Madrid, 1933); *ABC*, 3, 5 January; *El Socialista*, 2, 5 January; *Acción Española*, 15 January 1932.

21 *El Obrero de la Tierra*, 30 January; *La Mañana*, 1, 6, 7 April 1932.

22 *El Obrero de la Tierra*, 5, 13, 20 February, 5, 12, 26 March 1932.

23 *La Mañana*, 2, 6, 7, 16 April, 11 May, 24 June, 18 November 1932, 27 January, 18 February 1933, 16 January 1934; Pérez Yruela, *Córdoba*, 124–54; Actas, AH-20-1, 16 June 1932.

24 *El Obrero de la Tierra*, 8 October 1933.

25 *El Obrero de la Tierra*, 25 February 1933; Pérez Yruela, *Córdoba*, 128–9, 156; Macarro Vera, 'Sevilla', 137–41.

26 Gérard Brey and Jacques Maurice, *Historia y leyenda de Casas Viejas* (Madrid, 1976); Jerome R. Mintz, *The Anarchists of Casas Viejas* (Chicago, 1982);

Ramón J. Sender, *Viaje a la aldea del crimen* (Madrid, 1934); report of FNTT delegation, *El Obrero de la Tierra*, 15 July 1933.

27 *El Debate*, 14 January; *ABC*, 15 January 1933.

28 Actas, AH-20-2, 8 March 1933.

29 *El Obrero de la Tierra*, 13 May, 3, 10, 17 June, 15, 22, 29 July 1933; Pérez Yruela, *Córdoba*, 155–67.

30 *El Obrero de la Tierra*, 29 July, 12 August 1933; *Boletín de la UGT*, August– September 1933; Actas, AH-20-2, 11, 27 September, 11, 25, 27, 31 October 1933.

31 *El Obrero de la Tierra*, 30 September, 7, 19 October, 2, 23 December 1933; *Boletín de la UGT*, December 1933; Sevilla Guzmán, *Campesinado, 104;* Preston, *CSCW*, 94–5.

32 *Diario de sesiones de Cortes*, 12 December 1933; Pérez Yruela, *Córdoba*, 168–72, 362–5.

33 *El Obrero de la Tierra*, 6, 13, 20 January, 17 February 1934; Pérez Yruela, *Córdoba*, 175–90.

34 Actas, AH-20-2, 7 March 1934.

35 For a fuller account of the strike, see Preston, *CSCW*, 113–17; Pérez Yruela, *Córdoba*, 190–6; minutes of UGT executive meeting of 31 July 1934 in *Boletín de la UGT*, August 1934.

36 *El Obrero de la Tierra*, 29 February 1936; Pérez Yruela, *Córdoba*, 196–8.

37 For a fuller account of the election campaign, see Preston, *CSCW*, 146–50, 169–76.

38 *El Obrero de la Tierra*, 29 February, 7, 21, 28 March 1936; *La Mañana*, 9 April, 16, 17, 28 May, 13, 20 June 1936; Malefakis, *Agrarian Reform*, 368–74; Pérez Yruela, *Córdoba*, 201–14.

39 Cabrera, *La patronal*, 297; Preston, *CSCW*, 188–94.

40 Ronald Fraser, *Blood of Spain: The Experience of Civil War (1936–1939)* (London, 1979), 155–65; Anon., 'El comienzo: la "liberación" de Lora del Río (1936)' in *Cuadernos de Ruedo Ibérico*, nos. 46–8, July–December 1975; Larry Collins and Dominique Lapierra, *Or I'll Dress You in Mourning* (London, 1968), 88–99; Antonio Bahamonde y Sánchez de Castro, *Un año con Queipo* (Barcelona, 1938), 88–136.

41 Julio de Ramón-Laca, *Cómo fue gobernada Andalucía* (Seville, 1939), 151 ff.

8
The Basque question 1931–7
Juan Pablo Fusi

Had George Orwell gone to Bilbao instead of Barcelona and written a homage to Euzkadi – the Basque name for 'the fatherland of the Basques' – it would have been an altogether different book from the *Homage to Catalonia* that he published in 1938. For events turned out quite differently in both regions after July 1936. Indeed, the Basque country was perhaps the only Spanish region loyal to the Republic where the military uprising of 18 July 1936 was not followed by a working-class revolution. To begin with, Orwell would have encountered serious difficulties in joining a left-wing Marxist party like the POUM – the party he joined in Barcelona – or even in studying such a peculiar Spanish phenomenon as anarcho-syndicalism in the Basque Country. In contrast to Catalonia where anarcho-syndicalism had been the main force in the labour movement since the first decade of the century, socialism had become the dominant ideology of Basque workers since the end of the nineteenth century. Compared with the strength of both the Socialist Party and unions (PSOE and UGT) in the Basque region, the POUM, CNT, and even the Communist Party had been for many years almost non-existent. It was only after 1931, with the rise of the Basque Nationalist trade-union federation, the Solidarity of Basque Workers (SOV), that Socialist hegemony in the Basque Country was challenged. This was hardly a threat from the left: SOV was a moderate, Christian-inspired union movement with several priests prominent in its ranks and close links with the centre-right Nationalist Party (PNV). Its membership was restricted to workers and employees of pure Basque descent, its unions rejected ideas of class struggle and advocated a conciliatory line in labour disputes. Finally, SOV shared the PNV's ideal vision of social harmony for the Basque Country based on 'national' (meaning Basque) solidarity between workers and employers.[1]

The events of 18 July 1936 did not lead to a revolutionary process in Euzkadi. One of the three indisputably Basque provinces, Alava, supported Franco (let alone Navarre, the Francoist and Carlist bastion, where historical identity, whether Basque or not, has always been under strong dispute). There was no military rebellion in Vizcaya. In Guipúzcoa, the hesitations of the local *putschists* allowed the Republican loyalists to regain control of the situation after a brief, if intense, outbreak of street fighting in the provincial capital, San Sebastián.

After the Civil War broke out, the Madrid government finally took the decision to grant autonomy to the Basque provinces of Alava, Guipúzcoa and Vizcaya, thus putting an end to an issue which had been pending since 1931. The Basque statute of autonomy was passed by parliament on 1 October 1936. The left-dominated Provincial Defence Juntas set up in Vizcaya and Guipúzcoa as in the rest of Spain following the military rebellion, were immediately replaced by a Basque government, the first in history, presided over by the PNV leader, José Antonio de Aguirre. The PNV, with five portfolios out of a total of twelve, emerged as the axis of power of the newly elected autonomous government of the region. In a few months, from July to October, the political scenario had dramatically changed in the Basque Country: but what had taken place amounted, if anything, to a political counter-revolution. In the months that followed, until the final fall of the Basque Country in June 1937, not a single strike was recorded in the region, not one factory was collectivized, no bank was nationalized, despite Bilbao being the seat of two of the Spanish big banks and despite the Basque provinces being the centre of the Spanish steel industry. Churches remained open. Briefly, notwithstanding the events of 4 January 1937 in Bilbao, when following a Francoist air raid on the city, jails were attacked and more than 200 right-wing prisoners assassinated, President Aguirre was right in pointing out the extraordinary accomplishment of his government in the few months it had been in power, in preserving order and in 'civilizing' war.[2]

One fact seems unquestionable: the existence of a powerful Basque Nationalist Party had made Basque politics in the 1930s an altogether different matter from Spanish politics. This is precisely the object of this chapter: to study how, why, and to what extent Basque politics differed from Spanish politics. This seems the only way to understand why the Civil War also was different in the Basque Country.

It was in the general election of November 1933 that the PNV, with 30 per cent of the vote and twelve out of seventeen MPs, emerged as the indisputable first political party in the Basque provinces. The two years from 1931 to 1933 were also the key years in the rise of SOV: its membership grew from 7500 in the 1929 Congress to 40,342 in 1933 – a figure close to 30 per cent of the industrial labour force of the Basque provinces and only slightly behind UGT membership.[3]

The first two years of the Second Republic, with Azaña as head of several centre-left governments, all including a number of Socialist ministers, saw, therefore, a spectacular rise in the strength of Basque nationalism in the Basque provinces. There were a number of reasons for this. First, the coming of the Second Republic with its promise of autonomy for the regions led to a marked strengthening of the Basque sentiment of a separate identity. Indeed, the resurgence of such feeling had been evident in the massive support for Basque cultural activities in the last years of the dictatorship of Primo de Rivera (1923–30), a clear indication of the determination of the Basques to protect their own separate identity against the repressive policies of the dictatorship aimed against both Basque language and culture. Even if the PNV had not joined in the activities against the monarchy of Alfonso XIII, Basque Nationalists felt as legitimized as the Catalans in demanding what they regarded as the historical rights of the Basque people: only three days after the Republic had been proclaimed, a number of PNV mayors from the province of Vizcaya met in the town of Guernica to form without success, a Basque government within a Spanish Federal Republic.

Second, the PNV undoubtedly gained considerably from the collapse of the historical parties following the fall of both the dictatorship and the monarchy in 1930 and 1931. Basque Catholic opinion rallied towards nationalism as the swing of Carlist and monarchist votes towards the PNV registered in the middle-class districts of Bilbao and San Sebastián in the 1931 elections clearly showed. Lacking in organization and internally divided, right-wing parties (i.e. Traditionalists, Monarchists, Catholics, Fascists) were in no position to offer a viable political alternative to the PNV in Vizcaya and Guipúzcoa until the 1936 elections, even if the Carlists won the three elections of 1931, 1933, and 1936 in Alava. But for the rest, the PNV remained until 1936 as the best Catholic, moderate, and popular answer to the ascendancy of the left in the Basque provinces.

The Basque Church – or, at least, a substantial part of it – seemed to have shared this opinion. Basque priests (José de Ariztimuño, José Miguel de Barandiarán, Manuel Lecuona) had played a prominent role in the rebirth of Basque studies and culture in the 1920s and 1930s, a fact clearly related to the resurgence of Basque political consciousness. Other priests – such as Policarpo de Larrañaga, Alberto de Onaindía or the said Ariztimuño – helped considerably in the organization of SOV; prominent politicians in the leadership of the PNV (Aguirre, Leizaola among many others) came from Catholic Youth organizations and would always maintain their close relationships with the local clergy. A growing number of priests made no secret of their support for Basque nationalism.[4] The Bishop of Vitoria after 1928, the Basque-speaking D. Mateo Múgica, although himself not a nationalist, supported Basque cultural efforts, stood up to defend the philo-nationalist priests of his diocese and favoured the co-operation of all conservative and Catholic parties of the Basque Country – including the PNV – in a common political front. In 1933, he openly endorsed the PNV-inspired statute of autonomy for the Basque Country, despite strong opposition to the statute from ultra-Catholic and anti-nationalist right-wing parties and newspapers both inside and outside the Basque Country.

As the best-organized Catholic party of the region, the PNV was in a strong position to make political capital out of Basque discontent against the anti-clerical policies of the Azaña governments. The Bishop of Vitoria, Dr Múgica, was expelled from Spain on 17 May 1931 as, in 1933, were the Jesuits, the order founded by a Basque with its central house in Loyola, at the heart of the Basque Country. Throughout the Republic, the PNV was second to none in the defence of Church rights, proclaiming again and again the truly Christian values which inspired their policies and ideals. There was no great exaggeration in the words written in 1936 by one of the PNV's main ideologists, Engracio de Arantzadi: 'There has never been in this region as solidly Christian a movement as Basque nationalism.' The editorials of the party's main newspaper, *Euzkadi*, often reminded its readers that the PNV had been a Catholic party since the very beginning and that its doctrine and pro-grammes were but the doctrines of the Church: 'thanks to Basque nationalism', Arantzadi argued, 'Euzkadi has been the refuge of Cath-olic resistance in the Spanish State.'[5] The impressive vote gains won by the PNV in 1933 had much to do with such a political line.

What turned the PNV into the first political force of the Basque region, however, even more than all reasons mentioned above, was its determination to see some form of political self-government established in the Basque provinces. While this issue, the 'Basque question', remained unsolved – and it did remain unsolved until October 1936 – the PNV was able to play with the sentiments of frustration and dis-illusionment of many Basques and to keep the nationalist flame alive through a policy of almost permanent confrontation with Madrid.

It is far from easy to explain why the Basque way towards political autonomy turned out to be an almost intractable imbroglio. The Basque question was no simple matter. Unlike Catalonia, the Basque Country had never formed a homogeneous 'nationality'. First, the Basque Country had never been a political unity, let alone an independent state. Its different territories had had separate histories, Navarre as an independent kingdom until 1512, Alava, Guipúzcoa, and Vizcaya as part of the kingdom of Castile. Second, even the geographical definition of Euzkadi was questionable: Navarre, which retained its category of kingdom until 1840, was only partially Basque. Third, there were areas in the Basque territory which had been Castilian in origin as the Encartaciones in Vizcaya and a part of Alava. Moreover, Basque sentiment was far from universal in 1931. It was strong in Vizcaya and Guipúzcoa but weak in Alava – where the PNV reached in 1933 an electoral peak of only 20.5 per cent of the vote – and it was almost non-existent in Navarre.

The cultural environment of the provincial capitals and main industrial centres differed but little from the rest of Spain. Basque ethnoculture remained restricted to the Basque-speaking towns and villages in rural and fishing districts. Industrialization at the end of the nineteenth century had brought massive immigration of non-Basque workers: by 1900, 26.4 per cent of the population of Vizcaya had been born outside the province. In contrast with their Catalan counterparts, most Basque intellectuals and artists – as, for instance, Unamuno, Baroja, Maeztu, Zuloaga, Arteta – cherished strong Spanish sentiments, felt part of the Spanish culture and rejected the idea that reduced Basque culture to literature written in Basque and 'regionalist' art.[6] Basque capital had financed a considerable percentage of the growth of the Spanish economy after 1876. In the 1930s San Sebastián was still the traditional summer capital of Spain.

There were relevant points involved in all this. First, Basque nationalism was not based in a modern culture, a fact which certainly put a formidable limit to its social and intellectual aspirations. Second, there were strong historical, cultural, economic and emotional ties between the Basque Country and the rest of Spain. Third, Basque society was deeply divided in relation to the idea of a Basque separate identity. If the evolution of the intellectuals can be regarded as a symptom of a major social change, a split in the 'national' consciousness of the Basques can be traced back to the last third of the nineteenth century. The generation of Basque intellectuals born around 1863–73 and brought to cultural life around 1900 followed divergent paths. Part of them turned towards the recovery, study, and vindication of Basque language and culture: obsessed by the definition of Basque identity, they formed what might best be described as the 'first nationalist generation' in which the names of Sabino Arana, Evaristo Bustinza, Toribio Alzaga, R. M. Azkue and Domingo Aguirre should be included.[7] But part of the same generation – Unamuno, Baroja, Maeztu, Salaverría, Grandmontagne, to mention a few names – turned their attention towards Spain and the problems of Spain: most of them were prominent members of the Spanish 'generation of 98'. It was not that they ignored Basque questions: it was, rather, that they saw Basque identity and the Basque past as a substantial, constituent component of Spanish nationality. This fundamental division has remained an essential feature of Basque culture ever since. Basque society was a complex, modern society where a number of different, if not conflicting, cultures coexisted.

It was during 1931–6 that these internal conflicts of Basque society would become politically relevant. The Republican constitution of 1931 recognized, as is well known, the right of regions to political autonomy. Catalonia had obtained its statute of autonomy in 1932. The general conviction both inside and outside the Basque Country was that the Basques would also be granted a similar status. As said before, this did not happen and the Basque Country had to wait until October 1936 – i.e. until after the outbreak of the Civil War – for self-government. At first glance this may seem something of a paradox since both 'Madrid' (government and congress) and all Basque political parties appeared to support the idea of Basque autonomy. But there was nothing paradoxical about it. Indeed, what happened was that there began to be a growing rift between the Spanish (including Basque) left and Basque nationalism about the nature of Basque autonomy (apart from the intrinsic problems for the latter over conflicting issues such as Navarre).

The Republic had granted autonomy to Catalonia almost at once, in view of the many ideological and political links that had brought together Spanish republican parties and Catalan nationalism under the Primo de Rivera dictatorship. It did not grant autonomy to the Basques simply because such links with Basque nationalism had never existed. The PNV refused to join in the revolutionary conspiracy against the monarchy in 1930–1. One of its leaders Federico de Zabala wrote in *Euzkadi*, just a few months before the coming of the Second Republic, that the whole Spanish crisis of 1931 was but 'an anti-christian and anti-social revolution of free-masons, anti-clericals, socialists and communists'.[8]

Statements of this kind helped little in improving the essentially negative image that Spanish democrats had of Basque nationalism. It had been traditionally regarded as a right-wing, Catholic, and xenophobic movement on account of the ideas of ethnicity, social exclusivism, and exacerbated religiosity engrained in the thoughts of the PNV founder, Sabino Arana (1865–1903). And this interpretation seemed to be confirmed, as late as 1931–6, by the unmistakably racist and reactionary views found in the writings of PNV ideologists, such as the prolific Engracio de Arantzadi.

These manifestations were the more unfortunate since they did not reflect the true nature of Basque nationalism in 1931. For the PNV of 1931–6 had in many respects ceased to be the party founded by Arana in 1893. The PNV had experienced a gradual process of *aggiornamento* parallel to the process of modernization experienced by Basque society. One fact had been particularly significant: the coming to the party at the end of the first decade of the century of a new generation of militants of Christian and democratic background, the generation of Aguirre and Leizaola, leaders of the party in the 1930s. There were another two relevant factors: (1) the increasing concern of the PNV with social and labour matters as reflected in the growth of SOV after 1931; (2) the emphasis in a modernized Basque culture by some intellectuals and writers who also joined the PNV in the late 1920s and early 1930s (Ariztimuño, Lizardi, Lauaxeta). All this combined to make the PNV a multi-dimensional party. Together with the reactionary, anti-liberal legacy of the Aranist orthodoxy – which many regarded as permanent – there existed in fact inside the PNV modern and more democratic views and ideas, such as the following: a comprehensive, non-exclusive view of Basque society; a Christian idea of labour relations; a similarly Christian sense of education, family and life; a theory of Basque democracy which emphasized the role of municipalities; and a growing concern with culture (although Basque culture was still seen as the expression of ethnicity). Basque nationalism in 1931 wanted to turn

Euzkadi into a dynamic, egalitarian, and orderly society, kept together by a combination of Christian and ethno-cultural values.

The PNV of 1931 was, to all effects and purposes, a Christian and populist party. It was close to what would later become the Christian-democratic parties of Catholic Europe – it was much closer to this party model than, say, the CEDA of Gil Robles. And yet, the Spanish left, obsessed by the Aranist 'soul' of the PNV, failed to see in Basque nationalism a truly democratic force. This was an important mistake in historical perception. But it is also a fact that the PNV was not yet a liberal, laic party, that is, a party fully identified with the Republican project of the Spanish democrats. The PNV still had an excess of racist and ultra-Catholic overtones; it still retained too many links with a Church clearly divorced from the Republic. And its unions, SOV, still imposed a sort of racial exclusivism for new recruits and were too confessional for democratic tastes. The PNV was a Basque, Christian and democratic party. But their concept of a Basque Christian-democracy had little to do with the radical traditions of liberal democracy. There was no room in the Basque Country for left-wing, liberal nationalism along the lines, for instance, of the Catalan Esquerra. A small minority of left-wing nationalists had to leave the PNV in 1930 and formed an electorally irrelevant party, Basque Nationalist Action (ANV). The PNV's idea of democracy – as expressed, for instance, in the writings of the priest José de Ariztimuño – was essentially an organic view of democracy, a view which envisaged a Basque society built upon the traditional pillars of family, social corporations, and town councils with no mention of individual freedom, political parties, or labour unions.[9]

There were, moreover, in the PNV of 1931–6 too many ambiguities, too much vagueness and confusion in respect of the central question of 'autonomy or independence'. This was also a result of the vaguely independentist legacy of Arana which was still evident, for instance, in the frequent allusions by prominent party members to the Basque right to sovereignty (allegedly lost in 1839). And yet, the PNV was not that separatist ghost which haunted the dreams of the unitarian Spanish right, a prejudice which found its most hysterical expression in the passionate attack against the PNV launched in congress by José Calvo Sotelo on 5 December 1935. It was true that there was inside Basque nationalism an independentist wing led by Eli de Gallastegi and the weekly *Jagi-Jagi*. It is even likely that a part of the nationalist masses cherished platonic dreams of independence. But the obvious fact was that the leadership of the PNV, the influential daily *Euzkadi*, and the parliamentary group of the party played the card of autonomy to the very end. After all, the PNV would end in 1936 at the head of a Basque government with the least radical statute ever drafted.

Critics of the PNV were only partially right in one respect. Unlike Catalan nationalism, Basque nationalism lacked both a Spanish strategy and a Spanish vocation, that is, the PNV had neither sensitivity for nor an explicit interest in Spanish matters and affairs. Basque Nationalists quite simply wanted to recover for the Basque provinces that degree of self-government which would allow them to carry on with the educational, social, and cultural policies which they considered necessary to preserve Basque 'national' identity. They had but a slight interest in Spanish politics. Hence their lack of clear and sympathetic references to Spain. On the contrary, the PNV's highly explosive language was an open challenge to Spanish patriotism. Such was the case, for instance, with the insistence of Basque leaders on the right of its people to national sovereignty, even if PNV ideologists took care to distinguish sovereignty from independence. Basque Nationalists were sincere when they argued that in demanding the abolition of the law of 1839 – the key to Basque sovereignty – they were not asking for independence but for a radical autonomy legitimized by history. The language of the party had, above all, an instrumental value: Basque nationalism resorted to emotional semantics as an instrument both to reinforce internal unity and to foster the sentimental integration of the nationalist community.

But it is easy to understand why a language which combined frequent appeals to Basque rights with a disdainful ignorance of Spanish concerns would raise suspicion and hostile reactions. This was not a reaction confined to right-wingers and the military who saw in Basque nationalism a new threat to Spanish unity. A similar reaction of irritation with Basque nationalism did in fact grow inside the ranks of the Republican left, many of whose prominent leaders (such as Azaña, Prieto, or Sánchez Román), though sympathetic towards the cultural and political demands of both Basques and Catalans, saw Spain as a unitarian state, as a historical and cultural unity. The left might have made the mistake of seeing only the reactionary, negative side of Basque nationalism, its

'Aranist' soul, thus ignoring its democratic, social leanings. But the PNV itself must bear much of the responsibility. Basque Nationalists failed to realize the problems of Spanish democracy. Their uncompromising policies became an additional obstacle to the stability of the Republican regime. It seems likely to me that with a fully Republican, laic and liberal PNV no serious obstacle would have barred the path to Basque autonomy in April 1931.

This was not the case. On the contrary, it soon became evident that the Republican-Socialist left in power since April 1931 was not prepared to accept a Basque Country under the control of the PNV. Neither anti-Basque feelings nor hostility against the idea of political autonomy were involved here. There was a justified fear (particularly felt by the Basque left) that the Basque Country under PNV control – a possibility after the June 1931 elections – might become a conservative, theocratic, and traditionalist reservoir.

So, the divorce between the PNV and the left-wing Republic of 1931–3 was hardly surprising. It was almost inevitable in view of the deep discrepancies that existed between Basque Nationalists and Spanish democrats about questions as politically relevant then as education, civil marriage, and the Church. Moreover, other frictional issues came to make relations even worse.

There was, first, the fact that the PNV had not taken part either in the Pact of San Sebastián in August 1930 – the central event in the opposition to the monarchy of Alfonso XIII – or in the revolutionary movement which followed later in December. There was, second, the PNV's evident attempt after the proclamation of the Second Republic to ignore the dynamics of national politics in order to press for a Basque statute of autonomy even before the constitution had been approved. The first move had been the meeting in Guernica on 17 April 1931. Thus far, developments had been similar to those in Catalonia, but with two substantial differences. Catalan nationalists had signed the Pact of San Sebastián in 1930 when the Republicans had promised to grant them autonomy once the Republic was proclaimed; Catalan nationalists had won the elections on 14 April 1931 whereas in the Basque Country, the PNV had won only in rural areas and small villages, the left winning in the provincial capitals and big towns. Accordingly the meeting in Guernica – and the movement of Basque town councils launched there by the PNV – was seen by the left as an inadmissible, anti-democratic manoeuvre by Basque nationalism to gain control over the Basque autonomy process. Since its electoral strength in small villages and rural areas gave the PNV the control of a majority of localities – but not of the electorate – Basque nationalism quickly moved to put negotiations for autonomy in the hands of town councils and its representatives instead of MPs and political parties. With the support of Carlists and despite the opposition from Republicans and Socialists, the PNV managed to enlist a total of 427 town councils from the Basque provinces and Navarre (out of 548 local councils in the whole region). At a meeting in the Navarrese city of Estella on 14 June 1931, they voted in favour of the statute of autonomy for the Basque-Navarrese Country drafted by the prestigious Society for Basque Studies early in May. It was to no avail. The Spanish parliament rejected the statute later in September.

The municipalist movement was counter-productive and a mistake. The movement was hardly representative despite the spectacular figure of 427 local councils. Not one of the big centres of the region – Bilbao, San Sebastián, Vitoria, Eibar, Baracaldo, Irún, etc. – not even Guernica, spiritual capital of the Basques, joined in the movement. Its legitimacy was, therefore, disputable. The insistence of the PNV that only municipalities should take part in the discussions and definitive preparation of the statute, made it impossible to reach a final text which was supported by all political forces of the Basque-Navarrese area. Besides, the statute of Estella was both contrary to the constitution and undemocratic. It went against the constitution in securing for the future Basque government relations with the Vatican. It was hardly democratic in rejecting proportional representation – a fact which favoured the rural areas and the PNV to the detriment of big cities and the left – and in raising to seven, instead of two, the years of residence in the Basque Country necessary to exercise political rights in the region, again a move against the left, which found its support largely among immigrants. And finally, the PNV had entered into an open political alliance with Carlism and the Catholic right: they had joined forces in the municipalist movement, and they joined forces again in the June 1931 general elections when they sponsored common candidates with the statute of Estella as their electoral programme. This was the final mistake. Basque autonomy appeared to the eyes of the Republic as a political move against Spanish democracy. The PNV seemed, moreover, to ignore the mathematics of parliamentary politics: alliance with the right meant that there could not be enough votes for the statute of Estella in a congress largely dominated by the left.[10]

The mistakes of Basque nationalism and the growing tension between the PNV and the left – aggravated by the government's anti-clerical policies – led to the failure of the Basque autonomy process as early as 1931. And things changed but little until the general elections of November 1933 which saw the return to power in Madrid of right-wing and centrist parties. There was little change until then for several reasons. The left, in power all through 1931–3, tried to go ahead with the autonomy process without the PNV. So, a determined policy to reinforce Republican and Socialist parties in the Basque Country and to restrain the activities of Basque nationalism was followed by 'Madrid' after 1932. The idea was probably to delay Basque autonomy until the Basque left was in a position to gain control over the government of future Basque institutions. The result was hardly surprising: after a brief and unconvincing *détente* from December 1931 to the summer of 1932, tension between the PNV and the left grew to a peak in May 1933.[11] Before this, Basque aspirations had suffered a serious setback on 19 June 1932 when Navarre disengaged itself from Basque autonomy. This was mainly due to the strong 'Navarrese' sentiment of a majority of the population of the province. But it was also a result of the political turnaround by the Carlists, the indisputably dominant force in Navarre. The Carlists turned against the idea of Basque autonomy as soon as they realized that the PNV was ready to come to terms with the Republic in exchange for Basque autonomy.[12] Thereafter, Carlists would also share with the rest of the Spanish right the idea that both Catalan and Basque autonomies were but a step towards full separatism.

The breakdown of the autonomy process in 1931–3 meant the frustration of the many expectations raised by the coming of the Second Republic. The PNV made impressive political capital out of both its policy of confrontation with Madrid and the disappointment of a part of Basque opinion with the failure of Basque autonomy. The emotional manipulation of this frustration helped to obscure the many strategic mistakes made by the PNV leadership. The PNV made the ignorance of Madrid and the allegedly anti-Basque feelings of the local left responsible for the failure of Basque autonomy. Together with the outrage felt by Basque Catholics against the anti-clerical policies of Azaña and with social discontent fostered by governmental impotence in the face of economic crisis, this explains the shift towards the PNV and the defeat of the left which, as far as the Basque Country was concerned, marked the general elections held on 19 November 1933. A first warning had already come on 5 November: 84 per cent of the Basque electorate (but only 46.4 per cent in Alava) had come out in support of a new statute of autonomy which did not include Navarre and which was in tune with the constitution. On 19 November, the PNV swept to victory in the elections in Vizcaya, including Bilbao, and Guipúzcoa and came second in Alava: in all, it won twelve out of seventeen Basque seats.[13]

Such an impressive show of strength was to turn out to be, however, a Pyrrhic victory for the PNV. Autonomy was not granted to the Basques in the two years (1934-5) during which a number of centre-right coalition governments of the Radical Party of Lerroux and the CEDA of Gil Robles remained in power. There should have been little surprise in this: it was unrealistic to expect a statute of autonomy to be approved by a congress where the CEDA had 115 deputies out of a total of 471. Such a congress was prisoner of the right, which in line with the views expressed again and again by its leaders Calvo Sotelo, Maeztu, Víctor Pradera, and José Antonio – to give a few names – saw in Basque autonomy a separatist threat to Spanish unity. It was precisely against Basque nationalism that Calvo Sotelo coined his famous phrase: he preferred Spain 'better red than broken' (*roja antes que rota*). Radical and CEDA deputies, on the other hand, lacked a clear answer of their own to the Basque question. Radicals, their brief flirtation with the PNV come to an end by the spring of 1934, gave in to the CEDA. The CEDA leader, Gil Robles, made some occasional and vague references to 'foral restitution'.[14] There were also some contacts between Basque Nationalists and the more democratic members of the CEDA. But all amounted to nothing. Basque autonomy came to a standstill in 1934-5. Not until

1936, with the victory of the Popular Front at the February elections, would there emerge new hopes for Basque autonomy.

If anything, events in 1934 took a turn for the worse. The dialectics of confrontation between the Basques and 'Madrid' intensified. In February, there was an attempt to try in Alava the sort of manoeuvre of disengagement so successfully accomplished in Navarre in 1932: considering that the votes for autonomy in the 5 November referendum had been below the 50 per cent mark in Alava, congress passed a resolution asking for a new, separate referendum to be called in that province to decide upon its future. This the PNV could not accept. In the summer, a dispute about the right to introduce in the Basque provinces a new tax on wine which the Basques thought incompatible with their old fiscal autonomy, escalated into a serious confrontation between the central government and the Basque local councils.[15] The conflict had a new and significant dimension: the Republican and Socialist left joined forces with the PNV in the rebellion against the government. In defiance of Madrid orders, Basque local councils held elections on 12 August to appoint a committee which would negotiate Basque fiscal rights with the government. PNV and left-wing MPs supported the move in a special assembly held on 2 September also against government orders. On 4 September, most Basque mayors and councillors resigned in protest. Hundreds of them were either brought to trial or fined. The mayor and 31 councillors of Bilbao, most of them from the left, remained in jail for several days.

Basque autonomy was fatally wounded as a result. Moreover, the events of the summer of 1934 opened new perspectives for Basque politics which were to bear upon the events of 1936–9. It was not that an alliance between separatism and revolution was sealed in 1934 as the non-democratic right would hysterically declare. The alliance simply did not exist. What took place in the Basque rebellion of 1934 was a mere coincidence of Basque nationalism and left-wing forces in defence of both the Basque economic system and the administrative autonomy of the local councils. This was, besides, a mere transient coincidence which brought no ideological changes and no new approaches from either the PNV or the Basque left to the burning Basque issue, or towards political, economic and social questions.

It proved to be a coincidence without continuity. The alleged alliance was to collapse immediately after the summer of 1934 with the revolutionary attempt launched by the Socialists in October against the appointment of a number of ministers from the CEDA. The revolution was extremely violent in some parts of the Basque Country: sixteen people were killed in Bilbao, six in Eibar and four in Mondragón. But in the rest it took the form of a peaceful, non-violent general strike. The PNV neither supported nor joined in the revolution; SOV only went along with the strike action from 4 to 12 October and then ordered its members to return to work. Although it seems that there had been some contacts with the revolutionaries mainly because of the bitterness left within the whole nationalist movement by the rebellion of the local councils, during the week from 4 to 12 October both PNV and SOV played a stabilizing, pacifying role in line with the moderate and Catholic traditions of the party and the unions. The PNV deputies returned to congress as soon as it reconvened and gave their votes for the new Lerroux government with CEDA ministers. Despite the campaign of hatred against the PNV inspired by the right, October 1934 showed quite clearly that the PNV, as the party of the Basque Catholic bourgeoisie and the rural masses, and SOV as the moderate union federation of Catholic workers and employees, would by no means lend their support to a left-wing revolution.[16]

Be that as it may, the October revolution and its aftermath left lasting scars in Basque politics. It came to reinforce both the shift in political direction and the new political alignments that had begun to take shape as a result of the rebellion of the local councils in the summer. For there were a number of lessons to be learned from such developments. First of all, 1934 marked the final breakdown in the relations between the PNV and the non-democratic right (both Basque and Spanish); or, in terms of class, 1934 signalled the separation of the Basque and the Basque-Spanish bourgeoisies in the Basque Country. At the elections of February 1936, the non-nationalist Basque right with a vehemently anti-PNV electoral platform, won an impressive increase in votes of 37 per cent over 1933.

In a way, the events of 1934 condemned the PNV to political isolation. Following the failure of the revolution, Basque Nationalists suspended all co-operation with the revolutionary left (apart from supporting compassionate measures for prisoners and exiles). After

October 1934, the PNV was to answer right-wing criticisms with a determined effort to reaffirm its image as a Catholic party for order and moderation. It never went as far as it was to go in February 1936 in its attempts to conquer the Catholic and conservative vote. In January, a PNV delegation went to Rome with the overt purpose of winning the backing of the Church for the coming elections. The party went to the elections with a platform which put the defence of 'Christian civilization' on the front line (together, quite naturally, with the defence of 'Basque freedoms' and 'social justice'). Never before had its electoral propaganda been so full of right-wing connotations: 'If there is an anti-revolutionary content', an editorial from *Euzkadi* on 31 January 1936 read, 'this lies with the PNV'; 'only Basque nationalism and nothing but nationalism', *Euzkadi* argued on the following day, 'has made a truly anti-revolutionary effort'. And the mouthpiece of the PNV asked: 'who, apart from us, has fought against red extremism?' The ideologist Arantzadi reminded his readers in the same pages that the PNV had raised 'the flag of Christ' and how it had 'invaded with its Catholic masses' the Basque cities; another commentator assured *Euzkadi* readers that he was going to vote for the PNV because it was 'Basque, Catholic, and counter-revolutionary'.[17]

The Basque left also drew its own conclusions from experience. The Popular Front learned the lessons of 1933. They went into the 1936 general elections with the promise of a Basque statute of autonomy on their ticket. The Basque left was not prepared to abandon, as it appeared to have done in 1932–3, a cause largely supported by Basque society. In 1936 the Popular Front won 30,000 more votes than had been cast for the left in 1933. With seven deputies and 130,822 votes it was in a strong position to challenge the PNV hegemony (nine deputies and 138,627 votes).

In the Basque Country, therefore, the February 1936 elections saw the recovery of the left, the rise of the non-nationalist right, and a significant check to PNV aspirations. After the elections, the Popular Front took steps towards the resumption of the autonomy process. Prieto, the powerful Socialist leader of Bilbao, took the issue to congress. He wanted to avoid the mistakes of 1931–3 and had realized that any further delay in solving the Basque question would only be to the benefit of the PNV. Moreover, he saw that granting autonomy to the

Basque provinces was perhaps the only democratic way for the integration of Basque nationalism within the Spanish constitutional framework. Prieto had also come to the conclusion that Basque autonomy must be the result of consensus by all Basque political parties, not the imposition of one of them. Thus, he tried to reach some sort of understanding with the PNV managing to convince their leader, José Antonio de Aguirre, to become a member of the parliamentary committee which in the spring of 1936 began to draft a new statute of autonomy to be submitted to congress later. The moderate wing of the PNV seemed to have lost all initiative after the electoral setback of February and was in need of some tangible results to counter criticisms from independentist sectors; so they seized the opportunity raised by the offer of the Popular Front. The new Basque statute was ready before July 1936. But the congress summer recess made it impossible for the statute to be approved before 18 July.

The events of 1934, the confrontation between the PNV and the right, and the elections of 1936 all help to explain much of what took place in the Basque country after the military uprising of 18 July. Alava, the least nationalist of the three Basque provinces and the most inclined to the right, supported Franco.[18] The left took up the defence of the Republic against the military in the provincial capitals and main industrial centres of Vizcaya and Guipúzcoa, with the PNV in cautious second place. Guipúzcoa, where in February 1936 the right had polled 26 per cent of the vote – almost as many as the PNV and 3 per cent more than the Popular Front – soon fell to Franco's troops. Only Vizcaya resisted for some months.

The Civil War and the Republican need to win the support of the PNV against Franco gave a new turn to the process for Basque autonomy. After all, the PNV was still the main political party in the Basque area. The Basque statute was approved on 1 October, but even more important was the constitution, on 7 October, of a Basque government before elections to a Basque parliament had taken place – a Basque government where the PNV retained the main posts. This was the price that the Republic had to pay for Basque Nationalist support.

The PNV took office in the most unfavourable of conditions (and not without the scepticism of those who saw the Civil War as a Spanish, i.e. not Basque, affair): Basque Nationalists had finally realized that the free Euzkadi of their dreams was only possible within a democratic Spain.

The Basque government fought bravely for Euzkadi and for the Spanish Republic, even if at the time it took office only Vizcaya remained under Republican control. The Basque forces fought until the military superiority of Franco's troops made resistance untenable. Guernica remained as the symbol of Basque resistance to fascism. But the war had had special peculiarities in the Basque Country: it had brought to power a party that defended Christian civilization, that openly proclaimed its counter-revolutionary credentials, and one that only a few months before the Civil War had emphasized its role as the main alternative to the rise of Marxist extremism in the Basque provinces. The activities of the Basque government from 7 October 1936 to 17 June 1937 bore the mark of such a party, the mark of the PNV. Orwell would not have been a witness to the revolution had he gone to Euzkadi for one very simple reason: no revolution took place in 'the fatherland of the Basques'.

Notes

1 There is no complete study of SOV. See I. Olábarri, *Relaciones laborales en Vizcaya (1890–1936)* (Durango, 1978) and P. Policarpo de Larrañaga, *Contribución a la historia obrera de Euskalerría* (2 vols., San Sebastián, 1977). I dealt with immigrant socialism in *Política obrera en el País Vasco 1880–1923* (Madrid, 1975).

2 For the civil war in the Basque country and the Basque government see Aguirre's own account in *Veinte años de gestión del Gobierno Vasco (1936–1956)* (Paris, 1956); G. L. Steer, *The Tree of Guernica* (London, 1938); and L. M. and J. C. Jiménez de Aberásturi, *La Guerra en Euzkadi* (Barcelona, 1978).

3 Another 5000 families were affiliated to the Organization of Basque Farmers (*Euzko Nekazarien Bazkuna*) formed in 1933. See A. Elorza, *Ideologías del nacionalismo vasco 1876–1937* (San Sebastián, 1978), 163–232.

4 Fourteen Basque priests were shot by Franco's troops (Ariztimuño among them); another 200 were put in jail and around 70 went into exile.

5 E. Arantzadi's articles in *Euzkadi*, 4 and 5 February 1936.

6 See M. Unamuno, *Obras Completas*, vol. VI, *La raza y la lengua* (Madrid, 1958), 326–89; P. Baroja, *Nuevo ablado de Arlequín* (Madrid, 1917); and R. Maeztu, *Autobiografía* (Madrid, 1962).

7 Not all of them were nationalists but all shared the same interest in Basque ethnic culture. For Basque literature, see L. Michelena, *Historia de la literatura vasca* (Madrid, 1960) and I. Sarasola, *Historia social de la literatura vasca* (Madrid, 1976).

8 F. de Zabala ('Leonardo'), *Euzkadi*, 24 February 1931.

9 José de Ariztimuño, *La democracia en Euzkadi* (San Sebastián, 1934). For the PNV as a Christian-democratic party, see X. Tusell, *Historia de la democracia cristiana en España* (Madrid, 1975), vol. II.

10 The composition of congress was: Socialists, 116 deputies; Radicals, 90; Radical-Socialists, 56; left-wing Catalan nationalists, 36; Republican Action, 26; Basques, 14. There were only 26 deputies from the non-Republican right.

11 The PNV called a general strike in the Bilbao area when President Alcalá Zamora went to visit the town on 1–4 May 1933. I have considered the Basque question in the Second Republic in *El problema vasco en la II República* (Madrid, 1979).

12 The PNV had returned to congress in December 1931 and gave its votes to elect Alcalá Zamora as President of the Republic. For the 'Navarre question' see Víctor M. Arbeloa, *Navarra ante los Estatutos. Introducción documental (1916–1932)* (Pamplona, 1978) and Martin Blinkhorn, *Carlism and Crisis in Spain 1931–1939* (Cambridge, 1975).

13 There is no complete study of elections in the Basque country. Electoral figures used in this text are based on X. Tusell and G. García Queipo de Llano, 'Introducción a la sociología electoral en el País Vasco durante la II República', *Revista Española de la Opinión Pública*, no. 48, April–June 1977; A. Cillán Apalategui, *Sociología electoral de Guipúzcoa 1900–1936* (San Sebastián, 1975); Stanley G. Payne, *Basque Nationalism* (Reno, 1975), and in my own research through the Basque press.

14 'Foral restitution' meant a return to the old Basque system of *Fueros* (old laws), by which town councils in each province met annually in a big assembly (or *Junta*) to deal with fiscal and other matters. The foral system was finally abolished in 1876 after being considerably altered in 1839.

15 From 1878 the Basque provinces periodically signed an economic agreement with the central government. By this system each Basque province paid the central government an annual sum for their total provincial taxation; but individual taxes were raised and administered by local and provincial councils.

16 For the events of the summer and October 1934 see J. P. Fusi, *El problema vasco en la II República* (Madrid, 1979); for the campaign against the PNV, see *Gaceta del Norte* and *El Pueblo Vasco* (Bilbao), 12 October 1934 and ff.

17 *Euzkadi*, 5 February 1936. For the electoral campaign in February 1936 see *Euzkadi*, 7 January–23 February 1936.

18 In February 1936 the right had polled in Alava 42.8 per cent of the vote against 16.4 per cent by the Popular Front and 14.9 per cent by the PNV. For these and other figures given in the text, see note 13 above.

9
Soldiers, politics and war
Michael Alpert

The apparent readiness of the majority of Spanish army officers to over-throw civil government in July 1936 is sometimes taken for granted. It is probably too late now to investigate to what extent officers declined to take part in the uprising for reasons of conscience or how many officers would not have rebelled had they realized that their action would lead to a full-scale war against half of Spain.[1]

Was the rebellion of July 1936 a new type of putsch or was it a repetition of the traditional *pronunciamiento*? To attempt to answer this and similar questions requires some consideration of the historical nature of the Spanish army.

Politico-military studies have explained how the liberal and modernizing army of the nineteenth century reacted in a hostile way to the spread of both working-class and regionalist activities.[2] The former were perceived as a threat to law and order; the latter as a menace to Spanish national unity. Few Spanish officers in fact came from the advanced bourgeoisie of Catalonia and the Basque provinces.[3] Moreover, Spanish working-class and regionalist movements tended to be anti-militarist and to advocate strong civilian control over the army. This was unfortunate, for although regionalism has been associated with progressive views in Spain, it does not necessarily imply anti-militarism, as the Swiss example demonstrates. Nor are anti-militarist views necessarily paramount in every country's working class.[4]

The cause of Spanish anti-militarism was the peculiar position of the army at Spain's stage of historical development. Although the Spain of the late nineteenth and early twentieth centuries was a constitutional monarchy, its social system was out of phase with its political structure. The army represented something akin to a pre-revolutionary estate. Because of the failure of the Spanish bourgeoisie to establish strong institutions, the army had an influence out of proportion to its numbers. Whereas in France the Third Republic established the hegemony of the civil state,[5] in Spain almost the reverse took place. The 1906 *Ley de Jurisdicciones* gave the army power to court martial its own critics.[6] From 1916 onwards, the Juntas de Defensa – associations of army officers – made and unmade ministers of war and achieved an Army Act by which their special interests were satisfied.[7]

The army was not only an estate but also a caste. Army families were preserved by endogamous marriage and by sons who followed their fathers into the service. Outside blood entered through the promotion into the officer class of men from the ranks. The army was a regular upward path of social mobility.[8]

Even for the academy-trained officer of middle-class origin, the army was not just the place to spend some pleasant, youthful years. Spanish officers saw the service as a reward gained through competitive examination and hard work. The ranks they achieved became their property. Unless convicted of major offences they could not be deprived of their ranks and remained in the army until they reached the age for obligatory retirement, which for most officers was in the early sixties.

Since their livelihoods were affected by any change, officers were highly sensitive to attacks on the army, particularly when directed towards their military competence, as happened increasingly after the 1898 defeat at the hands of the United States. Attacks on the army would lead it into a state of acute defensiveness and a hypervaluation of traditional Spanish values.[9] This naturally increased the conflict with progressive sectors.

The anti-militarism of the working class was caused not only by the army's hostile view of what it saw as social indiscipline, but also because it was the working class which bore the brunt of the conditions of military service. Recruits were taken away from families which depended on their earnings. Badly fed and housed, negligibly paid and incompetently if bravely led, their conditions would never improve until young men of the middle class fulfilled their obligations in the same way. But until 1912 it was possible to buy oneself out of military service completely and even afterwards it would be usual for those with higher educational qualifications to do a minimum of service.[10] The result of this was to alienate the more influential middle classes from the army and vice versa. Thus progressive views included anti-militarism as a matter of course and the army in its turn was largely unaffected by modern trends.

Two further details complete the vicious circle. The lack of interest shown in the army by Spain's middle class in comparison with other countries[11] meant that Spain produced very few reserve officers. It was for this reason that the permanent officer corps was so large.

The isolation of the Spanish officer was further increased by his lack of general education. The age of entry into the military academy was usually below eighteen and many had entered much younger.[12] Officers had in fact undergone an experience not unlike trainee priests in a seminary. Much of their previous time had been devoted to cramming for the entrance examination. They had neither served in the ranks nor enjoyed any liberal education. Through no fault of his own but because of the general *desfase* of the Spanish social system, the army officer was out of sympathy with modern trends, though he had no reason to be so; was afraid of working-class and regionalist manifestations of progressivism, though the success of these threatened the army very little; and, because the army was all he had, was often forced into undisciplined defence of his personal career interests.

It was with these attitudes that the Spanish army had gained for itself the Army Act of 1918. The law had created extra posts and imposed strict seniority as the only cause for promotion. Having been successful in this, the army went on to act independently of the civil authorities in suppressing working-class activity until 1923 when the coup of General Primo de Rivera cut short a possible liberal reform of the army and an investigation of the disastrous 1921 defeat in Morocco.[13]

The army, however, was also internally divided over the question of promotion. Should promotion by selection or as a result of battlefield merit be allowed to override seniority? This would seem no more than a technical matter were it not that the political attitude towards it of Primo de Rivera and later of the reforming minister of the Second Republic, Manuel Azaña, were seen as reflections of general political views.[14]

Over promotions and other issues Primo de Rivera came into direct conflict with parts of the army. The attempted rebellions of 1926, 1929 and 1930 against Primo and the monarchy combined the interests of officers opposed to changes in their career structure with progressive trends among a small group.

A certain number of officers, outraged by Primo's machinations to stay in power, and infuriated by the 500 or so field promotions made as a result of the war in Morocco, took part in conspiracies to end the monarchy and bring in a republic. Some, such as Fermín Galán,[15] executed for his part in the 1930 Jaca rebellion, saw the army as spearheading a complete social revolution. Others, such as Ramón Franco, brother of the future dictator, shared with other young airmen an inchoate revolutionary view.[16] Yet others, such as Juan Hernández Saravia, Leopoldo and Arturo Menéndez and Segismundo Casado, were serious, intellectual officers who thought that only profound reform could save Spain.[17]

Much historiography suggests that the radical reform carried out by Manuel Azaña, Minister of War and for most of the time Prime Minister of the 1931–3 governments of the Second Republic, contributed to the army's willingness to rebel in 1936. But it is doubtful whether the Azaña reforms could have had more than a very indirect effect on a decision taken several years later.

Nevertheless, the reforms can be seen as part of a view of what Spain should be and what the army should represent in a liberal, bourgeois republic. Azaña, conscious of the political disarray of the army and of the moment of prestige for the Republic, tackled issues of reform which had come up against invincible parliamentary opposition in the past. He attacked the problem of the gross inflation of the officer corps by offering retirement on full basic pay. Over 8000 of the nearly 21,000 active-list officers accepted the offer. He closed the general military academy in which cadets studied before going to the specialized colleges, and sharply reduced the number of new entrants into the officer corps. He gave non-commissioned officers a special status and, while stopping their route into a second-class list of officers, reserved 60 per cent of academy places for them. He settled the promotions issue by combining the seniority criterion with one of professional examinations. He required all prospective cadets to serve in the ranks and to have passed some university examinations. He rationalized the structure of the army by consolidating half-manned regiments into a smaller number. Abolishing the viceregal remnants reflected in the posts of Captain-General, he took all judicial functions away from the army.[18]

In military circles, the undercurrent of resentment and opposition was, however, fierce. The removal of judicial functions from commanding generals, at a time when trade-union and street political activity and agitation was at its height, together with the government's rejection of the army's traditional role of pronouncing on issues of civilian life, created the excuse for a sustained attack on the reforms in general. It also stimulated the creation of the body of myth whereby the 1931–3 regime was sectarian, and its leader, Azaña, a pervert who nourished hatred for the virile virtues of the army, which he intended to destroy, leaving Spain defenceless and prey to freemasonry and Marxism. Though it may be doubted whether the majority of officers actually felt that they had individual cause for grievance – at any rate more than officers had ever had in the past – the accepted attitude amongst most of them, always excepting those who had progressive views, was that Azaña, and thus the Republic, was betraying the ideals of the army. Thus it was easy for them to readopt the sense of grievance which the army had cherished at least since 1898. In their view politicians were dishonest; the left wing was unpatriotic. The army was the only safeguard for traditional values; the regime, with its anti-clerical legislation, was destroying them. The army, traditionally centralist, saw regionalism gain the upper hand, so it thought, with the 1932 Catalan statute of autonomy. It was not hard to find quotations from excited Catalanists to prove that Catalans would refuse to serve in the Spanish army. Therefore, in military eyes, Catalonia was disloyal and the government was encouraging the treachery. When a group of monarchist military plotters was defeated in General Sanjurjo's rebellion in August 1932, Sanjurjo's consequent imprisonment in a convict prison instead of a military gaol where he would have enjoyed the privileges befitting his rank became another example of the conspiracy theory which the military developed. Yet, half-planned *coups* no longer had a chance of success. The level of political consciousness and of organization, together with the prestige of the Republic, meant that the old-style *pronunciamiento* had to give way to a properly planned simultaneous take-over in most of the garrisons, together with the immediate neutralization of the working-class movement. Accordingly, a divided officer corps was unlikely to succeed. This is generally stated to be the reason why General Franco did not lead a *coup* in 1935 when, under a centre-right government, commands were held by sympathetic generals and he himself was chief of staff, and even more so, in February 1936, after the victory of the Popular Front.[19] Certainly plotting had continued ever since the inauguration of the Republic.[20] It became serious and intensive, however, during the spring and summer of 1936.

The conspiracy of 1936 was carefully planned over many months. Though certain officers itched to take over power in the case of a Popular Front victory, there was not, in February, sufficient unity among the officer corps to justify the risk. It may well be questioned whether the army genuinely feared a cataclysm if there were a left-wing landslide, hence, perhaps, the lack of 'moral unity' of which Franco complained.[21] The historiography of this period speaks of the fear that the Civil Guard would be disbanded and that Azaña, elected President in the spring, would dissolve the army, replacing it with a Socialist militia.[22] Given Azaña's record, it is doubtful whether such moves would have met with his approval. There were certainly Socialist militia, but in spite of their uniforms and marching, flags and slogans, they did not reach even an elementary level of military efficiency.[23] Beyond the usual changes in commands, there were no anti-army measures.

The conspiracy organized by General Mola from Pamplona was slow to take form. In part, it required the acute increase in social disorder of the early summer, culminating in the assassination of the opposition leader Calvo Sotelo, to stimulate support for the rebellion. However, there are other important factors to consider in explaining the inertia of the army officers.

The expectation of success is important; most officers had seen the unsuccessful attempts at *coups* in 1926, 1929, 1930 and 1932 and suspected that the military were really not capable of a successful rising. But patient and detailed planning by Mola ended by his obtaining pledges of support from the Falange, the prestigious General Sanjurjo in exile in Portugal, the Carlists who would provide the first mass civilian support and, perhaps most importantly, agreement from Franco to assume the leadership of the professional forces in Morocco. Only when all these indications of support and reasonably competent planning became evident was confidence created that the *coup* had a chance of success. Even then, the level of commitment varied from garrison to garrison.[24] Nevertheless, there were enough garrisons with small groups of officers who managed to prevail upon their reluctant colleagues to join them. That it was not easy to do is shown by the need to circulate rumours of fictitious Red plots.[25]

There were two more aspects to consider. It had been usual for governments in Spain to use the army at times of public disorder and, though the Republic had tried to avoid this by creating a corps of Republican police – the Assault Guard – this was also paramilitary and commanded by officers seconded from the army. The declaration of states of siege, which brought troops onto the streets, was often judged less provocative than bringing in the ruthless and better trained Civil Guards.[26] Thus,the army expected to be called in. The other consideration, in the event crucial, was the sense of loyalty to fellow-officers fostered in cadets from their academy days. In conservative circles, the Republic was seen as impermanent and most officers could feel no emotional loyalty to it. They clung instead to the ideals of loyalty to the army and the territorial integrity of Spain.

It was with this ideological and emotional equipment that officers threw in their lot with the rebels. In those parts of Spain where the rebels were to be successful, officers felt little hesitation in aligning themselves with their fellows. Not more perhaps than two or three hundred officers who refused to join the rebels were imprisoned or executed by them in their zone.[27] The uprising would fail in many garrisons, however, often because many officers had remained loyal to the government. This was particularly true with the police forces in Barcelona who, together with the militant working class of that city, defeated the garrison. In Madrid, the defeat of the rebels was in no small measure due to loyal officers. While it is true to say that officers posted to the capital had often received that posting precisely because of their trustworthiness, it is also true that many officers in the garrisons in Catalonia, the Levante, the south-east and the north of Spain were unwilling to follow their colleagues.[28] In the Republican zone the behaviour of officers varied for many complex reasons, few of which corresponded to clear political motivations except in the case of the two hundred or so who belonged to the Unión de Militares Republicanos Antifascistas, a body which contrasted with the conservative Unión Militar Española.[29]

When war came, the rebels took over the zone covering nearly all the 5th (Zaragoza), 6th (Burgos), 7th (Valladolid) and 8th (La Coruña) administrative divisions of the Spanish army, as well as most of the garrisons of the 2nd (Seville) division, all the Moroccan army, the troops on the Canary Islands and the Balearics except for the sizeable base at Mahón on Minorca.[30] The divisions remained in operation with no more than a change in supreme command in the cases of Generals Villabrille, Batet, Molero, Salcedo and of Gómez Morato, who was High Commissioner in Morocco. Only a minority of generals in senior command joined the rebellion mainly because, as might be expected, the government had tried to appoint men it considered reliable. In fact, a large number of generals were imprisoned, dismissed or executed after the war began because their loyalty and often their actions were suspect. A considerable number of divisional generals – La Cerda, Riquelme, Peña, Masquelet and García-Gómez Caminero, served the Republic during the war as did many brigadier generals. But some – Patxot, García Aldave, de Miquel, Fernández Burriel, Lon, Fernández Ampón, Bosch Atienza, Legorburu, Araujo and Grijalvo (Civil Guard) – were shot in the Republican zone. Romerales, Campins and Caridad were executed by the rebels, as were the divisional generals Batet and Salcedo. The peculiar structure of the army ensured that only the exceptional divisional general was young enough to campaign actively. Some brigadier generals did occupy important commands in both armies for the rest of the conflict, but the majority were dismissed or retired compulsorily provided they were still at liberty in one or other part of Spain. The war would have to be a young man's one. Franco was one of the youngest generals. Fanjul and Goded, who were shot for their part in the failed *coup*, were among the younger ones. No brigadier generals except for Miaja, the 'saviour' of Madrid and Republican commander in central Spain for almost the whole of the war, played a significant part in high active command for more than a short time.[31]

As for the other professional officers, many in the rebel zone were not employed because of doubts about their political background or their professional capability. In the Republican zone, however, perhaps 4000 officers from the active or retired lists were imprisoned or executed for participation or suspicion of involvement in the rebellion. Many others would stay concealed or attempt to flee to the other side.[32] Others would fulfil their minimum military obligations, but with little enthusiasm. Their unwillingness would be noted and they would be shunted into office jobs or, often mistakenly, into officer-training schools or even more sensitive areas where they would sabotage the war effort. One senior officer who was in charge of an artillery repair workshop in Madrid turned out to be an important Franco agent.[33] Other officers served the Republic with great loyalty and self-denial. These were men such as Vicente Rojo, recently promoted major in 1936, who rose to be chief of the general staff and responsible for planning most of the Republic's initially successful offensives; or Juan Hernández Saravia, a retired lieutenant-colonel and close associate of Azaña, who ended the war in command of an army. There were low-ranking retired officers such as Juan Perea and Adolfo Prada, both of whom commanded armies, and there were perhaps 2500 other professional officers on the active list in 1936 who served in the Republican army.[34] There were certainly officers who were loyal to the Republic for obviously political reasons: members of the Communist Party such as the two Galáns, brothers of the Fermín who had become the proto-martyr of the Republic, and Catalan nationalist sympathisers such as Enrique Pérez Farrás, who had escaped execution in 1934 for his participation in the October rebellion.[35] Other officers served quietly and conscientiously throughout the conflict, organizing and administering from offices and staff headquarters. Some officers were known to have distinctly conservative views, such as Colonel Escobar, who led the Civil Guard against rebel army units in Barcelona in July 1936, would go on to command an army and be executed by the victorious rebels.

At the beginning of the war, the attitude of the Republican militias towards the professional officers was frankly unfavourable. They might accept them as advisers or '*técnicos*' but they refused to accept their orders and suspected them of treachery. Some officers, in attempts to prove themselves, or perhaps to try to pass over to the other side, risked their own lives. Only the Spanish Communist Party's Fifth Regiment took up the position that the professional officers were to be respected and obeyed, even if they were not politically on the left. This position was based on the experience of the use made by the Red Army of Tsarist officers during the Russian civil war.[36]

In order to check on the loyalty of professional officers, and to some extent to guarantee them and give them the confidence to lead militia columns and later regular units, the hurriedly reconstructed War Ministry organized the Committee of Investigation (Gabinete de Información y Control). This GIC classified officers as F (fascists), R (Republicans) or I (Indifferent). In the few months of the war there was indescribable chaos with officers not knowing which units to report to and no clear chain of command on the administrative side.[37] This would go on until the reconstruction of the general staff by Largo Caballero after he took office as Prime Minister and Minister of War on 4 September 1936. Throughout 1937 and 1938 the Gabinete de Información y Control would continue to classify professional officers who were then either confirmed in their commands and given retroactive promotions, or dismissed. The Gabinete's job was perhaps essential, but complaints that political bias was depriving the Republic of good officers were frequent.[38]

Officers were constantly criticized for incapacity or lack of enthusiasm. The problem was often that many of them were trying to hold commands which were beyond their capacity. This occurred partly because of the need to select commanders of large formations from amongst a considerable choice of low-ranking majors and captains. There was a real absence of suitable senior officers with infantry combat experience.[39] This contrasted sharply with the rebel army which enjoyed the services of most of the younger colonels such as Muñoz Grandes, Martín Alonso and García Escámez. Practically the only officer of the necessary quality serving with the government was José Asensio Torrado, a staff colonel whom Largo Caballero promoted to general and gave overall command of the theatre of operations in central Spain. A combination of bad luck, the loss of Málaga and Asensio's own inability to compromise with the demands of the political forces behind the army brought his downfall.[40] One unfortunate result of the freedom to make promotions through merit which the government gave itself was the consequent rivalry, on which President Azaña, who had tried to solve the problem in 1931, commented 'Rivalry and disputes over promotion; there is no end to it.'[41] All Republican NCOs, if favourably reported on, were promoted to the rank of lieutenant, and all officers obtained one 'loyalty' promotion. Some had brilliant war careers. Six generals of the Republican army (Rojo, Matallana, Jurado, Menéndez, Casado and Hidalgo de Cisneros) began the war as majors. This is in stark contrast with the rebel army where, perhaps because of the memory of the trouble caused in the past by battlefield merit promotions, officers were usually made up to an acting rank (*estampillado*), and only one major (García Valiño) became a general.

In the Republican army, ex-lieutenants of the Civil Guard, often promoted NCOs, were acting as brigade chiefs of staff, and sergeants were directing artillery batteries. The archives of the Republican army are full of reports by its own commanders attacking the inefficiency of the junior officers. Their inability to manoeuvre and to advance independently once the tactical breakthrough had been made, is an aspect of performance which is obvious in the battles of La Granja (June 1937) and Brunete (July 1937).[42] These battles, like those of Belchite, Teruel and the Ebro, were characterized by initial success, followed by inability to exploit it, especially if the resistance was obstinate. The battles then degenerated into slogging matches, until exhaustion set in or the Republican forces were obliged to withdraw. The chief of staff, Vicente Rojo, complained about careless talk, disobedience, lack of confidence, insistence on outdated tactics, unwillingness of the officers to stay close to their units and many other quite elementary matters.[43] So frequent was this kind of report that one can only conclude that the Republican army did in fact suffer from inefficiency which led to or stemmed from a lack of will and the breakdown of social authority.

The shortage of professional officers was made up not only by the massive promotions of loyal NCOs but also by the creation of a new officer corps. The Republican militia elected their own officers. Not until January 1938 were they allowed to advance beyond the rank of major even though some of them such as Modesto, Enrique Líster, and Valentín González 'El Campesino', among the Communists, and Cipriano Mera, Gregorio Jover and Miguel García Vivancos among the anarcho-syndicalists, were commanding divisions and army corps. A few would be promoted to lieutenant-colonel in 1938. Enrique Líster would become a colonel and Modesto, fleetingly, a general at the very end of the war. It was these militia leaders who were the subjects of the flowery writing of many politically motivated authors and journalists of the time. Later studies have cast doubt on their brilliance, also for political reasons, though it has to be said that they commanded through example and that the technical work was often done by capable and self-effacing professional staff officers. Given the circumstances, however, a fair conclusion is that the militia leaders showed remarkable ability.[44]

Militia officers and regulars were still insufficient to command an army which was growing fast. Early in the war, schools were established for the emergency training of temporary wartime officers, called *tenientes en campaña*. The schools included the emergency wartime staff college for training professional officers and civilians. The problem of untrained members of brigade and even divisional staffs was serious and multiplied by the Republican army's larger number of independent units. In the army of Extremadura, for instance, as late as April 1938, only the chief of staff had passed a staff course. The other staff officers were a *teniente en campaña* and militia officers.[45]

In spite of reorganizations, however, the officer schools of the Republican army would never provide sufficient temporary wartime officers.[46] The real reason was probably social. The type of young man who would be officer material in most armies, would be automatically under suspicion in Republican Spain because of his higher social class and education. He himself would be less likely to want to be an officer because of lack of sympathy for the breakdown of social order he had seen and because to be an officer was in itself a political statement in that it required a certificate of loyalty from a political party or trade union. Furthermore, the political orthodoxy required by authorities which in 1937 suppressed dissidents and the social revolution may also have contributed to reducing the number of young men who came forward to be officers of the Ejército Popular.

All this contrasts with the rebel army where temporary second-lieutenants (*alféreces provisionales*) were trained in increasing numbers in a total of twenty-eight academies providing a basic training for the command of platoons. In all nearly 30,000 *alféreces provisionales* were turned out.[47] And there was no shortage of competent professionals to command larger units.

The contrast between the two parts of Spain divided by the uprising cannot be more striking. In Republican Spain (Madrid, New Castile, Catalonia and the Levante, the Basque provinces, Santander and the Asturias), the conscript army units, though numerically nearly as large as in rebel Spain, were demoralized by the actions of their officers. In Madrid, in particular, where troops had abandoned their barracks and mingled with the triumphant militia, it was very difficult to assemble any coherent forces. The archives of the Republican War Ministry reveal the heterogeneity of these 'regular' troops, scattered in small packets among columns of political and trade union militia, commanded by improvised leaders or by NCOs and officers whom they did not know. It is true that the columns of militia were sometimes reinforced by paramilitary units but even these were largely composed of men recruited since the rebellion. Furthermore, after the sacking of the depots it was often hard even to find sufficient rifles which worked.

It was the immense enthusiasm, heterogeneity and military inefficiency of the militia which characterized Republican forces in the early weeks of the war. They numbered some 80,000 at their height, in addition to the 30,000 or so fighting on the Aragon front. The militia were heroic and inspired by dreams of social revolution, but untrained, ill-led and distrustful of the few professional leaders they had. They were easily put to flight by the experienced and highly trained though small units of the Moroccan army as it advanced north through Extrem-

adura and up to the capital.[48] Professional officers and NCOs had to
contend with the political demands for consultation made by the militia,
who would not accept orders without debate, yet required officers to
lead operations. Many loyal officers were placed in an impossible
quandary. They wanted to serve the Republic, but they could not function in charge of undisciplined, inexperienced men who might often
resist the superior skill of the rebel columns with great bravery but were
ideologically opposed to accepting a discipline which the revolutionary
moment could not possibly impose. This was the reason why so many
officers gravitated towards the Communist Party which in the pages of
Milicia Popular, the daily paper of the Fifth Regiment, stressed the
importance of formal military organization.

The rebel, insurgent or nationalist army also had its militias. But
their political creed included respect for the military hierarchy. There
were the Carlist *Requetés* and the men of the Falange. Attempts to
maintain Carlist and Falangist militias separate from the army were
summarily quashed. Militias were brought formally under military
jurisdiction on 20 December 1936, though this had already happened in
effect. Republican militias were also militarized in a decree which
appeared on 30 September 1936 but the militia spirit and the consciousness of belonging to a particular political background would remain a
feature of the Republican army throughout the conflict.

The essential difference between the Republican and the rebel zones
was the dominance in the latter of the army. The rebellion itself had
consisted of the declaration of a state of war by unilateral decision of the
army. A state of war was not declared in the Republican zone until very
late in the war, precisely because this meant giving the military full
control. The dominance of the army in the rebel zone was accompanied
by the swift establishment of unity, both military and political, under
Franco. In the Republican zone command would belong, constitution-
ally, to the ministers of war and later of national defence, who were
Largo Caballero, Prieto and lastly Negrín; the military command was in
the form of a chief of staff who had no civilian authority. In the rebel
zone, authority was immediately entrusted to officers or to civilians
whom they selected. Government was assumed by the Junta de Defensa
Nacional, composed of generals and colonels. On 29 September 1936
General Franco was made *generalísimo* and head of state by the Junta.

The war was run by Franco and his headquarters staff with no civilian interference.

At first the rebels fought in columns, of the kind familiar to them from the Moroccan campaigns. They were based on the existing administrative divisions. Though rebel army units in the Peninsula were composed of green conscripts, it has to be stressed that they marched out from their barracks in Burgos or Valladolid, Seville or La Coruña, with all their equipment, their own NCOs and officers, and free of the mass of undisciplined militia which, in Madrid, Barcelona, Valencia and other cities held by the Republic, had invaded military establishments.

Only when the rebel army grew with mobilizations and volunteers were the early columns formed into larger units and then into divisions and corps. In the Republican army, in contrast, the urge to militarize, restore the authority of the state and put order into the haphazard militia, meant that brigades, divisions and corps were formed at speed, without the benefit of existing administrative organization or bases. Units might be formed on paper, often without arms and frequently without officers to command them. Whereas in the rebel zone almost all divisional commanders had been on the active list before the war, many Republican commanders had had no military experience for several years. The rebel commanders had been pre-war generals and colonels. At divisional level they were usually senior officers, nearly always belonging to the infantry. Republican command lists show how frequently commanders had been only majors, captains or lieutenants in 1936. Brigades were commanded by militia officers or officers of the Civil Guard or *Carabiñeros*, but rarely by senior infantry officers.[49] In other words, one side used fully professional infantry officers to command units within their competence; the other had a few inexperienced men commanding large units for which they were not competent, looking over their shoulders all the time in case they were accused of disloyalty or political unreliability. Republican battalions were nearly always led by new men whereas in the rebel forces the *alféreces provisionales* were entrusted with the smallest units only. Their training, organized by the monarchist general Orgaz, was brief and efficient, while Republican training of officers was often over-theoretical.[50]

One consequence of rebel unity of command was the ease of decision-making. While the Republic, split between military and political considerations, argued about whether to strike in the insurgent rear by seaborne landings or not, Franco was able in March 1937 to desist from bloody attempts to take Madrid – attempts which had failed in the winter of 1936 and at the battles of the Jarama and Guadalajara in the following year – and to concentrate on the weak north, cut off because of the inability of the Republican fleet to gain command of the sea. Later in the war, Franco would make up his mind correctly to take the decision, doubtful at the time, of tackling a well-organized and well-equipped enemy on the Ebro. In spite of the three months' struggle put up by Republican forces, when they at last retired over the river, their two armies – of the Ebro and of the East – were so weakened that they could not resist Franco's thrust into Catalonia.

The movement of vast resources and men to different fronts at speed was only possible with centralized command and efficient logistics. Nationalist reaction to sudden Republican offensives, as at Brunete in July 1937, Teruel in December 1937, or on the Ebro in July 1938, was rapidly to bring up reserves from other fronts. On the other hand, garrisons and fronts were denuded to create forces for major assaults because it was evident that the Republic was not able to organize its strength in such a way as to take advantage of such weakened fronts. In contrast, the Republic found great administrative and logistic difficulty in massive and swift transfers of men to threatened points.

Manoeuvre at lower levels in Franco's army was not brilliant. Infantry tactics were probably no more advanced than those of the Great War. Nevertheless, once the enemy was in flight, pursuit was swift though the opportunities offered by the German and Italian fast tanks to envelop Republican forces in retreat were not taken. In fact, neither of the sides in the Spanish war was skilful nor experienced enough for any serious lesson to be drawn from the conflict on the ground. Neither side fought a war of swift movement; both engaged in long battles in which they fought to exhaustion.

After the initial inflow of volunteers and militia, both sides called up classes of conscripts. Half of the class of 1936 was already in the army. Much of the class of the second semester of 1935 was on summer leave. In the government zone the classes of 1934 and 1935 were immediately recalled. The classes of 1930 to 1939 were called during 1937. In early 1938 the classes of 1929 and 1940 were called up and in April 1938, with the great rout which led to the division of Republican Spain into two, came the turn of the classes of 1927 and 1928 and that of 1941. Soon afterwards even older men from the classes of 1923, 1924, 1925 and 1926 were called. In early 1939, in desperation, classes going back to 1915 were called. In all twenty-seven classes of conscripts were called up to the Republican army.[51] The problem was the absence of a reception system which could cope with these immense numbers of men. Centros de Reclutamiento, Instrucción y Movilización were set up in 1937 but evidence shows that political manipulation sometimes directed men into certain units.[52] Training appears to have been rudimentary. One cannot tell what amount of evasion of the draft there was, although in 1938 and 1939, evasion and desertion was widespread as a result of the great defeats in Aragon and the retreat through Catalonia. There was also considerable movement from one side to the other, probably more to the rebels than in the other direction.

The rebels called up fewer classes of men and did so having the organization to do it properly. In all, the classes of 1927 to 1940 were conscripted.

The initially heavier concentration of population in the Republican zone gave the government an advantage, though this was outbalanced by more efficient recruitment on the other side where the political militia were swiftly brought under military control. After the northern provinces had been taken by the rebels in 1937, Republican prisoners were incorporated into the Nationalist army. Rebel advances into Extremadura in late 1936, to Málaga in February 1937, and the overrunning of Aragon and parts of the Levante in 1938 increased the supply of recruits. By the end of the war, the rebels had 1,025,500 troops under arms.[53]

In discussing sheer weight of numbers, the non-Spanish contribution has to be considered. The most diverse figures have been given for the Republican army's International Brigades, but the most reliable indicate a total of 59,380.[54] The Brigades became more and more Spanish in composition after the rush of initial recruitment had eased and the battles around Madrid in 1937 had destroyed the original formations.

As for Russians, a few hundred Russian advisers, interpreters and, in the early months, tank drivers, pilots and certain specialists went to Spain.[55] Russian advisers were present at staff and large unit headquarters and may occasionally have taken over the direction of battle at difficult moments from Communist militia leaders. That they had any serious influence on organization or tactics is doubtful. The mixed brigade, the characteristic small independent unit of the Republican army, which is said to have been foisted on the Spaniards by their Soviet advisers,[56] was a unit which already existed in Spanish military organization. It was also the most convenient way of militarizing the militia battalions. In reality, whatever the role of the Soviet political advisers and the non-Russian Communists who appeared in Spain under diplomatic or International Brigade cover, the Russian military advisers seem to have been self-effacing.[57]

In the Nationalist army, there was a constant supply of men from the Moroccan protectorate, with possibly up to 70,000 soldiers serving.[58] Italian ground troops numbered 72,775.[59] These figures are totals and the figure at any one time was substantially less. The Legion or Tercio de Extranjeros was almost completely Spanish in composition.

Like other armies, both Spanish forces had élite units, which suffered high losses and were constantly replenished. For the Republic these were the International Brigades in the early part of the war. But individual Republican militia fought bravely if unskilfully and many later brigades and divisions achieved renown as crack units. They would be heavily used and also constantly replenished. For the rebels, élite formations included the Moors and the Legion as well as some of the ex-militias such as the Carlist *Requetés*.

The Spanish war was one of mass armies, unlike anything that Spain had ever experienced. Consequently many of the phenomena of such armies were present. These were more marked in the Republican army precisely because it was a formal structure grafted on to a revolutionary situation. It therefore had to undertake an immense amount of educational activity to convince politically conscious and naturally anti-militarist men that, though the professional officers were the rebels, professionalization and militarization in themselves were not wrong. The Communists grasped this at once and the pages of *Milicia Popular* were full of attempts to hammer home the message that military discipline and respect for professional competence was of the essence of victory. This contrasted with the atmosphere in other militia units where the military rebellion had made it seem obvious that the war could be won by revolutionary means only, without the outmoded and discredited forms of the traditional army such as uniforms and hierarchies of rank. This feeling was most marked among the anarchists. Gradually, however, they became convinced, after the sequence of militia defeats in 1936, that the 'discipline of indiscipline' did not work. It was also brought home to them that if they wished to preserve the character of their units they would have to accept militarization with uniforms, ranks, brigade and divisional organization and the rest. Otherwise the new organs of state defence would not supply them with arms. It was the anarchist political officers, or commissars, who persuaded their men to accept militarization.[60]

The commissar system arose naturally in such an army. The title should not lead to the assumption that it was a Soviet imposition. The Republican battalions of militia usually had political leaders who co-operated more or less with the professional NCOs and officers. As the militia were brought under military law, it became advisable to maintain the political officer and this was done by a decree at the beginning of Largo Caballero's leadership.[61] The role of the political commissar in instructing new recruits in the meaning and purpose of the war, in seeing to their welfare and general education and in both overseeing and co-operating with the officers was one which required the preparation of masses of paper instructions produced for and by the Comisariado de Guerra for the moral and physical welfare of the troops.[62] It was needed only because of the uncertain authority of the officers and NCOs. In the Nationalist army moral exhortation was the concern of the unit chaplain. Other matters came under the NCOs and the officers. It was unnecessary to explain why, for instance, rifles and one's body had to be kept clean, yet such exhortations are frequently found in Republican commissar literature.

This was the essential difference in the character of the two armies. The Republican army was revolutionary in that it believed in persuasion rather than compulsion; but it lacked the revolutionary fervour, the sense of common purpose and the ready acceptance of discipline that in real revolutionary armies has made up for the lack of military experience and often of material.

What is striking in the contrast between the two armies is that the 'revolutionary' one was often the more conservative. It created a paper army without having the men and arms, much less sufficient competent and trusted commanders, to run it.[63] The rebels used the existing structure and created units as they had the resources to do so. Franco's army always had fewer divisions and corps than its opponents, which meant great savings in services, officers and staffs.[64]

The absence of guerrilla forces is also surprising in the country which gave them their name. The rebels had none at all. The Republicans did organize a certain number of guerrilla units. Although they do not seem to have had the support of the civilian population, Republican guerrilla units appear to have been able, by relatively minor acts of sabotage, to have alarmed their enemy, and it may well be asked why this method of fighting was not expanded. The answer must be that, following the Great War, such methods of fighting seemed perhaps out of date for the 1930s. The essential independence of guerrillas was anathema both to the authoritarian centralists of government and to the conservative officers who organized the Republican army, let alone to the Communists who played such an important part in giving the army its tone.[65]

To conclude with some generalizations, both sides had politically conscious militia and non-political conscripts. For the Republic the militia were a source of strife; for the rebels they were on the contrary the source of their strength. Republican conscripts suffered from a fairly justified lack of confidence in their leadership. Nationalist soldiers were resigned and trusting, aware that the Legion and the Moors would tackle the toughest operations.

Styles of battle were different also. The tactical concepts of Vicente Rojo and the initial dash of the best Republican units contrasted with the solidity of the rebel forces, their steady pushes and their better logistics, all of which, aided by the better flow and management of their arms supply, brought victory to them and defeat and disgrace to their opponents.

Notes

1 There are few accounts by army officers, even of the simple 'to save Spain from Marxism' kind. Perhaps an exception is the aviator J. A. Ansaldo's *¿Para qué ?... De Alfonso XIII a Juan III* (Buenos Aires, 1951).

2 There is a growing number of works on the Spanish Army. See S. Payne, *Politics and the Military in Modern Spain* (Stanford, 1967); Carolyn Boyd,

Pretorian Politics in Liberal Spain (Chapel Hill, 1979); J. Busquets, *El militar de carrera en España* (Barcelona, 1967); F. Fernández Bastarreche, *El ejército español en el siglo XIX* (Madrid, 1978); M. Alpert, *La reforma militar de Azaña* (Madrid, 1982).

3 Fernández Bastarreche, op. cit., ch. 6, and Busquets, op. cit., 99.

4 For a discussion on this see the work on French military policy by Manuel Azaña, *Estudios de política militar francesa*, in *Obras Completas* (Mexico, 1966), vol. I.

5 See Azaña, op. cit., *passim* for a view of this.

6 See J. Romero-Maura, *The Spanish army and Catalonia: the Cu-Cut! incident and the law of jurisdictions 1915–1916*, Sage Research Papers in the Social Sciences, 5 (London, 1976).

7 See Boyd, op. cit., 44–113.

8 Busquets, op. cit., 85–8, 151. Fernández Bastarreche, op. cit., 110–17.

9 Romero-Maura, op. cit., 11. For the post-Civil War army's social isolation see Busquets, op. cit., 51–2.

10 Boyd, op. cit., 30.

11 There seems to have been a dearth of militarist-type literature in earlier twentieth-century Spain compared with other European countries. Proto- and pseudo-military organizations for boys also seem to have been lacking.

12 To take the rebel generals of 1936 as examples, Queipo de Llano and Saliquet entered the service at 16, Franco at 14 and Goded, incredibly, at 13 years 8 months. See *Anuarios Militares*, Madrid.

13 Boyd, op. cit., 236 ff.

14 Payne, op. cit., ch. 12. Alpert, op. cit., ch. 4.

15 For Galán see Payne, op. cit., 260–2.

16 For Ramón Franco and the airmen see Azaña, *Memorias políticas*, 5 July 1931, in *Obras*, vol. IV.

17 See R. Salas, *Historia del Ejército Popular de la República* (Madrid, 1973) and M. Alpert, *El ejército republicano en la guerra civil*, (Paris-Barcelona, 1977), biographical index. Many of Primo's opponents were also the beneficiaries of battlefield promotions.

18 For an account of the Azaña reforms see Payne, op. cit., Salas, op. cit., and Alpert, *La reforma militar de Azaña*.

19 Payne, op. cit., 88.

20 Examples of monarchist military plotting are given in Paul Preston, 'Alfonsist Monarchism and the coming of the Spanish civil war', *Journal of Contemporary History*, 7 (nos. 3 and 4), 91–2, 95.

21 Payne, op. cit., 312.

22 Payne, op. cit., 321, 326, collects examples of these fears.

23 Alpert, *El ejército republicano*, 16, 18.

24 This can best be seen in the tendentious but detailed work of J. Arrarás, *Historia de la Cruzada española* (Madrid, 1940–3) which examines events in

each garrison. Luis Romero, *Tres días de julio* (Barcelona, 1967) also gives a vivid picture of military indecision. Officers' motives are also illustrated in R. Fraser, *Blood of Spain* (Harmondsworth, 1979).

25 Payne, op. cit., 351.

26 Romero-Maura, op. cit., 8–9.

27 See Alpert, *El ejército republicano*, 132, n. 14, for a discussion of this.

28 See Arrarás, op. cit., and L. Romero, op. cit.

29 Alpert, *El ejército republicano*, 15, and Payne, op. cit., 317.

30 For brief accounts of the war effort on both sides, see *Revista de Historia Militar* (Madrid), 17, 59–117 and R. Salas, *Los datos exactos de la guerra civil* (Madrid, 1980). For the best war history, see the series of campaign monographs by J. M. Martínez Bande (Madrid, 1967 et seq.).

31 For an account of the vicissitudes of professional officers, see Alpert, *El ejército republicano*, 101–39.

32 ibid., app. 10 for a calculation of numbers imprisoned and killed.

33 S. Casado, *Así cayó Madrid* (Madrid, 1968), 209.

34 The question of how many regular officers served in the Republican army is still sensitive. The figure of 2000–2500 is based on the figures for artillery officers which have been calculated by comparing the provisional list of 1938 (Servicio Histórico Militar, Archivo de la Guerra de Liberación, Documentación Roja, leg. 506) with the list in the 1936 *Anuario Militar*. In 1938 14 per cent were still in the Republican army. The same percentage of the entire officer corps would give 2187 officers.

35 See the index to Salas, *Ejército Popular*, and Alpert, *El ejército republicano*, app. 13 (biographies).

36 For the Communist view, see *Milicia Popular* (rep. Barcelona, 1977).

37 See J. Martín Blázquez, *I Helped to Build an Army* (London, 1939).

38 For the Gabinete, see Salas, *Ejército Popular*, 1, 220.

39 A. Cordón, *Trayectoria: recuerdos de un artillero* (Paris, 1971), 71.

40 Martín Blázquez, op. cit., 316 and J. Asensio, *El general Asensio: su lealtad a la República* (Barcelona, 1938).

41 *Obras*, vol. IV, 889. 'Rivalidades y disputas por los ascensos; esto no tiene remedio.'

42 For published criticisms see R. Casas, *Brunete* (Madrid, 1967), app. 1, and Martínez Bande, *Brunete* (Madrid, 1972), documents 9–13.

43 See his *España heróica* (Buenos Aires, 1942), *passim*.

44 For these men see Alpert, *Ejército republicano*; Salas, *Ejército Popular*; and J. Modesto, *Soy del Quinto Regimiento* (Paris, 1969); E. Líster, *Nuestra guerra* (Paris, 1966); Valentín González, *Comunista en España* (Mexico, 1952); Cipriano Mera, *Guerra, exilio y cárcel de un anarcosindicalista* (Paris, 1976); and J. Peirats, *La CNT en la revolución española* (Toulouse, 1951–3).

45 For details of military education in the Republican army see J. M. Gárate, *Tenientes en Campaña* (Madrid, 1976).

46 The total trained was 13,339. Gárate, op. cit., 239.

47 J. M. Gárate, *Alféreces provisionales* (Madrid, 1976), 332.

48 See J. M. Martínez Bande, *La marcha sobre Madrid* (Madrid, 1968) and his *La invasión de Aragón y el desembarco en Mallorca* (Madrid, 1970), for accounts of the earlier battles. See also the account books of the *Comandancia de Milicias* and an abstract from it, together with a list of Basque militias, in Alpert, *El ejército republicano*, apps. 4 and 5.

49 ibid., app. 12 for comparative lists of commanders.

50 ibid., 167–79 and Gárate, *Tenientes en Campaña*.

51 For mobilization details see R. Salas, *Los datos exactos*, 288–9.

52 Peirats, op. cit., III, 91.

53 Salas, *Los datos exactos*, 289.

54 A. Castells, *Las brigadas internacionales de la guerra de España* (Barcelona, 1974), 383.

55 See Alpert, *El ejército republicano*, 251–8 and, for a contrasting view, J. M. Alcófar Nassaes, *Los asesores soviéticos en la guerra civil española* (Barcelona, 1971).

56 S. Casado, op. cit., 77.

57 For an account of their activity in Spain by the Russian advisers who survived the Stalinist purges and the Second World War see *Bajo la Bandera de la República española* (Moscow, n.d. [1967?]).

58 35,000 at the end of the war. Salas, *Los datos exactos*, 173. But many more must have served.

59 See J. Coverdale, *Italian Intervention in the Spanish Civil War* (Princeton, 1975), 396.

60 See Mera, op. cit. Also personal information from the González Inestal brothers, sub-commissars general nominated by the CNT.

61 For the text, see *Gaceta de Madrid*, 17 October 1936.

62 For a small selection of the bibliography of the literature see V. Palacio Atard, *Cuadernos bibliográficos de la guerra de España* (Madrid, 1966–9), series 2, vol. 1.

63 '. . . Hemos creado un Ejército con el nombre de tal, con toda la nomenclatura y sistema de mandos de un Ejército regular . . . pero olvidamos que . . . sólo hemos subido los primeros peldaños para alcanzar la cumbre.' From a report by the Republican chief of staff, Vicente Rojo dated April 1938 in Servicio Histórico Militar, Archivo de la Guerra de Liberación, Documentación Roja, leg. 507, carpeta 1.

64 At the end of 1937 the Republican forces comprised six armies, with nineteen corps, fifty-eight divisions and 168 brigades. See SHM, AGL, Documentación Roja, leg. 462. At approximately the same time the Nationalists had four armies with eleven corps or groups and thirty-seven divisions. Their brigades were not independent units.

65 See Alpert, *El ejército republicano*, 291–6, for a discussion of the question of guerrillas.

10
The popular experience of war and revolution 1936–9

Ronald Fraser

Within weeks of the start of the Spanish Civil War, deep divisions emerged in the Republican camp on the question of revolution and war. These divisions, which reflected different political concepts of the nature of the war, remained a source of bitter dissension throughout the conflict and undermined the Republican war effort. At stake was not only the indispensable task of implementing a politico-military strategy capable of winning the war but – arising directly out of this strategy – also the wider issue of the type of society which would emerge from a future victory. The question in essence was: what were people in the Republican zone fighting for?[1]

As presented in the slogans of the time, the divisions appeared as a question of priorities: victory in the war first to ensure the subsequent triumph of the revolution, or the triumph of the revolution to ensure victory in the war. The war must come first, argued the Spanish Communist Party (PCE), supported by right-wing Socialist and liberal Republicans. Losing the war meant losing the revolution. No, responded the mass of the anarcho-syndicalist CNT, left Socialists and dissident Communists of the POUM: if the revolution did not triumph the war could not be won. Losing the revolution meant losing the war. Polarized between war and revolution, revolution and war, the polemic in fact obscured rather more of the reality of the situation than it revealed.

To understand what was obscured, we must begin by looking at the revolution which was precipitated in large areas of the Republican zone by the military rising. The defeat of the insurgents at the *combined* hands of loyal police forces and political and trade-union militants in five of Spain's seven largest cities extinguished not only the military's hope of rapid success but effectively disarticulated existing Republican state institutions. With the people armed and the state deprived of its coercive forces – the police, Civil Guard and what remained of the army could no longer be counted on – state power virtually collapsed overnight.

The new situation took the leadership of the left's political parties and organizations by surprise. Of no organization was this truer than of the CNT. 'We had set out to defend ourselves, to defend the working class against the military, not to make the revolution', observed Andreu Capdevila, a leading Barcelona CNT militant. 'But the Catalan proletariat had been thoroughly inculcated with anarcho-syndicalist revolutionary propaganda, it had been ingrained in the workers that any possible chance to make the revolution must be seized, so that when the chance came they seized it.'

Significantly, no left organization issued calls for revolutionary takeovers of factories, workplaces or the land. Indeed, the CNT leadership in Barcelona, epicentre of urban anarcho-syndicalism, went further: fer of power presented to it by President Companys, it libertarian revolution must stand aside for collaboration lar Front forces to defeat the common enemy. The revolution that transformed Barcelona in a matter of days into a city virtually run by the working class sprang initially from individual CNT unions, impelled by their most advanced militants; and as their example spread it was not only large enterprises but small workshops and businesses that were being taken over. The effects of expropriating the petty bourgeoisie were, very shortly, to increase opposition to the revolution, but in the euphoria of the moment the anarcho-syndicalists were oblivious to the danger. The revolution was triumphant: factories were working, public transport was running, food supplies were arriving, gas and water supplies functioning, cinemas and even greyhound tracks open − all to one extent or another organized and run by their respective workers.

It was not only the anarcho-syndicalists who felt the profound revolutionary change. A Madrid Communist railwayman, Narciso Julián, who had reached Barcelona on the night before the rising, was swept up by the tidal wave.

> It was incredible, the proof in practice of what one knows in theory: the power and strength of the masses when they take to the streets. Suddenly you feel their creative power; you can't imagine how rapidly the masses are capable of organizing themselves. The forms they invent go far beyond anything you've dreamt of, read in books. What was needed now was to seize this initiative, give it shape.

In Madrid itself, the revolution appeared somewhat more muted, in part because the capital was less industrialized than Barcelona, in part because the Socialist-led UGT was the dominant trade union. None the less, great numbers of workplaces were taken over and run by their workers.

In the countryside, committees created in haste by local left-wing militants to run villages and townships, seized land and initiated a profound agrarian revolution that, within a year of the start of the war, included some 800 rural collectives grouping 400,000 day-labourers and peasants. Many of these collectives were run jointly by anarcho-syndicalist and Socialist trade-union members.

The revolution's armed expression, the militias, organized by the trade unions and political parties, set out with great rapidity to defeat the enemy. Hastily formed and poorly armed, they took the initiative in rushing from Madrid to conquer and hold not only the passes of the Guadarrama but the neighbouring provinces. From Barcelona, thousands of men, many of whom had never handled a rifle in their lives, poured westwards to liberate Aragon. There was little doubt at that moment of the major revolutionary task: to crush the enemy.

'The people's revolutionary instinct was amazing', reflected Wilebaldo Solano, secretary of the POUM's youth movement.

> They knew they had to inflict one defeat after another, move ahead every minute. The cry went up – 'To Zaragoza!' I remember Sgt Manzana, who later became famous alongside Durruti in the latter's column, saying to me: 'To Zaragoza? We're still surrounded by fascists here. We've got to consolidate first. . . .' He was right, of course; but the people were even more right. The movement to set off – and which was such madness in military eyes – came from the streets, from the revolutionary turmoil, no one knew from whom or how.

There could be no disputing the extent and depth of the revolutionary upheaval; there could, however, be more than some doubt as to whether this multi-faceted, centrifugal revolution could consolidate itself. At issue was the question of power.

The problem was most immediately apparent in Barcelona. There, while the CNT had officially refused the offer of power, it exercised almost total power through its domination of the Popular Front Antifascist Militia Committee while refusing to turn the latter into the sole organ of power. In Barcelona, as in Madrid, the legally instituted Republican governments continued to exist. The revolutionaries drove past these patently powerless governments as though they were corpses. Moribund they might be, having lost their freedom of action, credibility, even the use of their coercive forces, but they continued to breathe; and one day new life might be instilled into them.

Meanwhile, power was atomized in myriad committees throughout the Republican zone.[2] Such division of power, normal to an incomplete revolution, could not, in the crucible of a civil war, continue for long. And it was precisely at the front that the absence of a central revolutionary power made itself most rapidly felt. Each party and trade union continued to have its own militia headquarters, supply services, transport, etc., which attended to the requirements of its own columns with scant regard for the rest. Such central staff as there was, was in no way able to formulate a common strategy of action and allocate supplies of men and arms – the latter always scarce – according to an effective plan. Sufficient for the initial moments, the decentralized militias were proving inadequate for the task of fighting a sustained war. As they fell back in disarray before the insurgents' main fighting force, the army of Africa, in its advance on Madrid, the need for a different concept of war began, however slowly, to be driven home.

A 17-year-old Socialist peasant, Timoteo Ruiz, who had joined the Communist-led fifth regiment, recalled the bitter experience of constant retreat. 'The worst was feeling alone, exposed. You could never be sure whether the column to your right or left was still there, or whether you were in danger of being encircled. Although I didn't know anything about military problems, I could see that it couldn't continue like this. We had to have a single command.'

The revolution's most significant failure was thus its inability to fuse into a centralized power that would mobilize popular energies and resources for the revolutionary task of winning the war.[3] Both anarcho-syndicalists and left Socialists came to recognize the need for such a power – but neither acted resolutely or rapidly.[4] The failure had inevitably to lead to the establishment of a different sort of power if the war were not to be rapidly lost. In this sense, the argument about war and revolution had been decided within two months of the outbreak of the conflict.

The creation of such a different power was the aim pursued by the PCE, for which the proletarian revolution, even if underway, was not on the historical agenda. With its acute understanding that the Republic was facing a large-scale civil war rather than the sequel to a military *coup*, the PCE insistently called for a strong central government which would re-create state power to organize a coherent war effort and to build an army. To achieve this it would obviously be necessary to 'bring under control' the fragmented and fragmentary revolution – in the first instance its armed expression, the militias – by 'incorporating' the revolutionaries in the new government and ensuring that henceforth all energies were directed towards winning the war. But the cornerstone of the PCE's and Comintern's anti-fascist strategy, in Spain as elsewhere, lay in securing the widest possible alliances with the bourgeois democracies abroad and bourgeois democrats at home, who must not be alienated from the struggle by fear of revolution. It was a policy which understandably appealed to a Republican petty bourgeoisie threatened by the revolution and fearful that the war would be lost if the 'revolutionary chaos' continued.

The Popular Front government formed in September 1936, during the complicated early days of Non-Intervention, represented an initial victory for these new objectives. On the question of war and revolution there could now be little doubt. The new government was not fighting for socialism or a Soviet regime but to 'maintain the parliamentary regime of the republic as it was set up by the constitution', Largo Caballero stressed on assuming the premiership.[5] Or, as he told a British newspaper, 'first we must win the war and afterwards we can talk about revolution.'[6]

But even as it lost strength to the Popular Front government, the proletarian revolution continued to defy the PCE's Procrustean efforts to fit it into its correct historical stage: defence of the pre-war republic and the completion of the bourgeois democratic revolution. Communist Party militants at the front had no doubt about the depth and extent of the revolutionary upheaval. 'It was a thorough-going revolution', recalled Miguel Nuñez who, many years later, was to become a member of the PSUC leadership. 'The people were fighting for all those things which the reactionary forces of this country had for so long denied them. Land and liberty, an end to exploitation, the overthrow of capitalism. The people were not fighting for a bourgeois democracy, let's be quite clear about that.'

By February 1937, the PCE was forced to concede that the struggle had gone beyond the defence of the 1931 Republic to the establishment of a 'democratic, parliamentary republic' unlike that of any capitalist country. Whatever this might mean, it was accompanied by a clear statement from José Díaz, the party's secretary general, that the bases of capitalism on the land, in industry and finance had been destroyed; the Church, as a dominant power, had likewise ceased to exist. The guarantee that these conquests would never be lost lay in the fact that the 'genuine anti-fascist people' – the workers, peasants, intellectuals and petty bourgeoisie – were armed. 'Precisely for that reason, because we have the guarantee that our conquests will not be lost, we should not lose our heads . . . by trying to introduce experiments in libertarian communism and socialization.'[7]

If capitalism had been destroyed, what prevented the PCE from declaring for socialism? The same reasons as before: the party's and Comintern's determination to defend the Popular Front option.

But there was another unstated reason: in the Comintern's book the march towards socialism could only be led by a Communist party. The revolution which was taking root had not only advanced the 'historical stage' but failed to conform either ideologically or politically to Communist orthodoxy. Thus, until the PCE could gather sufficient strength to impose its type of revolution,[8] it stood to gain nothing from competing on a terrain already occupied by anarcho-syndicalists, Poumists and left-Socialists. Indeed, its Popular Front policy of defending a petty bourgeoisie terrified by the revolution, its indisputable dedication to the military effort, and the all-important fact of Soviet aid brought it far greater immediate gains in membership and influence.[9] Meanwhile, in alliance with liberal republicans and right-wing Socialists, its growing strength could be used to try to prevent the proletarian revolution from consolidating its gains.

It was the struggle for political hegemony which in large part now underlay the polemic of war and revolution. In the words of José Sandoval, Communist Party organizer of Líster's eleventh division and later a member of the commission which wrote the party's official war history, the polemic was little more than a 'play on words'. The real problem did not lie in the fact that one sector was bent on making the revolution at all costs and the other on devoting all its energies to the war but rather in 'what sort of revolution should be made and how could this revolution, given that the former ruling class's power had been destroyed, contribute to winning the war'.

This, I would argue, was entirely correct; it was not, however, the manner in which the PCE conducted its side of the polemic. As Sócrates Gómez, a junior left-Socialist member of the government, put it, the PCE

> tried to absorb, monopolize everything, acting with the wildest sectarianism. Instead of unity, there was the opposite. The war was

being fought for the freedom of Spain, not to win a victory which
would hand the country over to the Communists who, in turn,
served the interests of another nation. But from the propaganda,
the large posters of Stalin, etc., the impression was gained that
Spain was in the Soviets' hands. That only alienated large sectors of
the population on our side and helped the enemy.

By continually invoking the need to put the war before the revolution, the PCE justified its sectarian and often pitiless opposition to a
revolution it did not control, and undermined working-class unity. Its
concentration on building the instrument to achieve victory – the
Popular Army – was intimately linked to its concepts of both war and
revolution. In reaction to the uncoordinated militias, the new army was
to be a regular, disciplined, hierarchized force under professional command. At the same time, in Communist eyes, it was a vital instrument
for 'consolidating' the revolution once victory had been won.

'Having an army of proletarians formed in the war, with proletarian
officers in command, a proletarian police force, proletarian hegemony
would be assured (after victory) as long as there was no foreign intervention', explained Pere Ardiaca, editor of the PSUC's paper *Treball*.
What this hegemony meant was soon apparent: very rapidly the Popular Army's crack forces were Communist-led, the political commissariat
and police forces were Communist-dominated,[10] Soviet aid and influence were dominant political facts.

At the military level, the Popular Army pursued strategies that differed little from the traditional warfare waged by the Francoist army –
but with less ultimate success, for although the Popular Army fought
with great bravery and won some important battles, it gained no
decisive victories. Indubitably, the Popular Army represented the
people in arms, but it failed to develop a strategy of people's war. The
reasons were as much political as military: the Popular Front option, so
resolutely backed by the PCE and Comintern, precluded such revolutionary developments.[11]

As we have seen, the Popular Front option had twin goals: to keep
bourgeois democrats nationally and the bourgeois democracies internationally in the anti-fascist struggle. But were these goals of necessity
as inexorably linked as the PCE argued? It was certainly necessary, both

to the revolution and the war, to keep the republican petty bourgeoisie in the struggle by protecting their economic interests; where this did not happen, as in Catalonia, the disaffection of the middle classes created an important enemy of the revolution and markedly weakened the war effort. But such a policy did not automatically imply the further goal of assuaging the bourgeois democracies with the pretence that the revolution was not happening. While it made sense not to antagonize them unnecessarily, Non-Intervention had rapidly shown that the capitalist countries, Britain in particular, had few illusions about where their real interests lay. The evidence, however, had to be ignored in favour of Stalin's foreign policy: justifiable or not, his desire for an alliance with Britain and France against Hitler was made to justify PCE policy in Spain. Irrespective of the depth and extent of the revolution, it was, in Stalin's words, 'necessary to prevent the enemies of Spain considering her a communist republic'.[12]

The conflation of these two policies had a marked effect on the conduct of the war, for it meant that the PCE supported a bourgeois leadership (in mentality and politics if not sociologically) of the struggle. This became even more pronounced when the Popular Front option was consolidated by the removal of Largo Caballero and his replacement as premier by Juan Negrín in mid-1937.

At the front these questions of policy became matters of victory or defeat. Timoteo Ruiz, the young peasant who had suffered the militias' retreat on Madrid and yearned for a centralized command, began to feel uneasy about the course of events.

A great mistake was being made in thinking that the war could be waged with classic strategies. This wasn't a traditional war – it was a civil war, a political war. A war between democracy and fascism, certainly – but a *popular* war. Yet all the creative possibilities and instincts of a people in revolution were not allowed to develop.

By now an officer in Líster's division and a Communist Party member, he reflected that the Republic should have found other ways of fighting the war.

If we hadn't been convinced that the democratic countries would come to our aid, different forms of struggle would have developed.

It was as though we had to be ashamed of the revolution, as though we were frightened they would get wind of it abroad. If we had realized from the start that we were alone – even opposed to the bourgeois democracies which were boycotting us – it would have become a popular revolutionary war.

An indication of the traditional way in which the war was being waged was the failure to develop forms of irregular warfare, including guerrillas. How was it possible, he often asked himself, that, in the very country which had invented the word, a co-ordinated guerrilla movement was not being sustained in the enemy rearguard? Irregular warfare, supported by a popular revolution, instead of pitched battles, would also have considerably reduced the effectiveness of German and Italian aid, he believed.[13]

But a more revolutionary course would only frighten the democracies, many argued. 'What nonsense!' thought another Communist, Paulino García, who became one of the fifth regiment's first political commissars.

The capitalist countries were frightened enough already by what was happening in Spain. 'Stalin won't agree,' said others. But was that the case? Would Stalin not have had to do what he did anyway – and a lot more perhaps – if we had pursued a revolutionary course? Could he afford to be seen betraying a proletarian revolution?

But the PCE's main error, in his view, was to have failed to see how to overcome the ideological and organizational divisions in the Spanish working-class movement. By leaning towards the reformist sectors of the Socialist Party, in putting the war before everything else, the PCE poisoned its relationship with the CNT and lessened the possibility of unity.

It was necessary to explain to the more politicized sectors of the CNT, as well as to the revolutionary sectors of the UGT, that neither libertarian communism nor socialism were possible at that moment.[14] But *at the same time* we had to set ourselves firmly on a revolutionary course – a long term one. . . . Such a policy would have neutralized both the extremist elements [in the CNT] and the reformists [in the PSOE]. Instead, the Communist Party chose a way of posing the problem which ensured that a solution was impossible; or chose an even worse course, that of drowning its opponents – in blood, as often as not.

The PCE's near exclusive emphasis on the war at the front, on military victory, gave rise to another failure which, in civil war, no people's army could afford. 'The party sent its best militants to the front; its dedication to the war effort was admirable. But as a result – and I think this was its major error – the party at certain periods lost its very important ties with the masses in the rear', recalled José Sandoval.

This was particularly noticeable at the end of the war in Madrid; the links which the party had forged with the capital's population during the glorious days of November 1936, had been undone. Failure to understand the threat of defeatism in the rearguard was, ultimately, failure to understand the conditions of victory at the front.

Whatever reservations individual party members may have had, the PCE held to its Popular Front policy to the bitter end. Its strength was to have a consistent policy where others had none; to be monolithically united where others were split.

The anarcho-syndicalists lacked the rigorous certainties of the PCE on the crucial issues of war and revolution. This was hardly surprising since the leadership had joined the Popular Front government while other CNT militants continued to pursue their revolutionary aims. Durruti's famous statement, 'We renounce everything except victory', was often adduced to mean that the revolution must be sacrificed to win the war. Given his other statements of the time – 'We want the revolution here, in Spain, now and not perhaps tomorrow after the next European war' – it was dubious that he meant to go so far. None the less, as one of the first anarchist leaders to realize that the working class was facing a civil war, he was aware that sacrifices in traditional libertarian aspirations would have to be made if the war were to be won.

Although the CNT Minister of Industry, Joan Peiró, attempted unsuccessfully to push a collectivization decree through the Popular Front government, many anarcho-syndicalists were well aware that the total social revolution could not be made. 'The first aim had to be to win the war; the revolution could come later', thought Peiró's private secretary,

Joan Manent. 'The collectives which had been created stood as the libertarians' revolutionary stake in the future when the republic would emerge victorious.'

The anarcho-syndicalists were no less aware than the Communists of the need to stake out positions for the future and, on occasion, no less prepared to shed blood to defend those positions. But their very ideology deprived them of a concept of political power. None the less, they too had to confront the immediate question of what was needed to win the war.

'We knew – it was so obvious, we all said it – that if the war were lost everything would be lost', explained Macario Royo, a national CNT committee member.

> On the other hand, if we of the CNT came out and said that making the revolution was not our concern, the enthusiasm of libertarians in fighting the war would have been entirely dissipated. Why? Because, ideologically, all libertarians were convinced anti-militarists. To have to serve in an army was the biggest contradiction they could face. Their only hope, therefore, was that if the war were won thanks to their sacrifice society would be transformed. Everyone of us held these two images simultaneously in his mind.

Two images simultaneously held, but which did not fuse into a unified revolutionary strategy. While the anarcho-syndicalists spread their revolution in the rearguard of Aragon, Catalonia, parts of the Levante and Andalusia, the CNT militia forces at the front failed to develop forms of revolutionary war. The example of their Ukrainian hero, Nestor Makhno, whose partisans fought white and red armies separately and sometimes simultaneously for three years, appeared to have been forgotten. To say this is to say no more than that revolution and war remained, if not two separate concepts, then two separate practices. At the front 'war', in the rear 'revolution', such was the paradox of the anarcho-syndicalist position.

The question must also be raised as to whether the libertarian revolution's organizational forms (or its lack of them) were the adequate revolutionary response to the need of the moment: winning the war. To ask the question is not to impugn the revolutionary spirit of the

working class which, through every difficulty, including bitter inter-
necine political struggle, kept collectivized industry going for thirty
months. But was it necessary to take over more than large industrial and
commercial enterprises, transport and the banks in order to consolidate
the revolution and win the war? Did the Catalan revolution, for
example, serve itself and the war effort by expropriating the petty
bourgeoisie; by allowing, within a collectivized system, the continued
existence of a market economy, lack of controls, a variety of types of
self-management and large numbers of deficitary collectives? Many
libertarians came to question the forms collectivization had taken; but
one of the sharpest criticisms came from the politically independent secretary of the commission overseeing the Catalan collectivization decree.
A staunch supporter of the revolutionary experiment, Albert Pérez-
Baró wrote seven months after the start of the revolution:

> the immense majority of workers have sinned by their indiscipline;
> production has fallen in an alarming manner and in many instances
> has plummeted; the distance from the front has meant that the
> workers have not experienced the war with the necessary intensity.
> The former discipline, born of managerial coercion, is missing, and
> has not been replaced, owing to the lack of class-consciousness, by
> a self-imposed discipline in benefit of the collectivity. In an infantile
> manner the workers have come to believe that everything was
> already won.[15]

On the land many questions would also have to be asked of anarcho-
syndicalist collectivization. The core of the problem was to find an
agrarian structure which ensured the peasantry's allegiance to the anti-
Francoist cause *and* the highest possible agricultural production.

Rural collectivization in Aragon, one of the libertarians' major revolutionary stakes in the future, represented a revolutionary minority's
attempt to control both production and consumption for egalitarian
purposes and the needs of the war. It was thus both a form of libertarian
and war communism. Stemming from these dual objectives, there coexisted 'spontaneous' and 'forced' collectives. Forced collectivization,
however, not only ran counter to libertarian ideology but did little to
ensure the small peasantry's allegiance to the war effort; there were
other ways, co-operatives, for example, which would have met these

twin needs better. Here again, the absence of an anarcho-syndicalist strategy in relation to the petty bourgeoisie was evident. Again many libertarians came to recognize the problems and to see that the collectives worked better when they were totally voluntary. But even as a form of war communism, rural collectivization was bedevilled by the problem of localism, the difficulty of creating a coherent structure in which the collectives could operate.[16]

For the dissident Communist POUM in Barcelona, the war and revolution were 'inseparable'. Ignacio Iglesias, political editor of the POUM's paper, *La Batalla*, expressed the party's position. There could be no triumphant revolution unless the war were won; but the war could not be won unless the revolution triumphed. The POUM's opposition to the Popular Army was based on revolutionary postulates: it was wrong to create a regular army since to do so was to pose the war in the same terms as the enemy.

> This was what the PCE was doing. But it was not a classic war, the situation did not require a regular army with hierarchized commands which inevitably destroyed the revolutionary spirit of the working class, but a popular revolutionary army. If the premise were accepted that the war could be fought only in a traditional manner – which was why the question of guerrilla warfare was never properly considered – the simplistic but true conclusion had to be reached that the enemy was bound to win. He had an army, trained soldiers, superior arms. Moreover, the premise ignored the important question of self-reliance. Those who stood for making the war and revolution simultaneously could not expect aid from Britain and France. How could we? Logically, international capital stood closer to Franco than to us; and within the republican zone, closer to the republicans and Communists than to the anarchists and POUM.

But the anarchists, in his view, had failed to understand this. With their visceral aversion to 'authoritarian marxism' and their hostility to 'power', the libertarians paid no heed to the POUM's calls for the working class to take power to consolidate the revolution and win the war. But the POUM, already under attack from the PCE for its anti-Stalinism, was always frightened of being isolated from the CNT where the mass of the Catalan workers remained. Although critical of many aspects of the libertarian revolution, it followed the CNT into the reconstituted Generalitat government when the anarcho-syndicalists abandoned their power base in the Anti-fascist Militia Committee in September 1936. Unsupported by the anarcho-syndicalists, the POUM rapidly suffered the fate of its anti-Stalinism: expelled after two months from the Generalitat, its leaders were arrested – and Nin vilely assassinated – by Stalin's secret police five months later, after the May events.

The polemic of war and revolution was effectively determined by the May events in Barcelona. Frustrated by seeing their revolution curtailed – by its own contradictions (especially the belief that power lay in the seizure of the means of production alone), by the difficulties of the war and by the alliance of PSUC and petty bourgeois Esquerra – anarcho-syndicalist militants erupted in the streets in response to a Communist-led attempt to take over the CNT-dominated telephone exchange.

With no other plan than to take revenge on the Communists, the anarcho-syndicalists, supported by the POUM, engaged in five days of bloody street fighting before CNT ministers in the Popular Front government succeeded in getting their companions to lay down their arms. The outcome was to leave the central government, shortly to be reconstituted without the CNT under Negrín, and the Communist Party even more firmly in control.

But the victory of the Popular Front option stemmed from the revolutionaries' earlier ambivalent attitude to the question of power and the consequent failure to consolidate the revolution politically and militarily. This, and the PCE's inflexible defence of the Popular Front policy, exacerbated a polemic in which war and revolution came to appear as polarized terms. As such, there could be little hope of uniting them in a phrase – *revolutionary war* – which would have served to answer the vital questions: what sort of revolution? what sort of war?

Notes

1 Many of the conclusions drawn in this chapter – and developed at greater length in *Blood of Spain* (London, 1979) – were suggested to me by participants of different political tendencies in the Republican camp. Indeed, one privilege of oral history is that, from the vantage point of the present,

witnesses can reflect on the lessons of the past and illuminate new areas of historical investigation. However, I must absolve everyone but myself for the manner in which these conclusions are presented here.

2 Shared, though unequally, in Barcelona between the Anti-fascist Militia Committee and the Generalitat; divided between the former and the other committees in Catalonia; divided between Catalonia and Madrid, and between Madrid and the other regions of Republican Spain; divided within each region between scores of local committees.

3 There can be little doubt that the creation of a revolutionary power would have encountered serious difficulties: the historic divisions in the working-class movement, the absence of a revolutionary party with a widespread following, traditional localisms and, above all, the rapid internationaliz-ation of the war militated against it. Moreover, there can be no historical guarantee that a revolutionary government would have succeeded where the revolutionary organizations had failed.

4 'The masses hold out their hands to us; they ask us for government leader-ship, but we remain passive, we avoid responsibility, we remain inactive', Largo Caballero told Mikhail Koltsov on 27 August 1936, as reported in the latter's *Diario de la Guerra de España* (Paris, 1963), 58. Largo Caballero, it appears, mooted the idea of a working-class government a month after the start of the war. The newly arrived Soviet ambassador, Rosenberg, pointed out the serious international consequences of such a move and suggested a Popular Front government instead. As this was being formed, the CNT proposed at the national level a working-class government with Republican participation; by then it was too late. Such was the anarcho-syndicalist confusion on the question of working-class power that the Catalan CNT had meanwhile agreed to give up its power base in the Anti-fascist Militia Committee for a minority partnership in a reformed Gener-alitat. 'This was our first mistake, a very great mistake, because we allowed the most authentic organ of the revolution to be destroyed', Federica Montseny, who was herself to become one of the CNT's ministers in the central government, admitted recently (Granada TV interview, 1982).

5 See Burnett Bolloten, *The Spanish Revolution* (Chapel Hill, 1979), 155.

6 *Daily Express*, 25 September 1936.

7 Speech at an amplified plenum of the PCE central committee, as quoted in José Díaz, *Tres años de lucha* (Toulouse, 1947), 295–7.

8 It is historically abstract to speculate on what such a revolution would have involved – or even whether it would have happened – other than to say that Stalin's foreign-policy needs at the time would have largely deter-mined the outcome.

9 In the first eight months of the war the PCE more than doubled in size to 250,000 members. Between 40 per cent and 50 per cent of the members were petty bourgeois: peasant owners, artisans, shopkeepers, etc., who outnumbered industrial workers. See Guy Hermet, *Les Communistes en*

Espagne (Paris, 1971). In Catalonia, the PSUC's membership rose nearly tenfold to 50,000 in the first four months of the war; by the same date, the PSUC-controlled UGT, which at the start of the war had been barely one-tenth the size of the CNT, actually outnumbered the anarcho-syndicalists, thanks to the influx of the petty bourgeoisie and white-collar workers.

10 Jesús Hernández, Communist minister and later head of the political commissariat, said after leaving the PCE: 'Our officers were given categoric instructions to promote the maximum number of Communists to higher ranks, thus reducing the proportion of promotions open to members of other organizations. But it is my duty to state that while this reckless policy was being carried out, the Communists did not cease fighting the enemy and their resolution and discipline at the fronts showed them to be better than the best, a fact that facilitated the proselytizing work we had undertaken' (Bolloten, op. cit., 236).

11 As it did other revolutionary developments, such as declaring Spanish Morocco's independence to undermine the enemy's rearguard and disrupt one of Franco's major sources of recruitment, the legalization of revolutionary conquests on the mainland, etc.

12 Stalin's letter to Largo Caballero, 21 December 1936.

13 The Popular Army included a guerrilla corps which raided but did not form a *maquis*. (The latter did exist, in isolation, in some parts of Andalusia and later Asturias.) Many factors could have favoured its development: the terrain, the great length of sparsely manned fronts, the vulnerability of the enemy rearguard, Franco's traditional military thinking, the lack of anti-insurgent weaponry and, above all, historic memories. Togliatti, the Comintern's chief adviser in Spain, recognized the lack of guerrilla warfare as one of the major failures of the Popular Front zone. The government and all the political parties, including the PCE, 'forgot that there was a mass of peasants and workers in the [enemy] zone. . . . Had [political] work been done amongst them they could have played a decisive role in weakening the fascist regime and constituted the base for a guerrilla movement in the countryside.' Report of 23 May 1939 to the Comintern in *Escritos sobre la Guerra de España* (Barcelona, 1980). It must be stressed none the less that there existed no guarantee that a people's war – of which guerrillas would have been but one element – would have triumphed. International isolation, absence of bases outside the national borders, continuing lack of working-class unity, might have been too heavy a burden.

14 As, in effect, was done in Asturias where the initiative was taken by the UGT and CNT and the outcome applauded by the Communist and Republican parties. At the national level, the CNT – as usual reacting to rather than acting on events – began to make important ideological and organizational revisions when its influence was already waning. Thus, in June 1937, it agreed a political programme which included the creation of a single, strictly hierarchized military command, the setting-up of a national

council of war industries and of an economics council whose decisions would be rigorously applied; and, seven months later, agreed to the administrative centralization of all CNT-controlled industries and agrarian collectives. These measures are an indication that, had the PCE not stood so resolutely opposed to the libertarian revolution, some revolutionary compromise might have been attainable much earlier.

15 Prologue to a pamphlet, *Col·lectivitzacions i control obrer* (February, 1937), cited in Pérez-Baró, *Trenta mesos de col·lectivisme a Catalunya* (Barcelona, 1970), app. 1, 191.

16 Rural collectivization and the peasant question was one of the PCE's major areas of anti-libertarian attack. The PCE consistently argued for the peasantry's complete freedom in the production and sale of its crops, and staunchly defended even the most right-wing peasant owners. Whether peasant free enterprise rather than the controls, however defective, instituted by the anarcho-syndicalists was more likely to help the war effort seems highly arguable, especially when it is noted that the enemy camp found agricultural regulation necessary.

11
Reflex reaction: Germany and the onset of the Spanish Civil War

Denis Smyth

There is little dispute about the influence of Nazi intervention in Spain upon the course and result of the Civil War there from 1936 until 1939. It was the Italo-German transportation of Franco's army of Africa over the Straits of Gibraltar from Spanish Morocco to metropolitan Spain, during the period late July to September 1936, that rescued the geographically dispersed military insurgents against the Republic from isolation and piecemeal defeat.[1] Hitler was in no doubt about the significance of this airlift, as his later comment demonstrates: 'Franco ought to erect a monument to the glory of the Junker 52. It is this aircraft that the Spanish revolution has to thank for its victory.'[2] Moreover, although the Nazi regime did not, like Fascist Italy, commit large numbers of ground troops to the Spanish struggle, the quantity and quality of the German *matériel* and military personnel dispatched to sustain the Francoist Civil War effort were sufficient to make a major contribution to its eventual victory over the Republican camp.[3] In conversation with Italian Foreign Minister, Galeazzo Ciano, in September 1940, Hitler was prepared to share the victor's laurels in Spain: 'Italy and Germany had done very much for Spain in the year 1936. . . . Without the help of both countries there would be today no Franco.'[4] However, among his own aides, on 7 July 1942, the German leader was inclined to appropriate the entire credit for the triumph of the rebel cause in Spain. For, although Hitler noted that the Spanish Nationalists could 'consider themselves very lucky to have received the help of Fascist Italy and National-Socialist Germany in their . . . civil war', he also made this observation:

> People speak of an intervention from Heaven which decided the civil war in favour of Franco . . . but it was not an intervention on the part of the madam styled the Mother of God . . . but the intervention of the German General von Richthofen [who commanded, in the later stages of the Spanish conflict, the German air corps that supported the Nationalist army, the Condor Legion] and the bombs his squadrons rained from the heavens that decided the issue.[5]

If historians are ready to recognize the impact of German intervention upon the outcome of the Spanish Civil War, there is much less of an historiographical consensus over the reasons for which the Nazi state became, and remained for the duration, involved in that combat.[6] Some commentators have attributed this absence of agreement about the primary purpose of Nazi engagement in Spain to the deficient state of the extant documentary sources pertinent to this problem.[7] It has also been asserted that the diversity of views concerning the origins and aims of German intervention in Spain's civil strife derives from an excessively static conception of German policy towards that conflict. According to this view, Nazi goals in Spain changed over time as the Civil War there developed into a protracted struggle which, in its turn, evolved as part of a general international situation to which German foreign-policy makers had to formulate a global response. Thus, it has been doubted whether Germany's help to the Nationalist camp over the course of the three-year Civil War can be explained by reference to the factors which induced Hitler, on the night of 25–6 July 1936, to lend immediate small-scale military assistance to Franco.[8] Indeed, one historian, Wolfgang Schieder, has characterized Germany's engagement in Spain's internal struggles as a cumulative one, which Hitler failed to control.[9]

However, it will be argued, on the contrary, in this essay that German support for the Francoist cause during Spain's Civil War was the result of a deliberate decision by Hitler himself to assist the rebel Spanish general; that sufficient contemporary documentary evidence is available to sustain an adequate explanation of this Hitlerian resolution; and that the basic reason persuading the Führer to aid Franco, in the first instance, continued to govern Germany's relations with, and inform Nazi policy towards, Nationalist Spain for the remainder of the Civil War. It is, indeed, true that Hitler's favourable reply to Franco's plea for aid (delivered to the German leader, late in the evening of 25 July at Bayreuth, by Johannes Bernhardt and Adolf Langenheim, two Spanish-Moroccan-based members of the Nazi Party's foreign countries' organization, the *Auslandsorganisation*) was remarkably quick, with the Nazi chief making up his mind within a couple of hours to answer the Spaniard's cry for help.[10] But this very swiftness of reaction is revealing. Hitler's response was instantaneous because it was instinctive: it sprang from his fundamental ideological principles, his strategic preoccupations and his diplomatic priorities. It was a reflex reaction but not an inadvertent one. Moreover, the commitment to support Franco, once contracted, was maintained, despite the vicissitudes of Nazi-Spanish Nationalist relations during the Civil War, precisely because it continued to serve the essential foreign-policy interests of the Third Reich, as defined by Hitler. Yet, the scale of German intervention in Spain was also carefully calculated by the Führer, so as to remain in harmony with, and in proportion to, German concerns in the fight.

A distinguished British visitor to Berlin in late July–early August 1936 received a very definite impression as to the concerns of German foreign-policy makers in the immediate aftermath of the outbreak of the Spanish Civil War. Sir Robert Vansittart, the Permanent Under-Secretary of State at the British Foreign Office, found 'those in authority' in Germany to be very agitated over this Iberian development.[11] In seven conversations with the British diplomat, the German Foreign Minister, Baron Konstantin von Neurath 'spoke always of Spain', whilst Vansittart found Hitler to be 'particularly preoccupied with events in Spain'.[12] However, in a conversation with the Führer over Anglo-German relations, on 5 August 1936, only ten days after Hitler's decision to dispatch military assistance to Franco, Vansittart realized that the onset of civil war in Spain was less a cause of, than the focus for, Nazi apprehension concerning the international scene. For, when Vansittart sought to divert Hitler from a monologue justifying previous Nazi actions at home and abroad, by observing that the British as a 'practical and reasonable people . . . looked more to the future than the past', the German leader retorted that he 'preferred to consider the past with reference to Communism, and the future in the light of its manifestations in Spain and their repercussions on France'.[13] Moreover, the British diplomat found that this fixation with the Bolshevik menace was widespread within the ruling circles of the Nazi regime: 'this is the constant theme of every man and woman in Berlin; indeed they can think and talk of little else. The obsession is in any case endemic, but Spanish events have reinforced their thesis.'[14]

Still, before accepting Vansittart's contemporary testimony that what he termed 'the Russian aspect of Spain' was the crucial factor conditioning the response of Hitler's Germany to the Spanish Civil War, one should question whether the Führer was not merely raising the Communist bogy as a means of promoting British co-operation with, or at least acquiescence in, Nazi expansion in Europe.[15] Hitler always matched his words to his audience. So was he simply using his discussion with Vansittart to appeal to the largely anti-Communist instincts of Stanley Baldwin's Conservative-dominated National Government in Britain? Certainly, another foreign diplomat in Berlin in 1936, a resident one, namely André François-Poncet, the French Ambassador, was sure that the Nazis were employing such a tactic to court the British. He informed Paris of this Nazi ploy on 5 August 1936:

Rarely have I seen so strong an effort made by the National Socialist Government to influence Great Britain. It believes that the events in Spain will impress English conservatives and, by opening their eyes to the reality of the Bolshevik peril and the dangers of an over close friendship with an already contaminated France, will detach them from our country. It is lavishing attentions upon Sir Robert Vansittart who is in Berlin on a visit. Its hope that circumstances are working for an Anglo-German rapprochement keeps on growing.[16]

Indeed, as the French Ambassador correctly discerned, Hitler was well aware, at that time, of the diplomatic advantage that might be wrung from the other powers' fear of Communism. In the course of a talk with Ciano at Berchtesgaden, on 24 October 1936, Hitler proposed that Germany and Italy should open a diplomatic offensive against the democracies on 'the tactical field' of 'anti-Bolshevism'. He explained his rationale to the Italian Foreign Minister, thus:

In fact many countries which are suspicious of Italo-German friendship for fear of Pan-Germanism or of Italian imperialism . . . will be brought to group themselves with us if they see in Italo-German unity the barrier against the Bolshevik menace at home and abroad.[17]

Moreover, although deferring to Ciano's anti-British sentiments to the extent of describing Fascist Italy and Nazi Germany as 'the natural enemies of England', Hitler emphasized the beneficial effect an Italo-German anti-Communist propaganda campaign could have on Britain's foreign policy:

if England sees the gradual formation of a group of powers which are willing to make common front with Germany and Italy under the banner of anti-Bolshevism . . . not only will she refrain from fighting against us, but she will seek means of agreement and common ground with this new political system.[18]

However, even in this conversation with Ciano, when he displayed an opportunistic sense of the diplomatic profit to be gained from an anti-Communist crusade, the Führer also revealed a more principled commitment to confrontation with Bolshevism. There was a tactical dimension to Hitler's anti-Marxism but it coexisted with a real ideological antipathy to the Soviet Union and international Communism. Disclosing the reality of his antagonism towards Communism in 'violent outbursts when he spoke of Russia and Bolshevism', Hitler also noted, in the discussion of 24 October, that 'in Spain, Italians and Germans have together dug the first trench against Bolshevism.' Again, when Ciano defined Italian intervention in Spain as emanating from a desire 'to bar the road to Bolshevism which was attempting to install itself at the entrance to the Mediterranean', Hitler 'entirely' approved, declaring his own willingness 'to make any effort to ensure that the way is not left open to Moscow'.[19]

Of course, it has also been mentioned above that the French Ambassador to Germany, François-Poncet, was conscious of the manner in which the Nazis could exploit the Red scare to their diplomatic advantage as a result of the outbreak of violent social struggle in Spain. Yet, as early as 22 July 1936, France's representative in Berlin also warned his Foreign Ministry that opportunism and ideology were inextricably mixed in the reaction of Germany's ruling élite to the Spanish Civil War:

> The press which they [the German rulers] inspire openly accuses Moscow of being at the bottom of the anarchy and the civil war in Spain. . . . This relentless and persistent campaign is, doubtless, intended to justify national-socialism in the eyes of the German people: it is also intended to impress 'les pays d'ordre' and to dispose them favourably towards Germany. But it indicates also that hostility against Russia, the idea that the mission of Hitlerism is to purge Europe of the Russian peril, and that it is incumbent upon the Third Reich to organize the struggle against Bolshevism . . ., more and more dominate the mind of the Führer and his lieutenants.[20]

François-Poncet also notified the Quai d'Orsay, on 30 July, that the German press, 'skilfully directed' by Goebbels, was presenting a very 'partial and tendentious' version of the fighting in Spain which depicted the Spaniards as rallying behind their patriotic army officers in a 'national rising' to 'safeguard their independence, against the communist bandits at the orders of the Third International'. The French Ambassador also relayed to Paris the allegation, made by one German newspaper on the previous day, that Spain was 'the field of attack which Moscow has chosen against Europe'.[21] The Nazis might thus seem to have been dupes of their own propaganda, and of the fabrications of the Spanish insurgents, in apparently attributing responsibility for the outbreak of the Spanish Civil War to the Kremlin.[22] To be sure, Berlin was receiving reports, like that of 24 July 1936, from its consulate at Tetuán in Spanish Morocco, that the 'Nationalist uprising was necessary in order to anticipate a Soviet dictatorship, which was already prepared'.[23] Yet, in reality, the Soviet government was as surprised as most other European executives by the turn of events in Spain. Communist influence inside Republican Spain was a consequence, not the cause, of the Spanish Civil War. Refused aid by the democratic world, Republican Spain had to depend, from 1936 onwards, upon Soviet help to maintain its fight for survival, a reliance which allowed the Partido Comunista de Espana (a relatively minor group in the pre-Civil War period) to compete on advantageous terms with the large anarcho-syndicalist and socialist movements in the internal political rivalries of the Republican zone.[24] However, far from engineering the outbreak of the Spanish war, the Kremlin initially regarded it as an unwelcome complication of an already menacing international scene in Europe.[25] Fully involved in their massive effort to transform their country socially and economically, by their industrial revolution planned and led by the state, the Soviet leaders sought only a quiet international existence which would permit them to complete their gigantic domestic experiment without external distraction or interruption.[26]

However, during 1934–5, the increasing threat posed to Soviet security by Hitler's anti-Communist regime persuaded Stalin to discard ideological sectarianism and seek anti-Nazi allies among the bourgeois democratic parties and states.[27] The major result of this endeavour to create an international Popular Front of anti-fascist powers was the Soviet-French Treaty of Mutual Assistance, of 2 May 1935, by which both powers promised 'immediate' joint consultation if either were 'threatened with or in danger of aggression' and also pledged 'reciprocally' to rush 'to each other's aid and assistance' if either country were the victim of 'an unprovoked aggression on the part of a European State'.[28] Although right-wing reticence in France delayed the ratification of the Treaty until March 1936, its confirmation then was followed, within weeks, by the election victory of Léon Blum's Popular Front coalition. This happy coincidence seems to have rekindled the Soviet desire to form a genuine military alliance with France, a scheme that they pursued actively, from the early summer of 1936 until the spring of 1937, the same period during which they also had to form their basic reaction to developments in Spain. The prospect that France might align itself militarily with the Soviet Union seems to have been the major influence affecting the latter power's attitude towards the Spanish Civil War during the crucial months of later 1936 and early 1937. Of course, Moscow's hopes in this regard were eventually frustrated by the ambivalence or antipathy of many members of the French government and the army's general staff towards the Russian connection.[29]

Still, in the opening phase of Spain's Civil War, it was the need to protect the strategic position of the Soviet Union's potential ally, France, that led Stalin to abandon his initial inclination to stand aloof from the Spanish imbroglio. He explained his view, 'definitively', to Republican Spain's Ambassador to the USSR, Marcelino Pascua, in early 1937:

> Spain, according to them [the Soviet leaders] is not suitable for communism, nor prepared to adopt it, and [even] less to have it imposed on her, nor even if she adopted it or they imposed it on her, could it last, surrounded by hostile bourgeois regimes. In opposing the triumph of Italy and Germany, they are trying to prevent any weakening in France's power or military situation.[30]

The British Ambassador in Moscow, Viscount Chilston, had discerned, as early as 10 August 1936, the essence of the difficulty created by the international dimension of the Spanish Civil War for the Soviet government: 'any danger to France is a danger to the Soviet Union.'[31] Significant strategic opportunities could accrue to Nazi Germany and Fascist Italy for interdicting France's vital lines of communication with its North African empire, and for creating a military threat along the previously secure Pyrenean frontier, in the event of the victory for the Axis-backed insurgents in Spain. Anxious to shore up France's strategic position, the Soviet Union became involved on a large scale in the Spanish Civil War. Indeed, Ambassador Pascua perceived, in 1937, a great preoccupation on the part of the Soviet government with the 'visible and progressive diminution of the international personality of France, its principal ally'.[32]

Moreover, the defence of Republican Spain against fascist aggression might also have provided convenient ground for co-operation between the Soviet Union and the Western democracies, a working partnership that could have developed into a fully-fledged military alliance with Britain and France, thereby realizing the Kremlin's general design for the protection of the Soviet Union against the threat of Nazism. The role of Soviet advisers and Spanish Communists in restraining, and even reversing, the revolutionary process inside Republican Spain seems explained, in part at least, by Stalin's concern that its regime should present a moderate bourgeois democratic image to conservative politicians in Britiain and France, who might have been persuaded to mount a joint Anglo-French-Soviet rescue operation on its behalf.[33] Again, acute Spanish Republican observers detected a distinct Soviet unwillingness to support their cause on a scale greater than that which the British and French would complement or tolerate.[34] Thus, the President of the Spanish Republic, Manuel Azaña, was sure, in August 1937, that the Soviet Union would avoid any action in support of Republican Spain that could seriously damage Moscow's relations with Britain or jeopardize its pursuit of 'western friendships', an opinion that Pascua fully endorsed.[35] It was not socialist internationalism but Soviet national interest, as embodied in that Stalinist fusion of ideology and geopolitics, 'socialism in one country', which was the crucial influence in inducing the USSR to intervene in Spain.

However, it was not ill-informed fears of a Communist take-over in Spain but the strategic implications of the advent of a radical left-wing regime to power there that actually drew the Third Reich into the Spanish struggle. A 'geo-ideological' conception of the international system inspired German Nazi, as much as Soviet Communist, foreign policy towards the Spanish Civil War. Sir Robert Vansittart was convinced by his round of conversations with prominent Nazis in Berlin, in early August 1936, that it was the international strategic dimension of the Bolshevik peril that concerned the German leaders. He found that the Nazi 'ruling caste' had little 'real fear of an internal [Communist] recrudescence which would be ruthlessly crushed'. On the other hand, the British diplomat did discern considerable misgivings among the Nazi regime's ruling élite over the growth of international Communist influence: 'What it fears is an external convergence, that Communism will extend in Europe and round on, if not encircle, Germany.'[36] Indeed, to the German rulers, with their historic fears of being surrounded by hostile coalitions of powers, just such a formidable anti-Nazi constellation did seem to be forming from amongst the European States in 1936. For, not only were France, Soviet Russia and Czechoslovakia bound together by a set of interdependent mutual assistance pacts, signed in May 1935, but the ideological aversion to Nazism shared by these powers suggested that their strategic co-operation might be more than a mere alliance of convenience.[37] Indeed, Hitler confessed to Ciano, in their late October 1936 conversation mentioned above, that he was concerned about the ideological coherence of the diplomatic and strategic association developing between the democratic powers: 'The democracies have formed amongst themselves an automatic bloc which finds a sort of cement and yeast in Bolshevism.'[38] There was tangible cause for German concern, too, in that the Soviet Union had more than doubled its defence budget in 1936 from 6.5 thousand million to 14.8 thousand million roubles.[39] Moreover, by June 1936 there was a Popular Front government, led by Blum, installed in office in France, an administration which the Nazis mistakenly assumed would be all too eager to court the Soviet military colossus. The manner in which German strategic fears came to be crystallized by, and to focus on, the Spanish Civil War was revealed even by a diplomat of the old school, Ernst von Weizsäcker. Observing the onset of civil strife in Spain from afar, on 25 July 1936, von Weizsäcker was moved to express his hope that events there would culminate in a 'complete military dictatorship', but he also gave a particular form to his disquiet at the outbreak of the Spanish fighting: 'All we need is to be caught also in the Bolshevik pincers from the West. Already one notices how the weak Blum begins to waver in Paris.'[40] Actually, having acceded, at first, on 21 July to the request made by the government of the Spanish Republic for permission to purchase arms from France, Blum was forced on 25 July, under the pressure of vehement political opposition to this move inside and outside the French government, and possibly also by British disapproval, to suspend immediate and direct military assistance to the

Spanish Republic.[41] On that same day, Ambassador François-Poncet had reported home on the German alarm at reports of French help to the Republican Government in Spain:

> The alleged delivery by France of arms, aircraft and munitions to the Madrid Government is considered, in Berlin's political circles, as a very serious affair and one calculated to involve complications. . . . In national-socialist circles, where the Madrid government is identified with that of Moscow, it is let be understood that in assisting Moscow's cause, France would perform a grave act, which could have repercussions on the future of Franco-German relations.[42]

Certainly, Hitler was as concerned as his assistants about the possible impact of Spanish developments upon the French and general European strategic scene. Again, Vansittart was a contemporary witness of the Führer's worry. Hitler admitted his concern to the British visitor during their conversation on 5 August 1936:

> He [Hitler] thought the Left in Spain would eventually win. . . . If his prediction were verified, France would be infected dangerously, perhaps desperately, and the contagion would then spread to her associates like Czechoslovakia where the seed was already sown. Germany would then be caught between two, if not three, fires, and must be prepared.[43]

According to the recollection after the Second World War of the some-time Nazi Ambassador to Britain and Reich Foreign Minister, Joachim von Ribbentrop, Hitler voiced an identical fear to him on 26 July 1936:

> Germany could not tolerate a Communist Spain under any circumstances. As a National Socialist he had the obligation to do everything to prevent that eventuality. . . . If a Communist Spain actually does emerge, in view of the current situation in France the Bolshevisation of that country is also only a matter of a short time and then Germany can 'pack up' [*einpacken*]. Hemmed in between the powerful Soviet bloc in the East and a strong Franco-Spanish communist bloc in the West we could hardly do anything, if Moscow decides to act against Germany.[44]

As usual, however, apprehension and aggression were combined in Hitler's attitude towards Soviet Communism. This ambivalence is evident in one of the few memoranda which Hitler personally drafted when in power, that on the Four-Year Plan drawn up by the Führer in August 1936. This document was designed to justify the Nazi economic concentration upon rearmament against the criticisms of bureaucrats and businessmen.[45] Hitler fully emphasized, therein, the challenge of Communism: 'Marxism, through its victory in Russia, has established one of the greatest empires as a forward base for its future operations. . . . Germany will . . . have to be regarded as the focus of the Western world against the attacks of Bolshevism.'[46] The memorandum's conclusions show, however, that Hitler was determined to get his retaliation in first: 'I The German armed forces must be operational within four years. II The German economy must be fit for war within four years.'[47]

Indeed, if Hitler's reaction to the outbreak of the Spanish Civil War was defensive, then apparently this was only so in the sense that the Führer was intent on protecting the feasibility of future Nazi aggression. Although the historiographical debate concerning the internal coherence of Hitler's foreign policy has not been concluded, it does appear that the Nazi leader's *Weltanschauung* embodied certain long-term foreign-policy ambitions which informed his main diplomatic and strategic choices amid developing historical circumstances. As the vigour of the historiographical controversy aroused by this problem indicates, it is not always easy to establish clear connections between particular instances of Hitler's foreign-policy decision-making and his grand design for German expansion.[48] However, it seems that Hitler's resolution to come to Franco's aid in July 1936, and his subsequent determination to maintain that support for the duration of the Spanish War, become comprehensible when considered in the context of the Führer's aim of winning racial *Lebensraum* at the expense of the Soviet Union, after France had been defeated in the West. Hitler's intervention in Spain appears explicable by a desire to defend this expansionist scheme.

Hitler did not intend to implant a National-Socialist regime in Spain, an exercise that he acknowledged in a speech to Nazi party officials on 29 April 1937, would be 'totally impossible, not to mention superfluous and absurd'. His purpose he explained, was to prevent Spain from 'becoming Bolshevised and being converted, as a result, sooner or later, into an extension of France'. The French must not be allowed to improve their strategic position through the establishment of a Spanish 'Bolshevik State' which would 'constitute a land bridge for France to North Africa', and thus safeguard the passage of colonial troops to metropolitan territory in any future hour of need. France must be denied this opportunity to consolidate its power to block Nazi aggression, particularly as its Popular Front Government seemed likely to develop military co-operation with Hitler's main, future enemy, the Soviet Union.[49] Indeed, when Hitler took his decision to send immediate aid to Franco, he was probably acting under the impression that the French government was intent on helping the Spanish Republicans to quell the military insurgents.[50] A victory for the Popular Front forces in the Spanish Civil War would strengthen the resources and resolve of the embryonic bloc of leftist powers which were obstacles to, and targets of, Nazi imperialism.

The German Foreign Ministry received, in the early hours of 25 July 1936, a warning from its Madrid embassy that 'the consequences of a [Spanish] Government victory would be very grave for . . . foreign affairs. . . . Spain, ideologically and materially, would become closely allied to the Franco-Russian bloc.'[51] Hitler may, or may not have been aware of this particular admonishment when he determined, on the night of 25–26 July at Bayreuth, to back the Spanish army rebellion, but it appears that it was his perception of this potential menace that inspired his decision.[52] The German leader disclosed the motivation behind his intervention in Spain to General Faupel, his newly appointed diplomatic representative to the Spanish Nationalist administration, on 18 November 1936:

> His [Hitler's] exclusive object was that, after the end of the war, Spanish foreign policy would neither be influenced by Paris or London nor by Moscow and consequently in the inevitable and definitive conflict over the reordering of Europe Spain would not be found on the side of Germany's enemies, but if possible on that of its friends.[53]

It is true that the documentary record of this revealing encounter was not made until 7 July 1942, by Counsellor of Legation, Hans Stille, who had also been present along with von Neurath, at the Obersalzberg meeting.[54] It has been doubted whether a 'subsequent account' can support the view that 'such far-reaching considerations of strategic alliance' were decisive in making up Hitler's mind, during the night of 25–26 July 1936, to aid the military uprising in Spain. Moreover, it has also been claimed that the June 1942 memorandum is 'clearly' contradicted by a 'primary source of November 1936', namely, the record of a conversation held on 27 November between General Faupel and two officials of the Economic Policy Department of the German Foreign Ministry.[55] The official minute of this latter meeting does contain the following paragraph:

> General Faupel stated that he had received instructions from the Führer to concern himself particularly with the extension of commercial relations between Germany and Spain and to utilize the present favorable moment so that England, which was well provided with capital (*kapitalkräftige*), would not take the market away from us at a later stage.[56]

However, since this 27 November discussion was specifically 'about economic relations with Spain', it is hardly surprising that Faupel should only mention Hitler's directions concerning the economic aspect of his mission in this context. This by no means precludes the possibility of Hitler's having mentioned the other facets of German involvement in Spain at his meeting with Faupel, including his original and primary motive for becoming engaged there, in addition to the opportunity being afforded Germany for economic entrenchment in Spain, with the emergence of a protracted civil war in late 1936.[57] Again, there is the even more contemporary evidence of Hitler's conversation of 5 August 1936, cited above, to testify that the strategic significance of a potential bloc of democratic leftist powers was central to the German leader's considerations on the Spanish Civil War, at its outbreak.

As to the implication that the temptation to exploit Spain's economic resources, particularly its mineral wealth, may have been the chief attraction drawing Germany into the Spanish fray, it seems that Hans-Henning Abendroth is correct to reject this notion. Although Nazi Germany did mount a major effort (which experienced temporary and partial success) to direct Spanish iron ore and pyrites production away from Britain and France to supply the industries of the Reich, Abendroth views this operation, however ambitious, as a mere 'by-product' of German intervention in Spain's Civil War, 'never its aim'.[58] Indeed, as Hitler himself reminded German business interests in August 1936 in his memorandum on the Four-Year Plan mentioned above, the Nazi state had one overriding priority, 'the duty of securing her existence by every means' in the face of the Bolshevik menace. He made a categorical declaration on this issue in that document: 'In face of the necessity of warding off this danger, all other considerations must recede into the background as completely irrelevant.'[59] German intervention was maintained throughout the Spanish Civil War in order to fulfil a primordial Hitlerian purpose. That purpose was defined thus, by German Foreign Minister von Neurath, on 5 December 1936: 'In the Spanish conflict Germany has predominantly the negative goal of not permitting the Iberian Peninsula to come under Bolshevist domination, which would involve the danger of its spreading to the rest of Western Europe.'[60]

It is true that Hitler was often disappointed, and sometimes disillusioned, with Franco and the Nationalist Spaniards, who proved to be as resentful of German political dictation as they were resistant to Nazi economic exploitation. It was amidst a struggle with the Nationalist administration over the German effort to secure a permanent, and controlling influence over some Spanish mining enterprises, and at a time of Francoist *rapprochement* with the British, that Hitler uttered to his advisers, on 5 November 1937, his oft-quoted remark that 'a 100 per cent victory for Franco' was undesirable 'from the German point of view', since their 'interest lay rather in a continuance of the [Spanish Civil] war and in the keeping up of the tension in the Mediterranean'.[61] Yet, once Franco, again in urgent need of *matériel* to finish off the groggy Republicans after the bloody stalemate of the Ebro, made the requisite economic concessions to the Nazis in November 1938, he received enough German armaments to destroy the Spanish Republic in a few months.[62]

Further evidence of Hitler's willingness to sustain the rebel cause in Spain until its eventual triumph was supplied by exchanges, between the Spanish Nationalist and German Nazi authorities, in the spring of 1938, on the possibility of a withdrawal of the Condor Legion from the

Francoist forces. Interestingly, it was Franco who raised the topic. In early April 1938, he informed the Germans 'in a cautious manner' that the moment might be opportune for them to call their airmen and other troops home, since the end of the Civil War seemed imminent, in the wake of his successful Aragonese offensive begun the previous month. Franco even admitted that he was suggesting the repatriation of German military personnel partly out of 'regard for French and British sensibilities'. Franco conveyed the 'total impression' that he was 'trying to secure a free hand for himself'.[63] Hitler professed himself ready to pull his pilots and other military experts out of Spain, since he too believed that the Civil War was drawing to a close and, consequently, the German technicians 'could not learn anything more' from that conflict.[64] It is true that the Spanish hostilities had provided the Nazi state with the opportunity to fight what Franco later described as an 'experimental war', in which German military techniques and technology could be tested under combat conditions.[65] However, the irrelevance of this matter to the continuance of German support for Franco's cause was demonstrated within a few weeks. For, when renewed Republican resistance proved that Franco and Hitler had both underestimated the resilience of the Spanish left, the Nationalists found they could not afford to dispense with the services of their exacting German allies.[66] Moreover, instead of withdrawing his battle-tried experts and equipment from Spain, Hitler actually restored the 'full combat strength of the Condor Legion' deciding that there were 'weighty political reasons' compelling the German unit's retention in Spain.[67] The political reason that seemed to carry most weight with Hitler was the one noted on 22 November 1936 by the then Director of the Political Section of the German Foreign Ministry, Ernst von Weizsäcker: 'The German aim . . . is above all negative: we do not want a Soviet Spain.'[68] In order to avoid Spain's absorption into a burgeoning bloc of left-wing and anti-Nazi powers, Hitler was prepared both to assist the Francoist Civil War effort, and to maintain that support for going on three years, often against the wishes of his Foreign Ministry and the German army and navy.[69]

Still, Hitler's determination to see Franco's cause through to victory was moderated by a realization that it was not in Nazi Germany's interest to precipitate a general European war by an excessive involvement in

Spain's civil conflict. Von Weizsäcker defined Hitler's problem in this way, on 22 November 1936:

> The Führer's decision to prevent a victory for Communism in Spain. The Führer is prepared, if necessary for this also to mobilize infantry help on a larger scale. . . . Our problem now consists in reconciling the German aim in Spain with the simultaneous German interest and intention of the Führer, to avoid an all out European war for the present. The question whether and how the conflict can be localized and be confined to the theatre of war in Spain, is therefore posed.[70]

Although Hitler does appear to have considered sending a sizeable number of ground troops to Spain at one stage, he decided against such a course of action on 21 December 1936, despite Franco's personal request that a German division 'be placed at his disposal as soon as possible'.[71] On the other hand, the Führer did maintain his approximately 5000-man Condor Legion in Spain to provide Franco's forces with German air and tank support. Thus, it seems that Hitler did not keep his Spanish engagement within certain limits for an ulterior motive: that is, the distraction of the democracies from Nazi political penetration and military intimidation of Central and Eastern European countries.[72] Rather was Hitler concerned to avoid jeopardizing the very German strategic interests that had prompted him, initially, to help Franco. The commitment of a large German expeditionary force to the Spanish Civil War might well have crystallized that very democratic-Communist coalition of powers whose formation Hitler was endeavouring to impede. It could even have provoked that anti-Nazi alliance into united and immediate action against the German units in Spain who would have been fighting at a considerable disadvantage, surrounded by French land-power and British sea-power. Indeed, even the moderate French Foreign Minister, Yvon Delbos, warned the Germans on 23 December 1936 that 'the sending [to Spain] of further troop transports would necessarily lead to war'.[73]

Hitler, therefore, had to calculate the scale of his military assistance to Franco so as to ensure that it would achieve its essential purpose, the frustration of a Bolshevik take-over in Spain, and yet not over-alarm or antagonize the Western powers. Hitler revealed the strategy he had pursued throughout the Spanish Civil War, to the men of his Condor Legion, when he welcomed them home on 6 June 1939:

> In July 1936 I quickly decided to accede to the request for help directed to me by this man [Franco] and to help him to exactly the extent and for so long as the rest of the world would give its help to Spain's internal enemies.[74]

Again, Hitler's subscription, on 24 August 1936, to the Anglo-French sponsored international Non-Intervention Agreement on Spain seems explained, in some degree at least, by his wish to minimize the risks of German intervention there, by confining the Spanish *Kulturkampf* to the soil from which it sprang.[75] Thus, when the French and British Ambassadors in Berlin visited von Neurath on 5 December 1936 to present proposals 'concerning an intensification of the non-intervention measures', the German Foreign Minister acknowledged that the Nazi state had 'the greatest interest, as did Britain and France, in seeing that the conflagration in Spain did not spread to the rest of Europe'. However, even then von Neurath also alluded to the fundamental purpose of German intervention in Spain: 'We had already stated repeatedly that we would not tolerate the establishment of a new Bolshevist center in Spain because of the danger which this involved for all of Europe.'[76]

So, far from allowing himself to become embroiled in the Spanish Civil War in a casual fashion, Adolf Hitler deliberately contracted his commitment to the Francoists. Moreover, the Nazi chief also carefully determined the extent of his engagement in the Spanish struggle and employed only as much force as would attain his defined goal without radically alienating the major democracies or provoking them into counteraction. Like other foreign-policy moves made by Hitler elsewhere in Europe, around this time, his Spanish venture was a gamble, but the risk taken was a calculated one. When George Orwell came to reflect, a few years after the end of the Spanish Civil War, upon the conflict in which he had participated, he was still puzzled at the apparently ineffectual policies pursued by Britain, France and the Soviet Union towards that contest. However, he was sure about one feature of the international involvement in Spain from 1936–9: 'at any rate the Spanish Civil War demonstrated that the Nazis knew what they were doing'.[77] It was Hitler's instantaneous apprehension of the geo-ideological issues at stake in Spain that led him to make, and maintain, his measured contribution to the Spanish insurgent cause. It was not only a German Communist volunteer in the International Brigades who conceived that one might 'reach Berlin through Spain'.[78]

Notes

1 Hugh Thomas, *The Spanish Civil War*, 3rd (paperback) edn (Harmondsworth, 1977), 370; John F. Coverdale, *Italian Intervention in the Spanish Civil War* (Princeton, 1975), 85–7.

2 H. R. Trevor-Roper (ed.), *Hitler's Table Talk, 1941–44: His Private Conversations*, 2nd edn (London, 1973), 687.

3 Coverdale, op. cit., 392–8; Thomas, op. cit., 977–8; Raymond Carr, *The Spanish Tragedy: The Civil War in Perspective* (London, 1977), 139.

4 *Documents on German Foreign Policy* (hereinafter cited as *DGFP*), series D (1937–45), XI (London, 1961), 213.

5 Trevor-Roper (ed.), op. cit., 569.

6 See, for example, Angel Viñas, 'Dimensiones económicas e internacionales de la guerra civil: una presentación de la literatura reciente', in Manuel Tuñón de Lara, *et. al.*, *Historiografía española contemporánea: X Coloquio del Centro de Investigaciones Hispánicas de la Universidad de Pau. Balance y resumen* (Madrid, 1980), 367, 372–3.

7 Wolfgang Schieder and Christof Dipper (eds.), *Der Spanische Bürgerkrieg in der internationalen Politik (1936–1939)* (Munich, 1976), 18; Angel Viñas, *La Alemania nazi y el 18 de julio*, 2nd edn (Madrid, 1977), 352.

8 Schieder and Dipper (eds.), op. cit., 18; Viñas, op. cit., 352.

9 Wolfgang Schieder, 'Spanischer Bürgerkrieg und Vierjahresplan. Zur Struktur nationalsozialistcher Aussenpolitik', in Schieder and Dipper (eds.), op. cit., 168.

10 Hans-Henning Abendroth, 'Die deutsche Intervention Im spanischen Bürgerkrieg: Ein Diskussionsbeitrag', *Vierteljahrshefte Für Zeitgeschichte*, 1 (1982), 120.

11 W. N. Medlicott, Douglas Dakin and Gillian Bennett (eds.), *Documents on British Foreign Policy, 1919–1939* (hereinafter cited as *DBFP*), 2nd series, XVII (London, 1979), 67.

12 ibid., 64, 758.

13 ibid., 759–60.

14 ibid., 760.

15 ibid., 773; Viñas, *La Alemania nazi*, 362.

16 Ministère des Affaires Etrangères, Commission de Publication des

Documents Relatifs aux origines de la Guerre, 1939–1945, *Documents Diplomatiques Français, 1932–1939* (hereinafter cited as *DDF*), 2ᵉ série (1936–9), III (Paris, 1966), 139.

17 Malcolm Muggeridge (ed.), *Ciano's Diplomatic Papers*, trans. S. Hood (London, 1948), 57.

18 ibid., 58.

19 ibid., 57.

20 *DDF*, 2ᵉ série, III, 24.

21 ibid., 89.

22 Schieder, 'Spanischer Bürgerkrieg und Vierjahresplan', 168–9.

23 *DGFP*, series D, III, *Germany and the Spanish Civil War, 1936–1939* (London, 1951), 8.

24 See, for example, Pablo de Azcárate, *Mi embajada en Londres durante la guerra civil española* (Barcelona, 1976), 40.

Even Hitler admitted, some time after the end of the Civil War, that this was the true pattern of cause and effect in the internal political evolution of Republican Spain, 1936–9: 'as the Red Spaniards never cease explaining, they had not entered into co-operation with the Soviets on ideological grounds, but had rather been forced into it – and thence dragged into a political current not of their own choosing – simply through lack of other support.' Trevor-Roper (ed.), op. cit., 569.

25 Records of the British Foreign Office, FO 371 ('General Correspondence after 1906')/20530, W8628/62/41; Angel Viñas, *El oro de Moscú: Alfa y omega de un mito franquista* (Barcelona, 1979), 149–50, 183–4 n. 10; Herbert R. Southworth, 'Conspiración contra la República', *Historia 16* (June, 1978).

26 Viñas, *El oro de Moscú*, 320–1.

27 Isaac Deutscher, *Stalin: A Political Biography*, revised edn (Harmondsworth, 1966), 407–12; Fernando Claudín, *The Communist Movement: From Comintern to Cominform* (Harmondsworth, 1975), 174–9.

28 J. A. Grenville, *The Major International Treaties 1914–1973. A History and Guide with Texts* (London, 1974), 152–3.

29 John E. Dreifort, 'The French Popular Front and the Franco-Soviet Pact, 1936–37: a dilemma in foreign policy', *Journal of Contemporary History*, 11 (1976), 217–36; Robert J. Young, *In Command of France: French Foreign Policy and Military Planning, 1933–1940* (Cambridge, Massachusetts, 1978), 145–50; Anthony Adamthwaite, *France and the Coming of the Second World War, 1936–1939* (London, 1977), 47–50.

30 Manuel Azaña, *Obras Completas*, IV, *Memorias políticas y de Guerra* (Mexico, 1968), 618.

31 FO 371/20530, W8628/62/41.

32 Azaña, op. cit., IV, 734.

33 Claudín, op. cit., 223–42, 707–8 n. 49.

34 Viñas, *El oro de Moscú*, 322–3.

35 Azaña, op. cit., IV, 734.
36 *DBFP*, 2nd series, XVII, 761.
37 Adamthwaite, op. cit., 24; Grenville, op. cit., 154–6.
38 Muggeridge (ed.), op. cit., 56.
39 Hans-Henning Abendroth, *Hitler in der spanischen Arena: Die deutsch-spanischen Beziehungen im Spannungsfeld der europäischen Interessenpolitik vom Ausbruch des Bürgerkrieges bis zum Ausbruch des Weltkrieges, 1936–1939* (Paderborn, 1973), 35.
40 Leonidas E. Hill (ed.), *Die Weizsäcker-Papiere, 1933–1950* (Frankfurt/M, 1974), 98.
41 John E. Dreifort, *Yvon Delbos at the Quai d'Orsay: French Foreign Policy during the Popular Front, 1936–1938* (Lawrence, 1973), 34–41; Joel Colton, *Léon Blum: Humanist in Politics* (Cambridge, Massachusetts), 236–46; J.-B. Duroselle, *La Décadence, 1932–1939*, Collection 'Politique Etrangère de la France, 1871–1969' (Paris, 1979), 301–2.
42 *DDF*, 2ᵉ série, III, 56.
43 *DBFP*, 2nd series, XVII, 761.
44 Quoted by Abendroth, *Hitler in der spanischen Arena*, 32.
45 William Carr, *Arms, Autarky and Aggression: A Study in German Foreign Policy, 1933–1939* (London, 1972), 49–60; Gerhard L. Weinberg, *The Foreign Policy of Hitler's Germany*, I, *Diplomatic Revolution in Europe, 1933–36* (Chicago, 1970), 348–54.
46 Anthony Adamthwaite (ed.), *The Lost Peace: International Relations in Europe, 1918–1939* (London, 1980), 180–1.
47 ibid., 183.
48 See, for example, William Carr, 'National Socialism: foreign policy and Wehrmacht', in Walter Laqueur (ed.), *Fascism: A Reader's Guide: Analyses, Interpretations, Bibliography* (Harmondsworth, 1979), 115–39; Andreas Hillgrüber, 'England's place in Hitler's plans for world dominion', *JCH*, 9, 1 (1974), 5–22; Schieder, 'Spanischer Bürgerkrieg und Vierjahresplan', 162–5.
49 Max Domarus, *Hitler: Reden und Proklamationen, 1932–1945: Kommentiert von einem deutschen Zeitgenossen*, I, *Triumph* (Munich, 1965), 688; Viñas, *La Alemania nazi*, 359–64, 367–9; Abendroth, *Hitler in der spanischen Arena*, 31–7; Abendroth, 'Die deutsche Intervention', 122.
50 Viñas, *La Alemania nazi*, 361.
51 *DGFP*, series D, III, 7; Abendroth, *Hitler in der spanischen Arena*, 29–30, 333 n. 96.
52 Abendroth believes that this telegram, from Counsellor Schwendemann of the German Embassy in Madrid, was available in Bayreuth on the night of 25–26 July 1936 (ibid., 29–30). Viñas also holds that it was not 'improbable' that Schwendemann's report was under consideration there at that time (*La Alemania nazi*, 340, 360), whereas Schieder maintains that this possibility can be 'ruled out' ('Spanischer Bürgerkrieg und Vierjahresplan', 167, 187 n. 34).

53 Quoted by Abendroth, *Hitler in der spanischen Arena*, 36. Although Hitler did refer, on this occasion, to the possibility of collaboration with a victorious Spanish Nationalist regime in a future European war, this prospect was not the decisive influence impelling him to become involved in the Spanish Civil War. For, as one historian has noted, Hitler did not exploit Franco's predicament, in late July 1936, to obtain a formal promise of continuing diplomatic goodwill towards the Third Reich, in exchange for the urgently required German military help. (Hans-Henning Abendroth, 'Deutschlands Rolle im spanischen Bürgerkrieg', in Manfred Funke (ed.), *Hitler, Deutschland und die Mächte: Materialen zur Aussenpolitik des Dritten Reichs*, paperback edn (Düsseldorf, 1978), 480.) Moreover, although the Führer was presented with ample evidence, during the course of the Spanish Civil War, that Franco's Spain might prove an unreliable political partner for Nazi Germany in the future, German military assistance to the insurgent camp was not discontinued. The fact that a Francoist victory over the Spanish left would prevent Spain's alignment with the anti-Nazi powers was enough to persuade Hitler to support the Nationalist rebellion. Prevention was the mother of intervention.

54 Abendroth, 'Die deutsche Intervention', 122.

55 Schieder and Dipper (eds.), *Der Spanische Bürgerkrieg*, 19, 41 n. 61.

56 *DGFP*, series D, III, 142.

57 See, also, the points made against the Schieder-Dipper argument, on this matter, by Abendroth ('Die deutsche Intervention', 123).

58 Abendroth, 'Deutschlands Rolle', 481; Schieder, 'Spanischer Bürgerkrieg und Vierjahresplan', 172–84.

59 Adamthwaite, *The Lost Peace*, 182.

60 *DGFP*, series D, III, 153.

61 Jeremy Noakes and Geoffrey Pridham (eds.), *Documents on Nazism, 1919–1945* (London, 1974), 528.

62 Glenn T. Harper, *German Economic Policy in Spain During the Spanish Civil War, 1936–1939* (The Hague, 1967), 71–92, 96–118.

63 *DGFP*, series D, III, 630–1.

64 ibid., 634–5.

65 Ramón Serrano Suñer, *Entre el silencio y la propaganda, la historia como fue: Memorias* (Barcelona, 1977), 334.

66 *DGFP*, series D, III, 647, 651, 653–6.

67 ibid., 671, 673, 689–91, 695; Abendroth, *Hitler in der spanischen Arena*, 210–11.

68 Hill (ed.), op. cit., 103.

69 Abendroth, 'Deutschlands Rolle', 479.

70 Hill (ed.), op. cit., 102.

71 *DGFP*, series D, III, 162; Weinberg, op. cit., I, 297–9, II, *Starting World War II* (Chicago, 1980), 143–4; Abendroth, *Hitler in der spanischen Arena*, 107; Muggeridge (ed.), op. cit., 57–8.

72 See, e.g., Weinberg, op. cit., I, 298–9, II, 143–4.
73 *DGFP*, series D, III, 181.
74 Domarus, op. cit., II, *Untergang* (Munich, 1965), 1210.
75 *DGFP*, series D, III, 56–7.
76 ibid., 156–7.
77 George Orwell, 'Looking back on the Spanish War', in Sonia Orwell and Ian Angus (eds.), *The Collected Essays, Journalism and Letters of George Orwell*, II, *My Country Right or Left, 1940–1943*, paperback edn (Harmondsworth, 1970), 302.
78 Quoted by Raymond Carr (ed.), *The Republic and the Civil War in Spain* (London, 1971), 128.

12
The financing of the Spanish Civil War

Angel Viñas

From the first days of the Spanish Civil War, both the Republican government and the military rebels faced huge economic problems. The Republic found itself with two advantages: Spain's substantial gold reserves and
the control of the principal industrial cities of the country. Both were,
however, considerably vitiated by the hostility of international financial
circles which obstructed the Republic's foreign financial and commercial
transactions. In contrast, the Nationalists, who seemed initially to be at a
considerable disadvantage economically, enjoyed enormous goodwill
among international financiers and found credit easier to obtain. In
addition, they controlled much of Spain's food-producing agriculture.

The war economies of both sides had to be improvised. In varying degrees, both were forced to resort to foreign suppliers to make good their own production deficiencies. Accordingly, problems arose in finding the funds to meet these expenses. Both sides were drastically short of foreign currency and, within Spain, dealt with the problem in the same way by calling upon the Bank of Spain in each zone to make advances to their respective treasuries. Neither taxes nor other extraordinary revenues played an important role in covering government expenditure. The result was foreseeable. Inflation rocketed, although in the territory controlled by the Burgos government greater food supplies made it possible to keep the problem in check until 1939.

In neither case, however, did internal financing constitute a major handicap. The main difficulty was in the area of international payments. Yet, in this, the initial positions of the two belligerents were very different. The Republic had the nation's gold. The rebels, without it, were at first much more tightly constrained. Indeed, gold was to be the main, albeit not the only, source for generating the means with which to meet international payments. Other sources included foreign trade, aid in foreign currency (loans and donations), private gold and silver holdings, and assets held abroad by Spanish citizens, sale of which had a certain bearing on the balance of payments. Both sides, faced with the same need for foreign currency and counting on very similar personal skills and experience, adopted strikingly parallel policies. In the end the war was not lost for lack of foreign currency, nor won because of it.

At the outbreak of the Civil War on 18 July 1936, the volume of bullion in the Bank of Spain at Madrid which could be mobilized for war purposes amounted to 2188 million gold pesetas, equivalent to 635 tonnes of fine gold (715 million dollars). The Republican treasury, however, held only 726 kilograms of fine gold abroad. In terms of its gold reserves, Spain ranked fourth in the world (excluding the Soviet Union) behind the United States, France and Great Britain. Legislation then in force provided that exports of bullion could only be made for maintaining the peseta exchange rate in international markets, i.e. within the context of a foreign monetary policy destined to promote the stability of the Spanish currency. This was an important legal stumbling-block which Republican leaders sidestepped from the beginning by applying to the Bank of Spain for loans in gold, which they then sold first to the Bank of France and then to the USSR National Bank, while officially claiming to the former (which was not a state-owned bank) that the currency equivalent (countervalue) was being assigned to bolster exch̲ ̲ge stability. No one was duped, however, and the representatives of private shareholders of the Bank of Spain cautiously protested against the measures. With the countervalue of the gold, which it began selling to the Bank of France as early as 25 July 1936, the Republic obtained foreign currency. This was used to purchase war *matériel* and other supplies abroad. The operation went through several stages and lasted until March 1937, the French having acquired an estimated total of 174 tonnes of fine gold, equivalent to 27.4 per cent of the total bullion in the Bank of Spain in Madrid at the onset of the Civil War. Its minimum value amounted to 598 million gold pesetas, some 195 million dollars. No public mention of this operation was ever made officially or otherwise by the French authorities. This availability of gold initially removed the major financial obstacle encountered by the Republic. Since the Western democratic powers were reluctant to provide large-scale material support, there is no question but that the war would have ended very quickly had the nation's gold reserves not been available to the Madrid government.

However, the mobilization of the gold through sales to the Bank of France did not solve all their problems. The government had to establish a proper system for allocating the countervalue to the purchase of items needed to maintain and continue the war. The first attempts were not very promising. On 8 August 1936, the Republican Ambassador to Paris, Alvaro de Albornoz, naïvely signed a contract with a certain Société Européenne d'Etudes et d'Entreprises for the purchase of arms and other goods, granting it no less than exclusive rights of sale. The Republican government would only be able to operate through this firm which was to receive a 7.5 per cent commission on the value of purchases. This contract, however, was immediately rescinded by the appropriate Republican authorities, at the cost of subsequent friction with the French intermediaries.

A system was gradually organized for buying arms and other goods abroad, but the Madrid government then met with difficulties created by certain foreign banks (those presented by London's Midland Bank are very well documented) which sabotaged the transfer of funds urgently required by Republican agents and diplomats. These obstacles must have greatly annoyed government leaders. As a consequence it was decided in October 1936 to use channels controlled by the Soviet banking apparatus established in the West.

Operational difficulties then emerged. Luis Araquistaín, the new Republican Ambassador in Paris, complained on one occasion that the rate at which foreign currency remittances were made in order to buy war *matériel* was not, in his opinion, adequate. Equally, purchases were sometimes erratic, depending upon the haphazard results obtained by specific missions sent to various countries. Not until the autumn of 1936, and then only in certain Republican embassies, was centralization implemented. Financial attachés made their appearance and reinforced the foreign service whose personnel had deserted *en masse* to the insurgents. Lack of institutional liaison between financial policy (conducted by the Ministry of Finance) and the allocation of foreign currency by the Ministries of War, the Navy and the Air in response to demands made by the fighting services also had negative consequences. There was waste, and certain unscrupulous agents found it possible to channel funds for their own profit after the initial control measures proved inadequate. There was also friction between the central and the autonomous Basque and Catalan governments, which wanted to handle foreign currency funds to effect purchases abroad, and to dabble in international affairs.

It should be stressed that during this time the Republic's foreign financial policy was well known to the insurgents, who on various occasions attempted to block transfers of gold and use of its countervalue; this was first done through direct representations to the Bank of France, the French and English governments and the League of Nations. Later came diplomatic support from the Fascist powers at the Non-Intervention Committee in London.

While the Giral government established after the *coup* had set a pattern for mobilizing the gold in the wake of the July 1936 uprising it was the subsequent Largo Caballero government, in which Professor Juan Negrín held the finance portfolio, that created the legal and operational bases for the Republican war economy proper. Recognizing that the gold holdings were vital for the Republic's existence, the government took precautionary measures in September 1936 to transfer them from the Bank of Spain headquarters in Madrid to a safe place, namely the ammunition depots at the Cartagena naval base on the Mediterranean coast. The gold safely at Cartagena and the Republic's international prospects waning, both Socialist leaders came to the crucial decision to send most of the remaining gold reserves on deposit to the Soviet Union, a measure that gave rise to one of the most serious controversies of the Civil War. With the knowledge both of the insurgents and of Nazi diplomats, the gold began to arrive in Moscow on 6 November 1936. Despite claims to the contrary, it was expeditiously counted in the Soviet capital and by the end of February 1937 the exact composition of the deposit had been determined. The holdings were in a wide variety of coins of many different types, periods and countries.

Dr Marcelino Pascua, Republican Ambassador to Moscow, sought first to obtain credits backed by the deposit (consisting of 510 tonnes of alloyed gold equivalent to an estimated 460.5 tonnes of fine gold or some 518 million dollars), but the Soviet Union – which until then had furnished war *matériel* on credit – refused. Consequently, from 16 February 1937, Largo Caballero and Negrín began depleting the deposit, ordering partial sales of gold to obtain its countervalue in foreign currency – appraised according to London metals market quotations – or to cover still unpaid debts accumulated by the Republic.

The currency equivalent of gold sold to the Soviet State Bank for purposes other than the repayment of Republican debts was transferred to the Banque Commerciale pour l'Europe du Nord, a Soviet banking institution operating in Paris under French law, where the Republic had opened a network of accounts from which many of its international payments were met. This ensured that the insurgents as well as Western financial circles would remain in the dark about many of the devices used for spending foreign currency funds, although French financial authorities may have been aware of the nature of the operations. Between February 1937 and late April 1938, the Republicans ordered sales of a total of 426 tonnes of gold in Moscow, and received in exchange 245 million dollars, 41.5 million pounds sterling, and 375 million French francs. This entire currency equivalent was transferred to Paris except for 131.6 million dollars which the Soviets received in 1937 as payment for previous supplies.

Neither Negrín, by then Prime Minister, nor Pascua gave up negotiation of credits with the USSR. In October 1937 the former instructed his Ambassador officially to request a credit for 150 million dollars, but no agreement was reached until February 1938, when Stalin expressed willingness to grant credit facilities for 70 million dollars at 3 per cent interest, 50 per cent of which would be covered by a gold guarantee. According to a secret agreement dated 7 March of that year, 35 tonnes of alloy were separated to this end from the remaining gold deposit. Negrín immediately authorized payments amounting to 33.3 million dollars to be charged against the loan, while the remainder of the first deposit was being converted to cash. According to a communication from the People's Finance Commissar dated 1 August 1938, the Republic at that time had slightly under one and a half tonnes of fine gold. Since several months of war and Soviet supplies still lay ahead, it is difficult not to believe that this gold would eventually disappear. If my calculations are correct, there is only an accounting gap of 0.4 tonnes of fine gold, equivalent to some 450,000 dollars.

Once the gold, the main source of foreign currency, was substantially depleted, there were additional sources that could be tapped. Firstly, there was silver, the mobilization of which was contemplated in January 1938 and started in April, through sales to the United States Treasury. Five shipments of silver were made to New York, yielding in all some fifteen million dollars. In the summer of 1938 the Barcelona authorities diversified their sales of silver, contacting a number of private French and Belgian firms willing to buy. From then until January 1939, nine transactions have been identified which generated foreign currency worth almost five million dollars. These various transactions – about which there has been much conjecture – involved sales of 90 per cent of the total silver stocks held by the Bank of Spain in Madrid when the Civil War broke out.

At the same time another little-known operation was taking place: secret provisions dated May and July 1938 were made to enable the Republican Ministry of Finance and Economy legally to mobilize new resources for generating much-needed foreign currency. These resources were various: they had been created through a broad spectrum of legislative measures which compelled the population to turn over to the authorities any jewels, bullion, gold and silver coins, or foreign assets that they held. The Burgos government also implemented parallel measures in its zone. There were, in addition, the proceeds of the confiscation and requisition of property of declared enemies of the Republic, which were channelled in part through the so-called Reparations Fund. Resources from the appropriation of private deposits in the Bank of Spain belong in this same category. Lastly, there remained certain coins – old gold – held by the Bank which had not been sent to Paris or Moscow. It is difficult to estimate their countervalue. Until 17 November 1938 such transactions – conducted mainly with private French and Swiss firms – had generated some nine million dollars. In the following months, small remittances of precious metals continued to be made from Catalonia to Paris; these also were sold and raised at least two million dollars more.

The thirty-one million dollars obtained through these sales did not go very far towards alleviating the Republic's dire financial situation. Thus, from the summer of 1938, Negrín was interested in negotiating with the Soviets a new credit of about seventy-five to one hundred million dollars, to be paid for partly, at his suggestion, by Spanish goods such as mercury, salt, lead, potassium, citric fruits, and almonds, as well as by the sale of certain ships and a small volume of gold remaining in a deposit established in France in 1931. The delivery of this gold to the Republican authorities, however, was at that time already blocked by the French courts. In August 1938, Ambassador Pascua negotiated with the Soviets a credit of sixty million dollars which was implemented by Negrín himself. Just how this was done remains unknown.

Equally obscure are the details of the Republican export trade during the Civil War. I have found scattered data that provide a partial picture for the period December 1936–June 1938. Sales abroad of certain products such as lead, oranges, lemons, olive oil, peanuts, almonds, potassium chloride, tartaric acid, cork and textiles (with iron ore and mercury, two major export goods, excluded) amounted to an estimated seven million dollars. Two million dollars of this total were already accounted for by the need to pay for imports, and two more had still to be received, leaving three million dollars as the disposable amount raised by exports. Aside from Soviet credits, there is no reliable data for assessing the volume of foreign financial aid received by the Republic, which obviously took the form of foreign currency or goods.

One highly debated and very important question is the adequacy of resources mobilized to meet the Republic's needs. Of course, the war involved substantial foreign-currency needs: early in 1937, import requirements were put at approximately fourteen million dollars monthly. To this should be added purchases of armament: part of the war *matériel* bought from the USSR during the first year of the war amounted to 132 million dollars. If we assume that the rate of supplies other than armaments in the initial months was maintained until the fall of Vizcaya (when its industry and iron-mines were lost by the Republic), a minimum estimate would be that in the first year of the war the Republican government spent at least 314 million dollars. This did not include purchases of war *matériel* outside the Soviet Union at what must have been an extremely high cost.

As territorial losses involved the loss of internal resources, Republican dependence on foreign supplies must have increased considerably both in the war and non-war sectors of the economy. By the summer of 1938, monthly foreign currency requirements for the year were averaging twenty-seven million dollars, excluding expenditures on Soviet armament. By applying this rate to the period between the fall of the northern front and of Catalonia, minimum additional foreign currency needs in these sixteen months would then have reached a figure of 430 million dollars. The estimated overall amount (in which admittedly only a part of the expenditure on armament is computed) is merely a guide for quantifying with some certainty the minimum volume of foreign currency required by the war: 744 million dollars. As this exceeded the gold countervalue mobilized, the authorities must have had to generate additional foreign currency through the financial and commercial transactions described above.

If the Republic, which controlled Bank of Spain gold reserves, encountered such limitations in external financing, how could the Franco government, with hardly any gold, overcome the constraints of meeting international payments? The insurgents' foreign financial policy was soon established. From the very first they aimed to obtain as much aid in war *matériel* and products for the war sector of the economy as the Fascist powers would provide. The contribution made in this respect by

Mussolini's Italy was not only much more generous and consistent than that from Nazi Germany, but has also attracted less attention.

On 24 August 1936, an unidentified emissary from the National Defence Junta met in Rome with Count Galeazzo Ciano, Minister of Foreign Affairs. By then, Italian supplies of war *matériel* had been partially paid for with some of the modest foreign currency holdings in insurgent hands. These comprised certain funds deposited abroad, donations (among which those from King Alfonso XIII, then in exile, must have been very important), and foreign banknotes, securities and gold transferred abroad from zones held by the rebel authorities (for example, from Mallorca, through transactions conducted by financier Juan March).

The Italians had requested a deposit of five and a half million lire in order to meet payments for pending and future supplies. In the course of that meeting Ciano – unaware of the request – appeared to oppose it, saying: 'Pas un seul mot de plus sur des questions d'argent. Après la victoire on en parlera, pas maintenant!' ('Not another single word on money questions. We will talk of it after the victory, not now.') This was not strictly complied with, yet the truth is that only part-reimbursement for massive shipments of Italian war *matériel* and other goods was made during the conflict, settlement of the greater part being held over. Nevertheless, in the course of the Civil War, a number of secret agreements were entered into with Italy for the purpose of regulating bilateral trade and obtaining some reduction in the volume of war indebtedness being incurred by the Burgos government.

The first of these agreements was signed in Rome by Nicolás Franco on 29 April 1937, and is known as the 'Franco-Fagiouli Agreement'. The Burgos authorities undertook to pay the Italian Government – from 1 January 1938 – the annual sum of 150 million lire (in goods or convertible foreign currency) to pay for 'special shipments'. In 1937 Franco undertook to repay Italy seventy-five million lire in kind; in particular iron ore, Riotinto pyrites, wool, raw hides, olive oil, lead and copper. Following protracted negotiations over the decision to ship Spanish goods, a new accord, the 'Franco-Ciano Agreement', was reached on 11 August 1937; this repeated provisions contained in the previous agreement that 'special shipments' would be paid for within a maximum period of ten years. A mixed commission would establish the proper amount. Other shipments of Italian war *matériel* not subject to special agreements (concerning ships and aircraft) were to take place between 15 July and 31 December 1937 and would be paid for half in convertible currencies or in kind (metals and metallic minerals, hides, wool, anthracite, etc.) and the remaining half through a credit of up to 125 million lire to be granted by a consortium of Italian banks presided over by the governor of the Bank of Italy. These and other provisions related to the payment for shipments to the Spanish armed forces. Those destined for the Italian CTV (Corps of Volunteer Troops) would be entered separately, forming the so-called 'general account', payment of which would be arranged by other means.

As a result of these contacts, a well-known Spanish currency expert, Manuel Arburúa, travelled to Rome in November 1937 representing a consortium of the Bank of Spain in Burgos, the Banco Español de Crédito and the Banco Hispano-Americano, in order to define the system to be followed for the financial operations agreed on 20 November; according to these a rolling credit was established for an initial 125 million lire and increased to 250 million on 27 November. This amount was guaranteed by different kinds of Spanish National Debt and Treasury securities which amounted to slightly more than 153 million nominal pesetas. Funds deriving from the rolling credit enabled payments to be made for war expenses. Some friction resulted from the meagre amount of foreign currency delivered by the Spaniards (about 14 per cent of the value of the supplies in question), and with regard to the kind of goods exported, which were not those which the Italian government was most interested in acquiring.

Such friction, however, was overcome as had been anticipated by Ciano's statement in August 1936. Antonio Mosquera, Spanish Commercial Attaché in Rome, noted that this was due to the 'goodwill prevailing at the highest levels of the Italian government to which it was necessary to resort on numerous occasions in order to solve technical difficulties presented by the ministries concerned. Without top-level help to eliminate these difficulties, such good results could not have been obtained.'

Nevertheless, the Burgos government's growing dependence on Italian war supplies made it necessary to enter into a new agreement, signed in Rome on 23 May 1938 after lengthy discussions. Thereby, the period for applying measures to regularize pending transactions, and to begin to discharge the debt incurred, was extended. This agreement further provided a formula for effecting payment for war supplies during that year to be covered by existing money on call in the rolling credit (increased to 300 million lire) and by exports of Spanish products: Rif iron ore, ingots, pyrites, cocoa, olive oil, raw wool and coal. Franco was thus able to ensure acquisition of war *matériel* in order to pursue the war, precisely when the Republic was constrained and hampered in its purchases abroad once the sale to Moscow of the Bank of Spain gold reserves was concluded.

In September 1938 an exchange of letters between Spain and Italy agreed the manner of payment for other supplies. In general, the settlement was mixed and provision was made to transfer foreign currency, Spanish goods and even pesetas (to cover certain Italian expenses in Spain). The total reached thirty million lire. Simultaneously, Franco requested immediate delivery of abundant artillery spares and 117 howitzers, as well as other war *matériel*. By November, requests already totalled 400 million lire (although this was reduced to 300 million in view of difficulties in securing payment). The bargaining between Spanish and Italian officials was still to last a long time and was only partially resolved by the personal intervention of Mussolini himself.

This brief summary will perhaps have shown the mechanisms by which the Franco government overcame external financial problems in its relations with Italy: compensation based on certain export products, delivery of foreign currency and even pesetas and, above all, recourse to temporary indebtedness which would have to be finally settled once the Civil War ended. Financially the general tone of relations between the two governments was good, although major technical difficulties did arise at times.

Additionally, all this demonstrates that continued economic and military aid from Fascist Italy (only partially and to a hardly significant degree repaid during the conflict itself) was the principal way in which the Burgos government could manage to make the international payments necessary to strengthen the war sector of its economy. In contrast, except in the case of the Soviet Union and even then with the difficulties outlined, the Republic never had financial support which was so constant and so little subject to unforeseeable fluctuations. Moreover, the nature of economic and financial relations between Franco's Spain and Italy helped sweeten the rather sour taste of those maintained with Nazi Germany.

Indeed, the Germans proved to be more aggressive and anxious to extract benefits from aid given to General Franco, the economic value of which, however, was well beneath that given by Italy. To such an end, they wielded an instrument established from the early days of the conflict – HISMA – a firm created in Tetuán under Spanish law. One of its founders, the businessman Johannes E. F. Bernhardt, had previously conveyed to Hitler Franco's request for support, and later advised the insurgent military authorities to confiscate large amounts of copper ore for the purpose of paying for shipments of German war *matériel*. The military administration and Franco, initially overwhelmed by the complexities of economic management in wartime, gave HISMA a free hand from September 1936 to develop Spanish-German trade on the basis of systematic compensation by barter of goods, without using foreign currency. The fact that the rebels' scarce gold and foreign-currency holdings had to be allocated for payments to other countries may have contributed to that. However, it led the Third Reich to maintain and expand the pace of aid according to whether it could be offset with Spanish raw materials and products.

This compensation became more substantial when a counterpart to HISMA, known as ROWAK, was constituted in Berlin in October 1936. The initial purpose of this firm was to channel regular Spanish trade to Germany and to devise means for Franco's Spain to offset her incipient war indebtedness. Both firms were controlled by members of the National Socialist Party and subordinate to the Four-Year Plan headed by Goering. As a matter of fact, they played a vital role in bilateral relations between the two countries as appendages to the peculiar administrative framework being constructed in the Third Reich to prepare the German economy for war. All of this caused intense friction with ministries and officials who had until then controlled the process of foreign economic policy-making in the Third Reich.

The two responsibilities of the HISMA/ROWAK apparatus were closely interrelated, and the mechanism, which monopolized Spanish-German trade to the detriment of other established private interests, lasted throughout the Civil War. The reasons are to be found in the desire of Nazi Germany's top echelons to maintain it, since this ensured the acquisition not only of the greatest possible volume of Spanish raw materials, but also of those goods of most value to the German war economy. Consequently, trading relations of the incipient Fascist state with the Third Reich became ever more dependent. Spanish exports were diverted towards Germany, thereby reducing the Spanish ability to generate foreign currency elsewhere.

The HISMA/ROWAK compensation system has not been sufficiently analysed. While not all of its principles were established from the beginning, its operation did not vary essentially once the notion of barter was defined and set in motion. Spanish import possibilities depended on the previously recorded volume of exports to the Third Reich. The mechanism initiated a substantial trade diversion in favour of Nazi Germany. The HISMA/ROWAK apparatus operated as a monopoly in financing Spanish-German trade, and established a private bilateral pattern of payments. It also ensured that Spanish raw materials of interest to the Berlin authorities (iron, copper and lead ore; mercury; pyrites; okume lumber; wool and hides, fats, etc.) were channelled to Germany. Only a part of the export trade would compensate for debts which Franco was incurring with Nazi Germany for its support. Accordingly, the large quantity of pesetas held by HISMA was to lead the Reich economic authorities to a new and highly debated project: the creation of a German-owned network of enterprises which were to extract and acquire Spanish raw materials. An assortment of companies was thus set up, which acted in almost all sectors of the economy of the Franco zone. From commercial penetration, the next step would be direct investment, with important political and economic consequences. The Franco policy towards foreign investment during the 1939–59 period, the epoch of autarky, is traceable to the fending-off of German investment efforts in the Civil War.

The HISMA/ROWAK scheme fostered the diversion of Spanish exports to Nazi Germany; in so doing, possibilities of selling to other markets (England, the United States, Switzerland, etc.) from which convertible foreign currency could be obtained were drastically curtailed. Notwithstanding, foreign currency was generated in some measure, and by various arrangements was allocated to the purchase of products (not exactly war *matériel*) in third countries. Thus, during the course of the Civil War, supplies from these markets were mostly paid for in foreign currency. The much-touted support of certain sectors of the Anglo-Saxon business world – in sales to Franco's Spain of fuel, trucks and other products that did not fall within the category of war supplies – was more in the nature of ordinary international trade than extraordinary aid to the new regime.

Naturally, however, the Burgos authorities did not overlook possibilities for attracting foreign currency, not least for partially defraying the cost of Italian and German shipments. Nazi pressure was behind the important decree of 14 March 1937 which, paralleling measures adopted in Republican territory, compelled private persons to yield to the government all the foreign currency they held or owned, either in the 'liberated zone' or abroad; to hand over all the gold they had in or outside Spain, and to make available to the authorities all foreign government bonds as well as foreign or Spanish internationally quoted securities.

A similar measure was the so-called 'National Subscription', a collection which channelled a variety of resources to the authorities and has had an enduring impact on the Spanish mind because of the sentimental value of the objects to the people (charms, jewellery, gold coins, watches, etc.). Many handed them over enthusiastically but also because they wished to banish any suspicion that their feelings of loyalty to the Francoist cause were rather lukewarm. There is certainly no overall estimate of amounts collected in foreign currency through the 'National Subscription'; calculations have been made based on foreign-currency remittances abroad: these totalled almost one million pounds, six million francs, one and a half million dollars, nearly five million escudos and slightly over two million lire.

Once peace was restored, Spanish proclamations of alignment with the hard line maintained by the Fascist powers contributed to the Western democratic nations' unwillingness to lend assistance. Aside from certain trade credits from the United States, the Francoist government was able to find only modest financial support – one million pounds granted in April and June 1939 by the Société de Banque Suisse. As against this, it had to pay for loans obtained during the war and settle arrears incurred even before 1936, as well as those accumulated by the Republic with numerous countries during the Civil War (naturally excluding the Soviet Union). Above all, it was imperative to resolve the thorny problem of debts with Mussolini's Italy and the Third Reich. Negotiations with Italy, starting towards the end of the Civil War, were cordial. Discussions with Germany, on the other hand, initiated after the conflict was over, were tense and difficult and failed to reach a solution. They were conducted in the atmosphere of initial German victories in World War II, when the Fascist powers would greatly have welcomed General Franco's regime as an active ally. Agreements between the Spanish and Mussolini governments, on the other hand, preceded Italy's entry into the war by only a few months.

In economic terms, we can now briefly summarize the overall amount of foreign support for General Franco to show how he was able to resolve his lack of foreign-currency holdings in the Civil War. The basic mechanism was credit: credit amortized or repaid in very diverse ways over an extended period; credit that made it possible to mobilize an ample supply of foreign resources (precisely those which the zone lacked); credit that involved material support (war equipment, logistics), industrial goods allocated to the economy's war sector, services (freight, personnel) and foreign currency. Only because the insurgents were able to call on such a wide range of resources could the Francoist authorities exchange domestic goods for other supplies from third countries. They then used privileged relations with the Fascist powers (particularly Italy) to ensure shipments of war *matériel* and other items they might not have been able to obtain elsewhere, in the volume and at the rate needed.

A distinction has been made here between three major channels of foreign support: the Italian connection, German aid, and financial credits granted by Spanish and foreign capitalist groups. Figures for the first two may be estimated, at the most, at some 8300 million lire and 560 million marks respectively. The foreign-currency balances in the accounts of the Francoist authorities with the Third Reich and HISMA were, however, 371 and 20 million marks respectively, and Germany received 755 million pesetas in Spanish currency during the Civil War. Mention must also be made of the rolling credit (300 million lire) and its financing service (68 million).

For purposes of comparison it seems justified to apply lira and mark exchange rates as quoted in Francoist Spain for the greater part of the war: 45.15 pesetas/100 lire, and 3.45 pesetas/mark. Depending on the exchange rate used, the amount obtained through Italian support would range from a maximum of 8668 million lire to a minimum of 7868 million. In the case of Germany, the range would be between a maximum, as demanded by Berlin, of 560 marks and a minimum, acknowledged by the Nationalists, of 371 million marks, plus the 755 million pesetas actually paid. This would mean that Italian support ranged from a maximum of 3914 to a minimum of 3552 million pesetas. In the German case, the range was between Berlin's valuation of 1932 million pesetas and the Francoist acknowledgement of 2104 million pesetas, being 1349 owed and 755 actually paid. Thus the joint support given by the Fascist powers would have been 5846 million pesetas at the highest level, and 5656 million at the lowest. Obviously these are estimates. A more detailed reconstruction (which has not yet been attempted) might yield more specific figures. Notwithstanding, those established here show reasonably accurately the extent of foreign resources received by General Franco from Italy and Germany.

Conversion to dollars, using the exchange-rate quoted during the greater part of the Civil War – 8.58 pesetas/dollar – gives maximum and minimum figures for support from Mussolini's Italy added to that of the Third Reich of 681 and 659 million dollars. At all events, it should be borne in mind that the amount of foreign financial credits, as recognized in a secret law of 1 April 1939 which retroactively approved them at the highest level possible, should also be reduced to a common denominator. Interest payments apart, such credits represented a total of 35 million dollars which must be added to the previous figures. Accordingly, the three channels of foreign support mentioned earlier amounted to a maximum of 716 and a minimum of 694 million dollars.

I do not wish to enter the statistical game: while a more precise estimate of base data has not yet been made, it should at least be clear that the volume of resources and services received on credit by General Franco during the Civil War, considering only identified items, totalled approximately 700 million dollars. At no time have I taken into account supplies paid for during the course of the conflict on the basis of more or less regular commercial credits. Thus, without reductions agreed with Italy, the financial debt incurred by Franco's Spain in order to overcome problems of external finance would not have been much less than the amount obtained by the Republic from gold sales. As initially noted, reserves of such metal which could be mobilized in Madrid at the outbreak of the Civil War amounted to some 715 million dollars.

To summarize: without the assistance of the Fascist powers, the government of General Franco would simply have been unable to overcome the difficulties of external financing, nor could he have diverted exports to third countries to pay for supplies unobtainable on credit. On the other hand, there is a distinct parallel between the amount of foreign resources obtained (though in different ways) by either side during the Civil War. The resource endowment of each side varied according to their control of the raw materials and goods in the different zones. Changes in territorial control as a result of the gradual advance of the Francoist army meant the gain, and corresponding loss by the other side, of raw materials and other resources. Nevertheless, an examination of both sides' methods of acquiring external support illustrates the extent to which political considerations were able to overcome the material domestic constraints in allocating resources to the economy's war sector. Further, the evidence that the foreign resources obtained by the rebels were of the same order of magnitude as those received by the Republic goes some way towards wiping out the stigma inflicted by Francoism on the losers when dealing with the economic aspects of the Civil War.

Notes

This chapter is based on three previous books by the author:
El oro español en la guerra civil, Instituto de Estudios Fiscales, Ministerio de Hacienda (Madrid, 1976).
El oro de Moscú. Alfa y omega de un mito franquista (Grijalbo, Barcelona, 1979).
Política comercial exterior en España, 1931–1975 (with Julio Viñuela, Fernando Eguidazu, Carlos Fernández-Pulgar and Senén Florensa), Banco Exterior de España (2 vols., Madrid, 1979).
Comprehensive references to primary material and sources may be found in them.

Spanish archives explored were the following:

Central archives

1 Archivo General de la Administración, Alcalá de Henares
2 Bank of Spain, Madrid
    i General Files
    ii Auditing Department
    iii Confidential Files
    iv Foreign Department
    v Research Department
    vi General Secretariat
3 Instituto Español de Moneda Extranjera, IEME (Foreign Exchange Authority), Madrid
    i General Files
    ii Director-General's Files
4 Ministry of Commerce, Madrid
    i General Files
    ii Personal Files
5 Ministry of Finance, Madrid
    i General Files
    ii Confidential Files
6 Ministry of Foreign Affairs, Madrid
    i General Files
    ii Dirección de Tratados
7 Presidency of the Government, Madrid
    i Burgos Files
    ii Minister's Files
    iii Government Secretariat
8 Servicio Histórico Militar, Madrid
    i Files of the 'Liberation War'
        a 'Nationalist' documents
        b 'Red' documents

Provincial archives

9 Delegación de Hacienda, Burgos

Personal archives

10 Dr Marcelino Pascua, Republican Ambassador to Moscow and Paris.

Index